Early praise for *SQL Antipatterns, Volume 1*

A unique and brilliant book addressing the often overlooked craft of database programming. With clear examples and solid advice, the book takes the reader on a tour of antipatterns, some of which can severely impact your database performance or even your development flows. A great read and recommended for developers of all levels of experience.

➤ **Shlomi Noach**
   Database Engineer, PlanetScale

You must read this book if you develop with SQL. With clarity and thoroughness, Bill explains a wealth of knowledge and solutions that will significantly advance your proficiency with SQL.

➤ **Daniel Nichter**
   DBA, author of *Efficient MySQL Performance*, Block Inc.

I wish I had this book when I was first starting out. There are so many antipatterns in the book that had me shaking my head about my past mistakes. If only I had known.

➤ **Samuel Mullen**
   Senior Manager of Engineering, ActiveProspect

Chock full of useful techniques. Whether you're a novice or a veteran, you're sure to learn something new from this book. I did.

➤ **Steven Grimm**
   Technical Lead, Terraformation

This is a great book for SQL beginners, and it continues to be a useful reference whenever one of the antipatterns comes up. I love the "See No Evil" and "Diplomatic Immunity" chapters. They are perfect for someone trying to improve an engineering team's practices.

➤ **Max Tilford**
   Senior Software Engineer, Firstup

SQL Antipatterns by Bill Karwin is not only one of the best database books I've read. But also one of the best technical books I've read period. I have legitimately read it three times cover to cover and the things I've learnt from it help me everyday at work.

➤ **Pim Brouwers**
   Senior Software Architect, National Hockey League Player's Association

Bill Karwin does a great job of identifying the most common antipatterns in several aspects of working with databases, and provides clear advice for identifying these patterns and how to get away from them. If a person finds themselves designing databases or queries, that person should consider reading this book to ensure best practices are being followed.

➤ **Alex Ostrem**
   Database Reliability and Software Engineer, Etsy

Even for someone who is not a trained programmer, *SQL Antipatterns* provides a great foundation by focusing on how and why some programming approaches fail and by giving clear, narrative explanations and specific coding examples of better solutions.

➤ **Jennifer Pesek**
   Reference Librarian

SQL Antipatterns, Volume 1
Avoiding the Pitfalls of Database Programming

Bill Karwin

The Pragmatic Bookshelf

Raleigh, North Carolina

Many of the designations used by manufacturers and sellers to distinguish their products are claimed as trademarks. Where those designations appear in this book, and The Pragmatic Programmers, LLC was aware of a trademark claim, the designations have been printed in initial capital letters or in all capitals. The Pragmatic Starter Kit, The Pragmatic Programmer, Pragmatic Programming, Pragmatic Bookshelf, PragProg and the linking *g* device are trademarks of The Pragmatic Programmers, LLC.

Every precaution was taken in the preparation of this book. However, the publisher assumes no responsibility for errors or omissions, or for damages that may result from the use of information (including program listings) contained herein.

For our complete catalog of hands-on, practical, and Pragmatic content for software developers, please visit *https://pragprog.com*.

The team that produced this book includes:

CEO: Dave Rankin
COO: Janet Furlow
Managing Editor: Tammy Coron
Development Editor: Jacquelyn Carter
Copy Editor: Karen Galle
Indexing: Potomac Indexing, LLC
Layout: Gilson Graphics
Founders: Andy Hunt and Dave Thomas

For sales, volume licensing, and support, please contact *support@pragprog.com*.

For international rights, please contact *rights@pragprog.com*.

ISBN-13: 978-1-68050-898-7
Book version: P1.0—November 2022

To my wife Jan, my best supporter.

Contents

Part I — Logical Database Design Antipatterns

Part II — Physical Database Design Antipatterns

Part III — Query Antipatterns

Part IV — Application Development Antipatterns

Part V — Bonus: More Foreign Key Mini-Antipatterns

Acknowledgments

Many people helped me along the path to learn enough to write this book.

My parents recognized my passion for computer science when I was a teenager, and they sacrificed to get me a personal computer at a time when those were not common. Also thanks to my parents and my grandfather, I got my education at the University of California.

Many professors showed me the traditional computer science theory and practice, but I want to thank two in particular: Dr. Kevin Karplus and Dr. Dan Scripture. They created a class I took on Technical Writing, which showed me how important it is to practice writing in a field that requires so much care to communicate complex ideas.

I've been inspired by many managers and colleagues. Keith Reynolds gave me some early C code projects, which taught me that the practice of programming is mostly working on other people's code. David Bredenberg inspired me by his example to spend time helping other software developers. Rhea Barron's coaching took my technical writing to a new level.

I'm honored that the following technical reviewers offered their time for the second edition of this book: Ronald Bradford, Jean-François Gagné, Steven Grimm, Samuel Mullen, Alex Ostrum, Jennifer Pesek, Max Tilford, and Pim van der Wal. All their feedback made the book better. Thank you!

I also thank the numerous people who have given positive reviews and feedback since the first edition of my book was published.

My deepest thanks to my wife Jan Dwyer, who is an accomplished writer and a database developer in her own right. She was the first reviewer of every draft of both editions of this book. Her contributions and perspective have been invaluable, but her consistent support, encouragement, and inspiration were what made me able to finish this project.

Introduction

This book is about SQL, the popular language programmers use for data. Specifically, it's about the worst ways to use SQL.

Everyone makes mistakes, but experts try to learn from their mistakes, turning them into opportunities to improve their skills. You'll become a better software developer by studying the most common errors made by other developers, and how to fix them.

My first encounter with SQL involved turning down a job. I had just finished college, and I had been approached by a manager who worked at the university and knew me through campus activities. He had an idea for his own software startup company, and he wanted to develop a database management system portable between various UNIX platforms using shell scripts. He needed a programmer like me to write the code to recognize and execute a limited version of the SQL language.

He said, "I don't need to support the full language—that would be too much work. I need only one SQL statement: SELECT."

I hadn't been taught SQL in any of my college classes. But I had developed complete applications in shell, and I knew a little about parsers and domain-specific languages. So, I thought about taking the job. How hard could it be to parse a single statement of a specialized language like SQL?

As I started to read about SQL, I noticed immediately that this was a different sort of language from those I had used before. To call SELECT only one statement in that language is like calling an engine only one part of an automobile. Both statements are true enough, but they certainly belie the complexity and depth of their subjects. To support execution of that single SQL statement, I realized I would have to develop a fully functional relational database management system and query engine. I could tell it would take years for an experienced developer to do that, and I was still too junior to take on a big project like that by myself.

I declined this opportunity to code an SQL parser and RDBMS engine in shell script. The manager had underestimated the scope of his project, perhaps because he didn't understand what an RDBMS does.

My early experience with SQL seems to be a common one. Most developers are self-taught in SQL, learning it out of self-defense when they find themselves working on a project that requires it. Whether the person is a hobbyist or a professional programmer or an accomplished researcher with a PhD, SQL is a language that tends to be used by programmers without training. This leads to many common mistakes being made over and over.

Notes on the Second Edition

Since writing the first edition of this book, I've worked as an SQL consultant, trainer, developer, and database administrator. I've visited dozens of companies in all sorts of fields of business, all of which use SQL. I've talked with other expert developers and database administrators at conferences and meetups, hearing about their successes and failures.

All software developers still work with data, no matter what language or system they use, and SQL is still the dominant language used for data. Since the software development field in general keeps growing, the number of software developers using SQL is always increasing, even as alternative database technologies are also gaining popularity.

The second edition of *SQL Antipatterns* is updated with the latest observations about common mistakes of SQL and data-driven application development. Feedback about the first edition has been addressed. Internet resources are updated to reference current sites and the latest information.

A number of all-new "mini-antipatterns" appear in between the existing chapters. These briefly cover all-new types of blunders and describe "quick wins" you can use to avoid them.

The code examples are updated to be compatible with the latest versions of MySQL and Python, the most popular open source database and dynamic programming language in today's technology market.

Who This Book Is For

SQL Antipatterns is for any software developer who needs to use SQL—which is virtually all software developers. It doesn't matter whether you're a beginner or a seasoned professional. People at all levels of experience will benefit from the subjects in this book.

You may have read a reference on SQL syntax. Now you know all the clauses of a SELECT statement, and you can get some work done. Gradually, you increase your SQL skills by reading code, books, and blogs. In spite of this, it's hard to tell if you're learning best practices, or another way to paint yourself into a corner.

You may find some topics in *SQL Antipatterns* that are well known to you. You'll see new ways of looking at the problems, even if you're already aware of the solutions. It's good to reinforce your good practices by reviewing widespread programmer misconceptions, and the reasons we avoid them.

It's not uncommon for the relationship between developers and database administrators to be contentious. If you're a DBA, this book can help you explain good practices to the software developers you work with and the consequences of straying from that path.

About This Book

There are plenty of books and internet resources for the basics of the SQL language, so this book assumes the reader has learned enough SQL syntax already to use the language and get some work done.

Performance, scalability, and optimization are important topics for database-driven applications, especially on the web, but it's not the main focus of this book. Recommended books specifically about performance and scalability include *SQL Performance Tuning [GP03]*, *High Performance MySQL, 4th Edition [BT21]*, *Efficient MySQL Performance [Nic21]*, and *Effective MySQL Optimizing SQL Statements [Bra11]*.

Every brand of SQL database product has its own tools and commands, but this book is not a command reference or a collection of recipes.

Data access frameworks and object-relational mapping libraries are helpful tools, but these aren't the focus of this book either.

Database administration and operation tasks such as server sizing, capacity planning, installation and configuration, monitoring, backups, log analysis, and security are important and deserve a book of their own.

Conventions

The following sections describe some conventions in this book.

Typography

SQL keywords are formatted in all-capitals and in a monospaced font to make them stand out from the text, as in SELECT.

SQL tables, also in a monospaced font, are spelled with a capital for the initial letter of each word in the table name, as in Accounts or BugsProducts. SQL columns, also in a monospaced font, are spelled in lowercase, and words are separated by underscores, as in account_name.

Literal strings are formatted in italics, as in *bill@example.com*.

Terminology

SQL is pronounced "ess-cue-ell," not "see-quell." Both usages are common enough that everyone will know what you mean. In this book, the former is used. You will read phrases like "*an* SQL query," not "*a* SQL query."

In this book, the plural of *index* is *indexes*. In other contexts, it may be pluralized as *indices*. Both are correct according to most dictionaries.

In SQL, the terms *query* and *statement* are somewhat interchangeable, being any complete SQL command that you can execute. In this book, for the sake of clarity, *query* refers to SELECT statements and *statement* for all others.

Online Resources

The examples and source code shown in this book are under the source code link on the Pragmatic Bookshelf website.[1] You can also report any errors or suggestions using the errata link on the same site.

If you like this book and it serves you well, I hope that you will let others know about it—your reviews really do help. Tweets and posts are a great way to help spread the word. You can find me on Twitter at @billkarwin, or you can tweet @pragprog directly.

Bill Karwin
October 2022

---

1. https://pragprog.com/book/bksap1

An expert is a person who has made all the mistakes that can be made in a very narrow field.

> Niels Bohr

## CHAPTER 1

What's an Antipattern?

An *antipattern* is a technique that is intended to solve a problem but that often leads to other problems. An antipattern is practiced widely in different ways, but with a thread of commonality. People may come up with an idea that fits an antipattern independently or with help from a colleague, a book, or an article. Many antipatterns of object-oriented software design and project management are documented at the Portland Pattern Repository,[1] as well as in the 1998 book *AntiPatterns [BMMM98]*.

SQL Antipatterns describes the most frequent missteps software developers naively make while using SQL. I have talked to them in technical support and training sessions, worked alongside them developing software, and answered their questions on internet forums. Many of these blunders I've made myself; there's no better teacher than spending many hours late at night making up for one's own errors.

Types of Antipatterns

This book has four parts for the following categories of antipatterns:

Logical Database Design Antipatterns
> Before you start coding, you should decide what information you need to keep in your database and the best way to organize and interconnect your data. This includes planning database tables, columns, and relationships.

Physical Database Design Antipatterns
> After you know what data you need to store, you implement the data management as efficiently as you can using the features of your RDBMS technology. This includes defining tables and indexes and choosing data

---

1. https://wiki.c2.com/?AntiPattern

types. You use SQL's *data definition language*—statements such as CREATE TABLE.

Query Antipatterns

You need to add data to your database and then retrieve data. SQL queries are made with *data manipulation language*—statements such as SELECT, UPDATE, and DELETE.

Application Development Antipatterns

SQL is supposed to be used in the context of applications written in another language, such as C++, Java, PHP, Python, or Ruby. There are right ways and wrong ways to employ SQL in an application, and this part of the book describes some common blunders.

There are many other antipatterns related to general software development or operations, but this book focuses on the SQL language.

In addition, you'll find *mini-antipatterns* throughout the book, between chapters. These cover other mistakes commonly made by developers using SQL. Mini-antipatterns are covered more briefly than the main antipatterns.

Many of the antipattern chapters have humorous or evocative titles. It's traditional to give both positive design patterns and antipatterns names that serve as a metaphor or mnemonic.

The appendix provides practical descriptions of some relational database theory. Many of the antipatterns this book covers are the result of misunderstanding database theory.

Anatomy of an Antipattern

Each antipattern chapter contains the following subheadings:

Objective

This is the task that you may be trying to solve. Antipatterns are used with an intention to provide that solution but end up causing more problems than they solve.

The Antipattern

This section describes the nature of the common solution and illustrates the unforeseen consequences that make it an antipattern.

How to Recognize the Antipattern

There may be certain clues that help you identify when an antipattern is being used in your project. Certain types of barriers you encounter, or quotes you may hear yourself or others saying, can tip you off to the presence of an antipattern.

Legitimate Uses of the Antipattern

Rules usually have exceptions. There may be circumstances in which an approach normally considered an antipattern is nevertheless appropriate, or at least the lesser of all evils.

Solution

This section describes the preferred solutions, which solve the original objective without running into the problems caused by the antipattern.

Entity-Relationship Diagrams

The most common way to diagram relational databases is with *entity-relationship diagrams*. Tables are shown as boxes, and relationships are shown as lines connecting the boxes, with symbols at either end of the lines describing the cardinality of the relationship. The following are examples of entity-relationship diagrams:

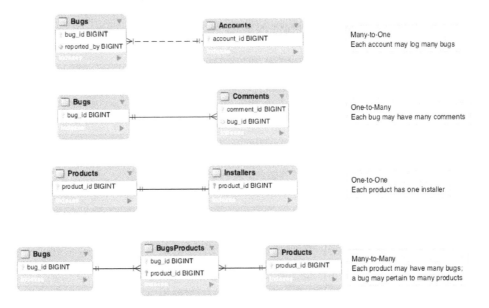

Example Database

Most of the topics in *SQL Antipatterns* are illustrated using a database for a hypothetical bug-tracking application.

The following data definition language shows the tables defined in SQL. In some cases, choices are made for the sake of examples later in the book, so they might not always be the choices one would make in a real-world application. Examples use only standard SQL so they are applicable to any brand of database, but some MySQL data types also appear, such as SERIAL and BIGINT.

```sql
Introduction/setup.sql
CREATE TABLE Accounts (
  account_id        SERIAL PRIMARY KEY,
  account_name      VARCHAR(20),
  first_name        VARCHAR(20),
  last_name         VARCHAR(20),
  email             VARCHAR(100),
  password_hash     CHAR(64),
  portrait_image    BLOB,
  hourly_rate       NUMERIC(9,2)
);

CREATE TABLE BugStatus (
  status            VARCHAR(20) PRIMARY KEY
);

CREATE TABLE Bugs (
  bug_id            SERIAL PRIMARY KEY,
  date_reported     DATE NOT NULL DEFAULT (CURDATE()),
  summary           VARCHAR(80),
  description       VARCHAR(1000),
  resolution        VARCHAR(1000),
  reported_by       BIGINT UNSIGNED NOT NULL,
  assigned_to       BIGINT UNSIGNED,
  verified_by       BIGINT UNSIGNED,
  status            VARCHAR(20) NOT NULL DEFAULT 'NEW',
  priority          VARCHAR(20),
  hours             NUMERIC(9,2),
  FOREIGN KEY (reported_by) REFERENCES Accounts(account_id),
  FOREIGN KEY (assigned_to) REFERENCES Accounts(account_id),
  FOREIGN KEY (verified_by) REFERENCES Accounts(account_id),
  FOREIGN KEY (status) REFERENCES BugStatus(status)
);

CREATE TABLE Comments (
  comment_id        SERIAL PRIMARY KEY,
  bug_id            BIGINT UNSIGNED NOT NULL,
  author            BIGINT UNSIGNED NOT NULL,
  comment_date      DATETIME NOT NULL DEFAULT CURRENT_TIMESTAMP,
  comment           TEXT NOT NULL,
  FOREIGN KEY (bug_id) REFERENCES Bugs(bug_id),
  FOREIGN KEY (author) REFERENCES Accounts(account_id)
);

CREATE TABLE Screenshots (
  bug_id            BIGINT UNSIGNED NOT NULL,
  image_id          BIGINT UNSIGNED NOT NULL,
  screenshot_image  BLOB,
```

```
  caption              VARCHAR(100),
  PRIMARY KEY        (bug_id, image_id),
  FOREIGN KEY (bug_id) REFERENCES Bugs(bug_id)
);
CREATE TABLE Tags (
  bug_id               BIGINT UNSIGNED NOT NULL,
  tag                  VARCHAR(20) NOT NULL,
  PRIMARY KEY        (bug_id, tag),
  FOREIGN KEY (bug_id) REFERENCES Bugs(bug_id)
);
CREATE TABLE Products (
  product_id           SERIAL PRIMARY KEY,
  product_name         VARCHAR(50)
);
CREATE TABLE BugsProducts(
  bug_id               BIGINT UNSIGNED NOT NULL,
  product_id           BIGINT UNSIGNED NOT NULL,
  PRIMARY KEY        (bug_id, product_id),
  FOREIGN KEY (bug_id) REFERENCES Bugs(bug_id),
  FOREIGN KEY (product_id) REFERENCES Products(product_id)
);
```

Here is the entity-relationship diagram for the example bug database:

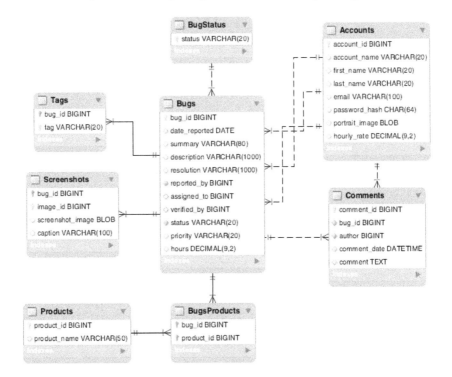

In some chapters, especially those in Logical Database Design Antipatterns, different database definitions appear, either to exhibit an antipattern or to show an alternative solution that avoids the antipattern.

This chapter has introduced antipatterns and you now know their field marks. Next we'll dive into studying each antipattern and the trouble they cause.

Part I

Logical Database Design Antipatterns

Before you start coding, you should decide what information you need to keep in your database and the best way to organize and interconnect your data. This includes planning database tables, columns, and relationships.

A Netscape engineer who shan't be named once passed a pointer to JavaScript, stored it as a string, and later passed it back to C, killing 30.

   Blake Ross

CHAPTER 2

Jaywalking

You're developing a feature in the bug-tracking application to designate a user as the primary contact for a product. Your original design allowed only one user to be the contact for each product. However, it was no surprise when you were requested to support assigning multiple users as contacts for a given product.

At the time, it seemed simple to change the database to store a list of user account identifiers separated by commas, instead of the single identifier it used before.

Soon your boss approaches you with a problem. "The engineering department has been adding associate staff to their projects. They tell me they can add five people only. If they try to add more, they get an error. What's going on?"

You nod, "Yeah, you can only list so many people on a project," as though this is completely ordinary.

Sensing that your boss needs a more precise explanation, "Well, five to ten— maybe a few more. It depends on how old each person's account is." Now your boss raises his eyebrows. You continue, "I store the account IDs for a project in a comma-separated list. The list of IDs has to fit in a string with a maximum length. If the account IDs are short, I can fit more in the list. So, people who created the earlier accounts have an ID of 99 or less, and those are shorter."

Your boss frowns. You have a feeling you're going to be staying late.

Programmers commonly use comma-separated lists to avoid creating an intersection table for a many-to-many relationship. This antipattern is called *Jaywalking*, because jaywalking is also an act of avoiding an intersection.

Objective: Store Multivalue Attributes

When a column in a table has a single value, the design is straightforward: you can choose an SQL data type to represent a single instance of that value, for example an integer, date, or string. It's not clear how you store a collection of related values in a column.

In the example bug-tracking database, you might associate a product with a contact using an integer column in the Products table. Each account may have many products, and each product references one contact, so there's a *many-to-one* relationship between products and accounts.

Jaywalking/obj/create.sql
```
CREATE TABLE Products (
  product_id    SERIAL PRIMARY KEY,
  product_name VARCHAR(1000),
  account_id    BIGINT UNSIGNED,
  -- . . .
  FOREIGN KEY (account_id) REFERENCES Accounts(account_id)
);

INSERT INTO Products (product_id, product_name, account_id)
VALUES (DEFAULT, 'Visual TurboBuilder', 12);
```

As your project matures, you realize that a product might have multiple contacts. In addition to the many-to-one relationship, you also need to support a one-to-many relationship from products to accounts. One row in the Products table must be able to have more than one contact.

Antipattern: Format Comma-Separated Lists

To minimize changes to the database structure, you decide to redefine the account_id column as a VARCHAR so you can list multiple account IDs in that column, separated by commas.

Jaywalking/anti/create.sql
```
CREATE TABLE Products (
  product_id    SERIAL PRIMARY KEY,
  product_name VARCHAR(1000),
  account_id    VARCHAR(100), -- comma-separated list
  -- . . .
);

INSERT INTO Products (product_id, product_name, account_id)
VALUES (DEFAULT, 'Visual TurboBuilder', '12,34');
```

This seems like a win, because you've created no additional tables or columns; you've changed the data type of only one column. However, let's look at the performance and data integrity problems this table design suffers from.

Querying Products for a Specific Account

Queries are difficult if all the foreign keys are combined into a single field. You can no longer use equality; instead, you have to use a test against some kind of pattern. For example, MySQL lets you write something like the following to find all the products for account 12:

```
Jaywalking/anti/regexp.sql
SELECT * FROM Products WHERE account_id REGEXP '\\b12\\b';
```

Pattern-matching expressions may return false matches. Performance is poor because the matching can't benefit from indexes. Since pattern-matching syntax is different in each database brand, your SQL code isn't vendor neutral.

Querying Accounts for a Given Product

Likewise, it's awkward and slow to join a comma-separated list to matching rows in the referenced table.

```
Jaywalking/anti/regexp.sql
SELECT * FROM Products AS p JOIN Accounts AS a
    ON p.account_id REGEXP '\\b' || a.account_id || '\\b'
WHERE p.product_id = 123;
```

Joining two tables using an expression like this one spoils any chance of using indexes, so again the performance will suffer. The query must scan through both tables, generate a cross product, and evaluate the regular expression for every combination of rows.

Making Aggregate Queries

Aggregate queries use functions like COUNT(), SUM(), and AVG(). However, these functions are designed to be used over groups of rows, not comma-separated lists. You have to resort to tricks, like calculating the length of the string of comma-separated values minus the length of that string with the commas removed. This can be used to count the elements in the list.

```
Jaywalking/anti/count.sql
SELECT product_id,
    LENGTH(account_id) - LENGTH(REPLACE(account_id, ',', '')) + 1
      AS contacts_per_product
FROM Products;
```

Tricks like this can be clever but never clear. These kinds of solutions are time consuming to develop and hard to debug. Some aggregate queries can't be accomplished with tricks at all.

Updating Accounts for a Specific Product

You can add a new ID to the end of the list with string concatenation, but this might not leave the list in sorted order.

Jaywalking/anti/update.sql
```
UPDATE Products
SET account_id = account_id || ',' || 56
WHERE product_id = 123;
```

To remove an item from the list, you have to run two SQL queries: one to fetch the old list and a second to save the updated list.

Jaywalking/anti/remove.py
```
import mysql.connector

cnx = mysql.connector.connect(user='scott', database='test')
cursor = cnx.cursor()

product_id_to_search = 2
value_to_remove = '34'

query = "SELECT product_id, account_id FROM Products WHERE product_id = %s"
cursor.execute(query, (product_id_to_search,))
for (row) in cursor:
    (product_id, account_ids) = row
    account_id_list = account_ids.split(",")
    account_id_list.remove(value_to_remove)
    account_ids = ",".join(account_id_list)
    query = "UPDATE Products SET account_id = %s WHERE product_id = %s"
    cursor.execute(query, (account_ids, product_id,))

cnx.commit()
```

That's quite a lot of code just to remove an entry from a list.

Validating Product IDs

What prevents a user from entering invalid entries like *banana*?

Jaywalking/anti/banana.sql
```
INSERT INTO Products (product_id, product_name, account_id)
VALUES (DEFAULT, 'Visual TurboBuilder', '12,34,banana');
```

Users will find a way to enter any and all variations, and your database will turn to mush. There won't necessarily be database errors, but the data will be nonsense.

Even if the values are at least integers, you can't be sure they are integers that occur in the Accounts table. The standard way to ensure this is to use a foreign key constraint, but foreign keys can only validate the whole column, not individual elements in a list.

Choosing a Separator Character

If you store a list of string values instead of integers, some list entries may contain your separator character. Using a comma as the separator between entries may become ambiguous. You can choose a different character as the separator, but you can't guarantee that this new separator will never appear in an entry.

List Length Limitations

How many list entries can you store in a VARCHAR(30) column? It depends on the length of each entry. If each entry is two characters long, then you can store ten (including the commas). If each entry is six characters, then you can store only four entries:

Jaywalking/anti/length.sql
```
UPDATE Products SET account_id = '10,14,18,22,26,30,34,38,42,46'
WHERE product_id = 123;

UPDATE Products SET account_id = '101418,222630,343842,467790'
WHERE product_id = 123;
```

How can you know that VARCHAR(30) supports the longest list you will need in the future? How long is long enough? Try explaining the reason for this length limit to your boss or to your customers.

How to Recognize the Antipattern

If you hear phrases like the following spoken by your project team, treat it as a clue that the Jaywalking antipattern is being employed:

- "What is the greatest number of entries this list must support?"

  This question comes up when you're trying to choose the maximum length of the VARCHAR column.

- "Do you know how to match a word boundary in SQL?"

  If you use regular expressions to pick out parts of a string, this could be a clue that you should store those parts separately.

- "What character will never appear in any list entry?"

  You want to use an unambiguous separator character, but you should expect that any character might someday appear in a value in the list.

Legitimate Uses of the Antipattern

You might improve performance for some kinds of queries by applying *denormalization* to your database organization. Storing lists as a comma-separated string is an example of denormalization.

Your application may need the data in a comma-separated format and have no need to access individual items in the list. Likewise, if your application receives a comma-separated format from another source and you simply need to store the full list in a database and retrieve it later in exactly the same format, there's no need to separate the values.

Be conservative if you decide to employ denormalization. Start by using a normalized database organization, because it permits your application code to be more flexible, and it allows your database to help preserve data integrity.

Some brands of SQL database products extend SQL data types with some kind of array type. PostgreSQL, Oracle, IBM DB2, and Informix each have some kind of array support. Depending on the implementation, they mitigate some of the difficulties described earlier in this chapter. For example you may specify the scalar data type of the array elements. But they won't solve all of the problems. They are complex to use, and you have to study how they work in each brand of SQL.

Solution: Create an Intersection Table

Instead of storing the account_id in the Products table, store it in a separate table, so each individual value of that attribute occupies a separate row. This new table Contacts implements a *many-to-many* relationship between Products and Accounts:

Jaywalking/soln/create.sql

```
CREATE TABLE Contacts (
  product_id  BIGINT UNSIGNED NOT NULL,
  account_id  BIGINT UNSIGNED NOT NULL,
  PRIMARY KEY (product_id, account_id),
  FOREIGN KEY (product_id) REFERENCES Products(product_id),
  FOREIGN KEY (account_id) REFERENCES Accounts(account_id)
);

INSERT INTO Contacts (product_id, account_id)
VALUES (123, 12), (123, 34), (345, 23), (567, 12), (567, 34);
```

When the table has foreign keys referencing two tables, it's called an *intersection table*. Some people use a join table, a many-to-many table, a mapping table, or other terms to describe this table. The name doesn't matter; the concept is the same. This implements a *many-to-many* relationship between the two referenced tables. That is, each product may be associated through the intersection table to multiple accounts, and likewise each account may be associated to multiple products. Here's a diagram of the entity relationship:

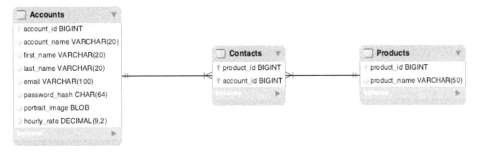

An intersection table resolves all the problems in the "Antipattern" section.

Querying Products by Account and the Other Way Around

To query the attributes of all products for a given account, it's more straightforward to join the Products table with the Contacts table:

```
Jaywalking/soln/join.sql
SELECT p.*
FROM   Products AS p JOIN Contacts AS c ON (p.product_id = c.product_id)
WHERE c.account_id = 34;
```

Some people resist queries that contain a join, thinking that they perform poorly. However, this query uses indexes much better than the solution shown earlier in the "Antipattern" section.

Querying account details is likewise easy to read and easy to optimize. It uses indexes for the join efficiently, instead of an esoteric use of regular expressions:

```
Jaywalking/soln/join.sql
SELECT a.*
FROM   Accounts AS a JOIN Contacts AS c ON (a.account_id = c.account_id)
WHERE c.product_id = 123;
```

Making Aggregate Queries

The following example returns the number of accounts per product:

```
Jaywalking/soln/group.sql
SELECT product_id, COUNT(*) AS accounts_per_product
FROM Contacts
GROUP BY product_id;
```

The number of products per account is just as simple:

```
Jaywalking/soln/group.sql
SELECT account_id, COUNT(*) AS products_per_account
FROM Contacts
GROUP BY account_id;
```

Other more sophisticated reports are possible too, such as the product with the greatest number of accounts:

```
Jaywalking/soln/group.sql
SELECT product_id, COUNT(*) AS accounts_per_product
FROM Contacts
GROUP BY product_id
ORDER BY accounts_per_product DESC
LIMIT 1;
```

Updating Contacts for a Specific Product

You can add or remove entries in the list by inserting or deleting rows in the intersection table. Each product reference is stored in a separate row in the Contacts table, so you can add or remove them one at a time.

```
Jaywalking/soln/remove.sql
INSERT INTO Contacts (product_id, account_id) VALUES (456, 34);

DELETE FROM Contacts WHERE product_id = 456 AND account_id = 34;
```

Validating Product IDs

You can use a foreign key to validate the entries against a set of legitimate values in another table. You declare that Contacts.account_id references Accounts.account_id, and so you rely on the database to enforce referential integrity. Now you can be sure that the intersection table contains only account IDs that exist.

You can also use SQL data types to restrict entries. For example, if the entries in the list should be valid INTEGER or DATE values and you declare the column using those data types, you can be sure all entries are legal values of that type (not nonsense entries like *banana*).

Choosing a Separator Character

You use no separator character, since you store each entry on a separate row. There's no ambiguity if the entries contain commas or other characters you might have used as a separator.

List Length Limitations

Since each entry is in a separate row in the intersection table, the list is limited only by the number of rows that can physically exist in one table. If it's appropriate to limit the number of entries, you should enforce the policy in your application using the count of entries rather than the collective length of the list.

Other Advantages of the Intersection Table

An index on Contacts.account_id makes performance better than matching a substring in a comma-separated list. Declaring a foreign key on a column implicitly creates an index on that column in many database brands (but check your documentation).

You can also create additional attributes for each entry by adding columns to the intersection table. For example, you could record the date a contact was added for a given product or an attribute noting who is the primary contact vs. the secondary contacts. You can't do this in a comma-separated list.

> Store each value in its own column and row.

Mini-Antipattern: Splitting CSV Into Rows

Assuming you're stuck using data formatted in comma-separated strings, like in the Jaywalking antipattern, another challenge you're likely to face eventually is expanding that comma-separated string of values into multiple rows, as if it had been stored with one value per row to begin with. You might not be at liberty to change the way the data is stored, because a lot of existing code depends on the current format, but you still need to change the display of the data, at least for the result of a specific query.

For example, you may need the query to list the accounts one per row, so that the result of the query can be passed to some other software, such as a spreadsheet. For whatever reason, you need a solution in SQL to split the string, but you can't count on SQL to have a convenient function to do that.

Some brands of SQL do have a function to do this. PostgreSQL has a non-standard function string_to_array() that converts the comma-separated string into an array type. Then the array can be the input to the unnest() function which expands an array into multiple rows:

Jaywalking/mini/unnest.sql
```
SELECT a FROM Products
CROSS JOIN unnest(string_to_array(account_id, ',')) AS a;
```

Microsoft SQL Server 2016 has its own non-standard operations too:

Jaywalking/mini/cross-apply.sql
```
SELECT product_id, product_name, value
FROM Products CROSS APPLY STRING_SPLIT(account_id, ',');
```

Another solution is to join the comma-separated list with a predefined set of integers, one integer per row. For each of the resulting joined rows, use a substring expression to extract the *Nth* element from the comma-separated list, as shown in the following example:

Jaywalking/mini/int-table.sql
```
SELECT p.product_id, p.product_name,
  SUBSTRING_INDEX(SUBSTRING_INDEX(p.account_id, ',', n.n), ',', -1)
  AS account_id
FROM Products AS p
JOIN Numbers AS n
 ON n.n <= LENGTH(p.account_id) - LENGTH(REPLACE(p.account_id, ',', ''));
```

This query is harder to understand. You need a table, Numbers, that has a column n populated with integers from 1 on up. Then join the table of numbers to Products so there are as many rows as needed to equal the number of comma-separated items. Calculate the number of commas by the difference between the length of the string and the length of the string without the commas. Finally, in the select-list, use MySQL's SUBSTRING_INDEX() function to extract substrings up to the nth item, and then use the function again with a -1 argument to keep only the last item in the list.

You don't always have a table with a series of integers handy. You might need to generate that series dynamically. You can do that with UNION:

Jaywalking/mini/int-union.sql
```
SELECT p.product_id, p.product_name,
  SUBSTRING_INDEX(SUBSTRING_INDEX(p.account_id, ',', n.n), ',', -1)
  AS account_id
FROM Products AS p
JOIN (
  SELECT 1 AS n UNION SELECT 2 UNION SELECT 3 UNION SELECT 4 -- and so on
) AS n
 ON n.n <= LENGTH(p.account_id) - LENGTH(REPLACE(p.account_id, ',', ''));
```

Finally, you could use a recursive solution to return each item from the list one by one:

Jaywalking/mini/recursive.sql
```
WITH RECURSIVE cte AS (
  SELECT product_id, product_name,
    SUBSTRING_INDEX(account_id, ',', 1) AS account_id,
    SUBSTRING(account_id, LENGTH(SUBSTRING_INDEX(account_id, ',', 1))+2)
    AS remainder
  FROM Products
```

```
  UNION ALL
  SELECT product_id, product_name, SUBSTRING_INDEX(remainder, ',', 1),
    SUBSTRING(remainder, LENGTH(SUBSTRING_INDEX(remainder, ',', 1))+2)
  FROM cte
  WHERE LENGTH(remainder) > 0
)
SELECT product_id, product_name, account_id FROM cte;
```

This task seems like it's harder than it should be. Some of these solutions only work in certain brands or certain verions of SQL databases. The best solution, which works in any database, is to store data the way you need to use it, instead of making the mistake of the Jaywalking antipattern.

If I had five minutes to chop down a tree, I'd spend the first three
sharpening my axe.

> Anonymous

## CHAPTER 3

Naive Trees

Suppose you work as a software developer for a famous website for science and technology news.

This is a modern website, so readers can contribute comments and even reply to each other, forming threads of discussion that branch and extend deeply. You choose a simple solution to track these reply chains: each comment references the comment to which it replies.

Trees/intro/parent.sql
```sql
CREATE TABLE Comments (
  comment_id    SERIAL PRIMARY KEY,
  parent_id     BIGINT UNSIGNED,
  comment       TEXT NOT NULL,
  FOREIGN KEY (parent_id) REFERENCES Comments(comment_id)
);
```

It soon becomes clear, however, that it's hard to retrieve a long chain of replies in a single SQL query. You can get only the immediate children or perhaps join with the grandchildren, to a fixed depth. If the threads can have an *unlimited* depth, you would need to run many SQL queries to get all the comments in a given thread.

The other idea you have is to retrieve *all* the comments and assemble them into tree data structures in application memory, using traditional tree algorithms you learned in school. Unfortunately, the publishers of the website have told you that they publish dozens of articles every day, and each article can have hundreds of comments. Sorting through millions of comments every time someone views the website is impractical.

There must be a better way to store the threads of comments so you can retrieve a whole discussion thread simply and efficiently.

Objective: Store and Query Hierarchies

It's common for data to have recursive relationships. Data may be organized in a treelike or hierarchical way. In a tree data structure, each entry is called a *node*. A node may have a number of children and one parent. The top node, which has no parent, is called the *root*. The nodes at the bottom, which have no children, are called *leaves*. The nodes in the middle are simply *nonleaf nodes*.

In the previous hierarchical data, you may need to query individual items, related subsets of the collection, or the whole collection. Examples of tree-oriented data structures include the following:

Organization chart: The relationship of employees to managers is the textbook example of tree-structured data. It appears in countless books and articles on SQL. In an organizational chart, each employee has a manager, who represents the employee's *parent* in a tree structure. The manager is also an employee.

Threaded discussion: As seen earlier in this chapter, a tree structure may be used for the chain of comments in reply to other comments. In the tree, the children of a comment node are its replies.

This chapter uses the threaded discussion example to show the antipattern and its solutions.

Antipattern: Always Depend on One's Parent

The naive solution commonly shown in books and articles is to add a column parent_id. This column references another comment in the same table, and you can create a foreign key constraint to enforce this relationship.

```
Trees/anti/adjacency-list.sql
CREATE TABLE Comments (
  comment_id    SERIAL PRIMARY KEY,
  bug_id        BIGINT UNSIGNED NOT NULL,
  author        BIGINT UNSIGNED NOT NULL,
  comment_date  DATETIME NOT NULL DEFAULT CURRENT_TIMESTAMP,
  comment       TEXT NOT NULL,
  parent_id     BIGINT UNSIGNED,
  FOREIGN KEY (parent_id) REFERENCES Comments(comment_id),
  FOREIGN KEY (bug_id) REFERENCES Bugs(bug_id),
  FOREIGN KEY (author) REFERENCES Accounts(account_id)
);
```

This design is called *Adjacency List*. The entity-relationship diagram for this kind of table is shown on page 23.

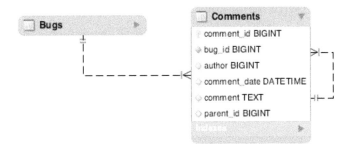

This is the most common design software developers use to store hierarchical data. The following figure illustrates this tree-structured data.

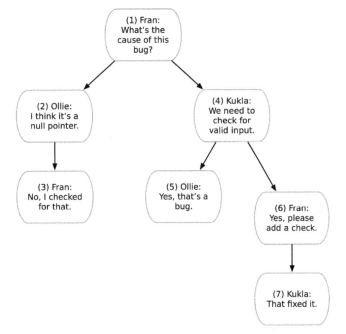

And here's the same data in a tabular format.

comment_id	parent_id	author	comment
1	NULL	Fran	What's the cause of this bug?
2	1	Ollie	I think it's a null pointer.
3	2	Fran	No, I checked for that.
4	1	Kukla	We need to check for invalid input.
5	4	Ollie	Yes, that's a bug.
6	4	Fran	Yes, please add a check.
7	6	Kukla	That fixed it.

Querying a Tree with Adjacency List

Adjacency List is a proper way to store the reference from child node to parent node, but developers often use the wrong approach when they have to do a most common task: query all descendants.

You can retrieve a comment and its immediate children using a relatively simple query:

Trees/anti/parent.sql
```
SELECT c1.*, c2.*
FROM Comments c1 LEFT OUTER JOIN Comments c2
  ON c2.parent_id = c1.comment_id;
```

This returns only two levels of the tree. One characteristic of a tree is that it can extend to any depth, so you need to be able to query the descendents without regard to the number of levels. For example, you may need to compute the COUNT() of comments in the thread or the SUM() of the cost of parts in a mechanical assembly.

This kind of query is awkward when you use Adjacency List, because each level of the tree corresponds to another join, and the number of joins in an SQL query must be fixed. The following query retrieves a tree of depth up to four but cannot retrieve the tree beyond that depth:

Trees/anti/ancestors.sql
```
SELECT c1.*, c2.*, c3.*, c4.*
FROM Comments c1                        -- 1st level
  LEFT OUTER JOIN Comments c2
    ON c2.parent_id = c1.comment_id  -- 2nd level
  LEFT OUTER JOIN Comments c3
    ON c3.parent_id = c2.comment_id  -- 3rd level
  LEFT OUTER JOIN Comments c4
    ON c4.parent_id = c3.comment_id; -- 4th level
```

This query is also awkward because it includes descendants from progressively deeper levels by adding more columns. This makes it hard to compute an aggregate such as COUNT().

Another way to query a tree structure from Adjacency List is to retrieve all the rows in the collection, without trying to use SQL to fetch a subset of rows like ancestors or descendants.

Trees/anti/all-comments.sql
```
SELECT * FROM Comments WHERE bug_id = 1234;
```

You would be responsible for writing code in your client application to fetch these rows and build a tree data structure incrementally. This means you would fetch more rows than required for the subtree you need. Your code would discard any rows that are not part of that subtree.

Copying a large query result set from the database to the application before you can analyze it is wasteful of network and computing resources. For example, your application might need only a subtree, so your query probably returns a lot more rows than you need. You might require only aggregate information about the data, such as the COUNT() of comments.

Maintaining a Tree with Adjacency List

Admittedly, some operations are simple to accomplish with Adjacency List, such as adding a new leaf node:

Trees/anti/insert.sql
```
INSERT INTO Comments (bug_id, parent_id, author, comment)
  VALUES (1234, 7, 12 /* Kukla */, 'Thanks!');
```

Relocating a single node or a subtree is also easy:

Trees/anti/update.sql
```
UPDATE Comments SET parent_id = 3 WHERE comment_id = 6;
```

Deleting a node from a tree is more complex. If you want to delete an entire subtree, you have to issue multiple queries to find all descendants. Then remove the descendants from the lowest level up to satisfy the foreign key integrity.

Trees/anti/delete-subtree.sql
```
SELECT comment_id FROM Comments WHERE parent_id = 4; -- returns 5 and 6
SELECT comment_id FROM Comments WHERE parent_id = 5; -- returns none
SELECT comment_id FROM Comments WHERE parent_id = 6; -- returns 7
SELECT comment_id FROM Comments WHERE parent_id = 7; -- returns none

DELETE FROM Comments WHERE comment_id IN ( 7 );
DELETE FROM Comments WHERE comment_id IN ( 5, 6 );
DELETE FROM Comments WHERE comment_id = 4;
```

You can use a foreign key with the ON DELETE CASCADE modifier to automate this, as long as you know you always want to delete the descendants instead of promoting or relocating them.

If you instead want to delete a nonleaf node and promote its children or move them to another place in the tree, you first need to change the parent_id of children and then delete the desired node.

Trees/anti/delete-non-leaf.sql
```
SELECT parent_id FROM Comments WHERE comment_id = 6; -- returns 4
UPDATE Comments SET parent_id = 4 WHERE parent_id = 6;
DELETE FROM Comments WHERE comment_id = 6;
```

These are examples of operations that require multiple steps when you use the Adjacency List design. That's a lot of code you have to write for tasks that a database should make simpler and more efficient.

How to Recognize the Antipattern

If you hear a question or a statement like the following, it's a clue that the Naive Trees antipattern is being employed:

- "How many levels do we need to support in trees?"

  You're struggling to get all descendants or all ancestors of a node, without using a recursive query. You could compromise by supporting only trees of a limited depth, but the next natural question is, how deep is deep enough?

- "I dread having to touch the code that manages the tree data structures."

  You've adopted one of the more sophisticated solutions of managing hierarchies, but you're using the wrong one. Each technique makes some tasks easier, but usually at the cost of other tasks that become harder. You may have chosen a solution that isn't the best for the way you need to use hierarchies in your application.

- "I need to run a script periodically to clean up the orphaned rows in the trees."

  Your application creates disconnected nodes in the tree as it deletes nonleaf nodes. When you store complex data structures in a database, you need to keep the structure in a consistent, valid state after any change. You can use one of the solutions presented later in this chapter, along with triggers and cascading foreign key constraints, to store data structures that are resilient instead of fragile.

Legitimate Uses of the Antipattern

Even if you still use a version of SQL database that doesn't support recursive queries, the Adjacency List design might be just fine to support your application. If you only need to support trees of limited depth, and do not need to query all descendants, then Adjacency List can work well for you.

Don't Over-Engineer
I wrote an inventory-tracking application for a computer data center. Some equipment was installed inside computers; for example, a caching disk controller was installed in a rackmount server, and extra memory modules were installed on the disk controller.

I needed an SQL solution to track the usage of hierarchical collections easily. I also needed to track each individual piece of equipment to produce accounting reports of equipment utilization, amortization, and return on investment.

The manager said the collections could have subcollections, and thus the tree could in theory descend to any depth. It took quite a few weeks to perfect the code for manipulating trees in the database storage, user interface, administration, and reporting.

In practice, however, the inventory application never needed to create a grouping of equipment with a tree deeper than a single parent-child relationship. If my client had acknowledged that this would be enough to model his inventory requirements, we could have saved a lot of work.

Solution: Use Alternative Tree Models

You can use any one of the following solutions to work with hierarchical data in SQL. Each has strengths and weaknesses, and any of them might be the right choice for a given application.

Recursive Queries

Some brands of RDBMS implement SQL syntax features to support hierarchies stored in the Adjacency List format. The SQL-99 standard defines recursive query syntax using the WITH keyword followed by a recursive *common table expression*.

Trees/soln/cte.sql
```
WITH RECURSIVE CommentTree
    (comment_id, bug_id, parent_id, author, comment_date, comment, depth)
AS (
    SELECT comment_id, bug_id, parent_id, author, comment_date,
      comment, 0 AS depth
    FROM Comments
    WHERE parent_id IS NULL
  UNION ALL
    SELECT c.comment_id, c.bug_id, c.parent_id, c.author, c.comment_date,
      c.comment, ct.depth+1 AS depth
    FROM CommentTree ct
    JOIN Comments c ON (c.parent_id = ct.comment_id)
)
SELECT * FROM CommentTree WHERE bug_id = 1234;
```

Here is a list of the most popular SQL database brands that support recursive queries, and the version in which they introduced this feature:

- Oracle 11g
- MySQL 8.0
- Microsoft SQL Server 2005
- PostgresSQL 8.4

- IBM DB2 UDB 8
- SQLite 3.8.3

Oracle 9i and 10g support the WITH clause, but not for recursive queries. Instead, those versions offered proprietary syntax: START WITH and CONNECT BY PRIOR. You can use this syntax to perform recursive queries:

Trees/legit/connect-by.sql
```
SELECT * FROM Comments
START WITH comment_id = 9876
CONNECT BY PRIOR parent_id = comment_id;
```

There are several alternatives to the Adjacency List model of storing hierarchical data, including *Path Enumeration*, *Nested Sets*, and *Closure Table*. The following three sections show examples using these designs to solve the scenario in the "Antipattern" section, storing and querying a tree-like collection of comments.

These solutions take some getting used to. They may seem more complex than Adjacency List at first, but they make some tree operations easier that were very difficult or inefficient using the Adjacency List design. If your application needs to perform those operations, and using recursive queries with common table expressions seems too complex, then these designs are a better choice than the Adjacency List.

Path Enumeration

One weakness of Adjacency List is that it's expensive to retrieve ancestors of a given node in the tree. In Path Enumeration, this is solved by storing the string of ancestors as an attribute of each node.

You can see a form of Path Enumeration in directory hierarchies. A UNIX path like /usr/local/lib/ is a Path Enumeration of the filesystem, where usr is the parent of local, which in turn is the parent of lib.

In the Comments table, instead of the parent_id column, define a column called path as a long VARCHAR. The string stored in this column is the sequence of ancestors of the current row in order from the top of the tree down, just like a UNIX path. You can even choose / as a separator character.

Trees/soln/path-enum/create-table.sql
```
CREATE TABLE Comments (
  comment_id    SERIAL PRIMARY KEY,
  path          VARCHAR(1000),
  bug_id        BIGINT UNSIGNED NOT NULL,
  author        BIGINT UNSIGNED NOT NULL,
  comment_date  DATETIME NOT NULL DEFAULT CURRENT_TIMESTAMP,
  comment       TEXT NOT NULL,
```

```
  FOREIGN KEY (bug_id) REFERENCES Bugs(bug_id),
  FOREIGN KEY (author) REFERENCES Accounts(account_id)
);
```

comment_id	path	author	comment
1	1/	Fran	What's the cause of this bug?
2	1/2/	Ollie	I think it's a null pointer.
3	1/2/3/	Fran	No, I checked for that.
4	1/4/	Kukla	We need to check for invalid input.
5	1/4/5/	Ollie	Yes, that's a bug.
6	1/4/6/	Fran	Yes, please add a check.
7	1/4/6/7/	Kukla	That fixed it.

You can query ancestors by comparing the current row's path to a pattern formed from the path of another row. For example, to find ancestors of comment #7, whose path is *1/4/6/7/*, do this:

Trees/soln/path-enum/ancestors.sql
```
SELECT *
FROM Comments AS c
WHERE '1/4/6/7/' LIKE CONCAT(c.path, '%');
```

This matches the patterns formed from paths of ancestors *1/4/6/%*, *1/4/%*, and *1/%*.

You can query descendants by reversing the arguments of the LIKE predicate. To find the descendants of comment #4 whose path is *1/4/*, use this:

Trees/soln/path-enum/descendants.sql
```
SELECT *
FROM Comments AS c
WHERE c.path LIKE '1/4/%';
```

The pattern *1/4/%* matches the paths of descendants *1/4/5/*, and *1/4/6/*, and *1/4/6/7/*.

Once you can easily select a subset of the tree or the chain of ancestors to the top of the tree, you can perform many other queries easily, such as computing the SUM() of costs of nodes in a subtree or simply counting the number of nodes. For example, to count the comments per author in the subtree starting at comment #4, do this:

Trees/soln/path-enum/count.sql
```
SELECT c.author, COUNT(*)
FROM Comments AS c
WHERE c.path LIKE '1/4/%'
GROUP BY c.author;
```

Inserting a node is similar to inserting in the Adjacency List model. You can insert a leaf node without needing to modify any other row. Copy the path from the new node's parent, and append the ID of the new node to this string. If your primary key generates its value automatically during the insert, you may need to insert the row and then update the path once you know the ID value for the new row. For example, if you use MySQL, the built-in function LAST_INSERT_ID() returns the most recent ID value generated for an inserted row in the current session. Get the rest of the path from the parent of your new node.

Trees/soln/path-enum/insert.sql
```
INSERT INTO Comments (bug_id, author, comment)
VALUES (1234, 56 /* Ollie */, 'Good job!');

UPDATE Comments AS c
CROSS JOIN Comments AS c7 ON c7.comment_id = 7
  SET c.path = CONCAT(c7.path, LAST_INSERT_ID(), '/')
WHERE c.comment_id = LAST_INSERT_ID();
```

Path Enumeration has some drawbacks similar to those shown in Chapter 2, Jaywalking, on page 9. The database can't enforce that the path is formed correctly or that values in the path correspond to existing nodes. Maintaining the path string depends on application code, and verifying it is costly. No matter how long you make the VARCHAR column, it still has a length limit, so it doesn't strictly support trees of unlimited depth.

Path Enumeration allows you to sort a set of rows easily by their hierarchy, as long as the elements between the separator are of consistent length. On the other hand, this may smell too much like the Jaywalking antipattern, because it is a string of character-separated id values.

Nested Sets

The Nested Sets solution stores information with each node that pertains to the set of its descendants, rather than the node's immediate parent. This information can be represented by encoding each node in the tree with two numbers, which you can call nsleft and nsright.

Trees/soln/nested-sets/create-table.sql
```
DROP TABLE IF EXISTS Comments;

CREATE TABLE Comments (
  comment_id   SERIAL PRIMARY KEY,
  nsleft       INTEGER NOT NULL,
  nsright      INTEGER NOT NULL,
  bug_id       BIGINT UNSIGNED NOT NULL,
  author       BIGINT UNSIGNED NOT NULL,
  comment_date DATETIME NOT NULL DEFAULT CURRENT_TIMESTAMP,
  comment      TEXT NOT NULL,
```

```
    FOREIGN KEY (bug_id) REFERENCES Bugs (bug_id),
    FOREIGN KEY (author) REFERENCES Accounts(account_id)
);
```

Each node is given nsleft and nsright numbers in the following way: the nsleft number is less than the numbers of all the node's children, whereas the nsright number is greater than the numbers of all the node's children. These numbers have no relationship to the comment_id values.

An easy way to calculate these values is by visiting all the nodes of the tree in a depth-first traversal. As you descend down the left side of each branch, assign numbers incrementally to nsleft. As you ascend back up the right side of the branch, assign numbers to nsright. Do the same on each of the branches, from left to right. It may be easier to visualize the pattern in the following figure:

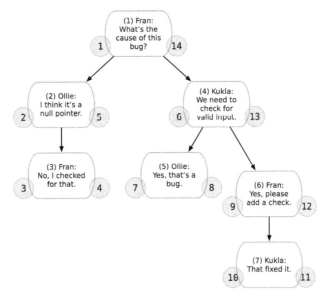

In the table, each comment is stored on a row that has an nsleft column and an nsright column. The values were set in the order of the depth-first traversal.

comment_id	nsleft	nsright	author	comment
1	1	14	Fran	What's the cause of this bug?
2	2	5	Ollie	I think it's a null pointer.
3	3	4	Fran	No, I checked for that.
4	6	13	Kukla	We need to check for invalid input.
5	7	8	Ollie	Yes, that's a bug.
6	9	12	Fran	Yes, please add a check.
7	10	11	Kukla	That fixed it.

Once you have assigned each node with these numbers, you can use them to find ancestors and descendants of any given node. For example, you can retrieve comment #4 and its descendants by searching for nodes whose numbers are between the current node's nsleft and nsright.

Trees/soln/nested-sets/descendants.sql
```sql
SELECT c2.*
FROM Comments AS c1
  JOIN Comments as c2
    ON c2.nsleft BETWEEN c1.nsleft AND c1.nsright
WHERE c1.comment_id = 4;
```

You can retrieve comment #6 and its ancestors by searching for nodes whose numbers span the current node's numbers. For example:

Trees/soln/nested-sets/ancestors.sql
```sql
SELECT c2.*
FROM Comments AS c1
  JOIN Comments AS c2
    ON c1.nsleft BETWEEN c2.nsleft AND c2.nsright
WHERE c1.comment_id = 6;
```

One chief strength of the Nested Sets design is that when you delete a nonleaf node, its descendants are automatically considered direct children of the deleted node's parents. Although the right and left numbers of each node shown in the illustration have values forming a continuous series and the difference is always 1 compared to adjacent siblings and parents, this is not necessary for the Nested Sets design to preserve the hierarchy. So when gaps in the values result from deleting a node, there is no interruption to the tree structure.

For example, you can count the depth of a given node and delete its parent, and then when you count the depth of the node again, it seems to have decreased depth by one level.

Trees/soln/nested-sets/depth.sql
```sql
-- Reports depth = 4
SELECT c1.comment_id, COUNT(c2.comment_id) AS depth
FROM Comments AS c1
  JOIN Comments AS c2
    ON c1.nsleft BETWEEN c2.nsleft AND c2.nsright
WHERE c1.comment_id = 7
GROUP BY c1.comment_id;

DELETE FROM Comments WHERE comment_id = 6;
```

```
-- Reports depth = 3
SELECT c1.comment_id, COUNT(c2.comment_id) AS depth
FROM Comments AS c1
  JOIN Comments AS c2
    ON c1.nsleft BETWEEN c2.nsleft AND c2.nsright
WHERE c1.comment_id = 7
GROUP BY c1.comment_id;
```

Some queries that are simple in the Adjacency List design, such as retrieving the immediate child or immediate parent, are more complex in the Nested Sets design. The direct parent of a given node c1 is an ancestor of that node, but no other node can exist in between them. So, you can use an additional outer join to search for a node that is both an ancestor of c1 and a descendant of the parent. Only if no such node is found (that is, the result of the outer join is null) is the ancestor truly the direct parent of c1.

For example, to find the immediate parent of comment #6, do this:

Trees/soln/nested-sets/parent.sql
```
SELECT c2.*
FROM Comments AS c1
  JOIN Comments AS c2
    ON c1.nsleft > c2.nsleft AND c1.nsleft < c2.nsright
  LEFT JOIN Comments AS c3
    ON c1.nsleft > c3.nsleft AND c1.nsleft < c3.nsright
    AND c3.nsleft > c2.nsleft AND c3.nsleft < c2.nsright
WHERE c1.comment_id = 6
  AND c3.comment_id IS NULL;
```

Manipulations of the tree, inserting and moving nodes, are generally more complex in the Nested Sets design than they are in other models. When you insert a new node, you need to recalculate all the left and right values greater than the left value of the new node.

This includes the new node's right siblings, its ancestors, and the right siblings of its ancestors. It also includes descendants, if the new node is inserted as a nonleaf node. Assuming the new node is a leaf node, the following statement should update everything necessary:

Trees/soln/nested-sets/insert.sql
```
-- make space for NS values 8 and 9
UPDATE Comments
  SET nsleft = CASE WHEN nsleft >= 8 THEN nsleft+2 ELSE nsleft END,
      nsright = nsright+2
WHERE nsright >= 7;

-- create new child of comment #5, occupying NS values 8 and 9
INSERT INTO Comments (nsleft, nsright, bug_id, author, comment)
  VALUES (8, 9, 1234, 34 /* Fran */, 'Me too!');
```

The Nested Sets model is best when it's more important to perform queries for subtrees quickly and easily, rather than operations on individual nodes. Inserting and moving nodes is complex, because of the requirement to renumber the left and right values. If your usage of the tree involves frequent insertions, Nested Sets isn't the best choice.

Closure Table

The Closure Table solution is a simple and elegant way of storing hierarchies. It involves storing all paths through the tree, not just those with a direct parent-child relationship.

In addition to a plain Comments table, create another table TreePaths, with two columns, each of which is a foreign key to the Comments table.

```
Trees/soln/closure-table/create-table.sql
CREATE TABLE Comments (
  comment_id    SERIAL PRIMARY KEY,
  bug_id        BIGINT UNSIGNED NOT NULL,
  author        BIGINT UNSIGNED NOT NULL,
  comment_date DATETIME NOT NULL DEFAULT CURRENT_TIMESTAMP,
  comment       TEXT NOT NULL,
  FOREIGN KEY (bug_id) REFERENCES Bugs(bug_id),
  FOREIGN KEY (author) REFERENCES Accounts(account_id)
);

CREATE TABLE TreePaths (
  ancestor     BIGINT UNSIGNED NOT NULL,
  descendant BIGINT UNSIGNED NOT NULL,
  PRIMARY KEY(ancestor, descendant),
  FOREIGN KEY (ancestor) REFERENCES Comments(comment_id),
  FOREIGN KEY (descendant) REFERENCES Comments(comment_id)
);
```

Instead of using the Comments table to store information about the tree structure, use the TreePaths table:

ancestor	descendant	ancestor	descendant	ancestor	descendant
1	1	1	7	4	6
1	2	2	2	4	7
1	3	2	3	5	5
1	4	3	3	6	6
1	5	4	4	6	7
1	6	4	5	7	7

Store one row in this table for each pair of nodes in the tree that shares an ancestor/descendant relationship, even if they are separated by multiple levels in the tree. Also add a row for each node to reference itself. See the following illustration of the tree.

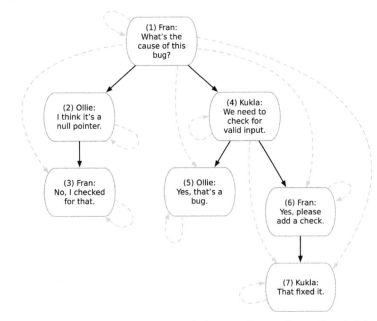

The queries to retrieve ancestors and descendants from this table are even more straightforward than those in the Nested Sets solution. To retrieve descendants of comment #4, match rows in TreePaths where the ancestor is 4:

Trees/soln/closure-table/descendants.sql
```
SELECT c.*
FROM Comments AS c
  JOIN TreePaths AS t ON c.comment_id = t.descendant
WHERE t.ancestor = 4;
```

To retrieve ancestors of comment #6, match rows in TreePaths where the descendant is 6:

Trees/soln/closure-table/ancestors.sql
```
SELECT c.*
FROM Comments AS c
  JOIN TreePaths AS t ON c.comment_id = t.ancestor
WHERE t.descendant = 6;
```

To insert a new leaf node, for instance a new child of comment #5, first insert the self-referencing row. Then add a copy of the set of rows in TreePaths that reference comment #5 as a descendant (including the row in which comment #5 references itself), replacing the descendant with the number of the new comment:

Trees/soln/closure-table/insert.sql

```
INSERT INTO TreePaths (ancestor, descendant)
  SELECT t.ancestor, 8
  FROM TreePaths AS t
  WHERE t.descendant = 5
 UNION ALL
  SELECT 8, 8;
```

To delete a leaf node, for instance comment #7, delete all rows in TreePaths that reference comment #7 as a descendant:

Trees/soln/closure-table/delete-leaf.sql

```
DELETE FROM TreePaths WHERE descendant = 7;
```

To delete a complete subtree, for instance comment #4 and its descendants, delete all rows in TreePaths that reference comment #4 as a descendant, as well as all rows that reference any of comment #4's descendants as descendants:

Trees/soln/closure-table/delete-subtree.sql

```
DELETE t1 FROM TreePaths AS t1
JOIN TreePaths AS t2 ON t1.descendant = t2.descendant
WHERE t2.ancestor = 4;
```

Notice that if you delete rows in TreePaths, this doesn't delete the comments themselves. This seems odd for this example of Comments, but it makes more sense if you're working with other kinds of trees, for instance categories in a product catalog or employees in an org chart. You don't necessarily want to delete a node when you change its relationship to other nodes. When you store paths in a separate table, it helps make this more flexible.

To move a subtree from one location in the tree to another, first disconnect the subtree from its ancestors by deleting rows that reference the ancestors of the top node in the subtree and the descendants of that node. For instance, to move comment #6 from its position as a child of comment #4 to a child of comment #3, start with the following deletion. Make sure not to delete comment #6's self-reference.

Trees/soln/closure-table/move-subtree.sql

```
DELETE t1 FROM TreePaths AS t1
JOIN TreePaths AS t2 ON t1.descendant = t2.descendant
JOIN TreePaths AS t3 ON t1.ancestor = t3.ancestor
WHERE t2.ancestor = 6 AND t3.descendant = 6
  AND t3.ancestor != t3.descendant;
```

By selecting ancestors of #6, but not #6 itself, and descendants of #6, including #6, this correctly removes all the paths from #6's ancestors to #6 and its descendants. In other words, this deletes the paths (1, 6), (1,7), (4, 6), and (4, 7). It does not delete (6, 6) or (6, 7).

Then add the orphaned subtree by inserting rows matching the ancestors of the new location and the descendants of the subtree. You can use the CROSS JOIN syntax to create a Cartesian product, generating the rows needed to match ancestors of the new location to all the nodes in the subtree you need to move.

Trees/soln/closure-table/move-subtree.sql

```
INSERT INTO TreePaths (ancestor, descendant)
  SELECT supertree.ancestor, subtree.descendant
  FROM TreePaths AS supertree
    CROSS JOIN TreePaths AS subtree
  WHERE supertree.descendant = 3
    AND subtree.ancestor = 6;
```

This creates new paths using the ancestors of #3, including #3, and the descendants of #6, including #6. So, the new paths are (1, 6), (2, 6), (3, 6), (1, 7), (2, 7), (3, 7). The result is that the subtree starting with comment #6 is relocated as a child of comment #3. The cross join creates all the needed paths, even if the subtree is moved to a higher or lower level in the tree.

The Closure Table design is more straightforward than the Nested Sets design. Both have quick and easy methods for querying ancestors and descendants, but the Closure Table is easier to maintain the hierarchy information. In both designs, it's more convenient to query immediate child or parent nodes than in the Adjacency List or Path Enumeration designs.

You can improve the Closure Table to make queries for immediate parent or child nodes easier. Add a TreePaths.path_length attribute to the Closure Table design. The path_length of a node's self-reference is zero, the path_length of its immediate child is 1, the path_length of its grandchild is 2, and so on. Finding the children of comment #4 is now straightforward:

Trees/soln/closure-table/child.sql

```
SELECT *
FROM TreePaths
WHERE ancestor = 4 AND path_length = 1;
```

Which Design Should You Use?

Each of the designs has its own strengths and weaknesses. Choose the design depending on which operations you need to be most efficient.

In the table shown on page 38, some operations are marked as easy or hard with each respective tree design.

Design	Tables	Query Child	Query Tree	Insert	Delete	Ref. Integ.
Adjacency List	1	Easy	Hard	Easy	Easy	Yes
Recursive Query	1	Easy	Easy	Easy	Easy	Yes
Path Enumeration	1	Easy	Easy	Easy	Easy	No
Nested Sets	1	Hard	Easy	Hard	Hard	No
Closure Table	2	Easy	Easy	Easy	Easy	Yes

You can also consider the following strengths and weaknesses of each design:

- *Adjacency List* is the most conventional design, and many software developers recognize it. It has the advantage over the other designs that it's normalized. In other words, it has no redundancies, and it's not possible to create conflicting data.

  Recursive queries using WITH or CONNECT BY PRIOR make it more efficient to use the Adjacency List design, provided you use a version of SQL database that supports the syntax.

- *Path Enumeration* is good for breadcrumbs in user interfaces, but it's fragile because it fails to enforce referential integrity and stores information redundantly.

- *Nested Sets* is a clever solution—maybe too clever. It also fails to support referential integrity. It's best used when you need to query a tree more frequently than you need to modify the tree.

- *Closure Table* is the most versatile of the alternative designs, and the only design in this chapter that allows a node to belong to multiple trees. It requires an additional table to store the relationships. This design also uses a lot of rows when encoding deep hierarchies, increasing space consumption as a trade-off for reducing computing. Like many denormalized solutions, it gives good performance for certain query cases.

There's more to learn about storing and manipulating hierarchical data in SQL. A good book that covers hierarchical queries is *Joe Celko's Trees and Hierarchies in SQL for Smarties [Cel04]*. Another book that covers trees and even graphs is *SQL Design Patterns [Tro06]* by Vadim Tropashko. The latter book has a more formal, academic style.

> A hierarchy consists of entries and relationships. Model both of these in a way that supports the queries you need to make against the hierarchy.

Mini-Antipattern: It Works on My Computer

"What does this error mean? My SQL query works fine while I'm developing code on my machine, but I get this error when I deploy my application to production."

> Error: 1064 (42000): You have an error in your SQL syntax; check the manual that corresponds to your MySQL server version for the right syntax to use near 'WITH'

In this example, the cause of the error is that the developer wrote an SQL query that uses the WITH keyword, for a common table expression. MySQL first implemented this syntax feature in in version 8.0. If the code attempts to run this query on an older version of MySQL Server, it returns the preceding error.

It's easier in a development environment to update to a newer version of database software than in production. Most projects are reluctant to risk any downtime in production, whereas that's not an issue on an individual developer's workstation or laptop.

Newer versions of any software have features that were not implemented in the earlier version. In the case of an SQL database, there might be enhanced SQL syntax, new built-in functions, or even new data types. New SQL features are usually quite attractive and powerful, but if you develop code that relies on them, you'll be surprised when you deploy to production and your code doesn't work the same.

These surprises are costly and hard to debug. You might be forced to redesign a lot of code that was assuming features of the database would work like they do in the version of the software you use in development.

To avoid this problem, be careful to equip your local development environment with the same version of database software that you use in production. The closer you can get to an exact version match the better, because sometimes even a minor software release contains new features, bug fixes, or breaks in backward compatibility.

Database servers also have optional features, so you should make your development server match the production server as closely as possible. This includes:

- Configuration options that affect data treatment or query behavior
- Configuration options that affect global defaults
- Database users, roles, and SQL privileges (but good security practices discourage using the same password across environments)

It's common practice to ensure the same versions are used in development and production when it comes to programming language, libraries, frameworks, and other dependencies. This is enforced automatically as you build and package your application code. However, in spite of the rise of popularity of containerized deployment, the database software isn't typically included in a deployable package.

The creatures outside looked from pig to man, and from man to pig,
and from pig to man again; but already it was impossible to say which
was which.

> George Orwell, Animal Farm

## CHAPTER 4

ID Required

Recently I answered a question that I see frequently, from a software developer trying to prevent duplicate rows. At first I thought he must lack a primary key. That wasn't his problem.

In his content management database, he stored articles for publishing on a website. He used an intersection table for a many-to-many association between a table of articles and a table of tags.

ID-Required/intro/articletags.sql
```
CREATE TABLE ArticleTags (
  id          SERIAL PRIMARY KEY,
  article_id  BIGINT UNSIGNED NOT NULL,
  tag_id      BIGINT UNSIGNED NOT NULL,
  FOREIGN KEY (article_id) REFERENCES Articles (id),
  FOREIGN KEY (tag_id)     REFERENCES Tags (id)
);
```

He was getting incorrect results from queries when counting the number of articles with a given tag. He knew that there were only five articles with the "economy" tag, but the query was telling him there were seven.

ID-Required/intro/articletags.sql
```
SELECT tag_id, COUNT(*) AS articles_per_tag
FROM ArticleTags WHERE tag_id = 327;
```

When he queried all the rows matching that tag_id, he saw that the tag was associated with one particular article in triplicate; three rows showed the same association, although they had different values for id, as shown in the table on page 42.

This table had a primary key, but that primary key didn't prevent duplicates in the columns that mattered. One remedy might be to create a UNIQUE constraint over the other two columns, but given that, the id column isn't needed at all.

id	tag_id	article_id
22	327	1234
23	327	1234
24	327	1234

Objective: Establish Primary Key Conventions

The objective is to make sure every table has a primary key, but confusion about the nature of a primary key has resulted in an antipattern.

Everyone who has been introduced to database design knows that a primary key is an important, even mandatory, part of a table. This is true; primary keys are integral to good database design. A primary key is guaranteed to be unique over all rows in the table, so this is the logical mechanism to address individual rows and to prevent duplicate rows from being stored. A primary key is also referenced by foreign keys to create table associations.

The tricky part is choosing a column to serve as the primary key. The value of any attribute in most tables has the potential to belong on more than one row. Textbook examples such as a person's first name and last name are clearly subject to having duplication. Even an email address or administrative identification numbers such as a United States Social Security number or taxpayer ID number aren't strictly unique.

A new column is needed in such tables to store an artificial value that has no meaning in the domain modeled by the table. This column is used as the primary key, so you can address rows uniquely while allowing any other attribute column to contain duplicates, if that's appropriate. This type of primary key column is sometimes called a *pseudokey* or a *surrogate key*.

To ensure rows can be given unique pseudokey values even when concurrent clients are inserting new rows, most databases provide a mechanism to generate unique integer values serially, outside the scope of transaction isolation.

The following is an example of standard SQL:2003 syntax for a pseudokey (tested on PostgreSQL, but MySQL does not support this syntax):

```
ID-Required/obj/sql:2003.sql
CREATE TABLE Bugs (
  bug_id   BIGINT GENERATED ALWAYS AS IDENTITY,
  summary  VARCHAR(80)
  -- other columns...
);
```

Before pseudokeys were standardized in SQL:2003, each database had to implement its own extension to SQL to implement them. Even the terminology for pseudokeys is vendor-dependent, as shown by the following table:

Feature	Supported by Database Brands
AUTO_INCREMENT	MySQL
GENERATOR	Firebird, InterBase
IDENTITY	DB2, Derby, Microsoft SQL Server, Sybase
ROWID	SQLite
SEQUENCE	DB2, Firebird, Informix, Ingres, Oracle, PostgreSQL
SERIAL	MySQL, PostgreSQL
SQL:2003 standard	DB2, Derby, Firebird, Ingres, Oracle, PostgreSQL

Pseudokeys are a useful feature, but they aren't the only solution for declaring a primary key.

Antipattern: One Size Fits All

Books, articles, and programming frameworks have established a cultural convention that every database table must have a primary key column with the following characteristics:

- The primary key's column name is id.
- Its data type is a 32-bit or 64-bit integer.
- Unique values are generated automatically.

The presence of a column named id in every table is so common that this has become synonymous with a primary key. Programmers learning SQL get the false idea that a primary key always means a column defined in this manner.

ID-Required/anti/id-ubiquitous.sql
```
CREATE TABLE Bugs (
  id          SERIAL PRIMARY KEY,
  description VARCHAR(1000),
  -- . . .
);
```

Adding an id column to every table causes several effects that make its use seem arbitrary.

Making a Redundant Key

You might see an id column defined as the primary key simply for the sake of tradition, even when another column in the same table could be used as the natural primary key. The other column may even be defined with a UNIQUE constraint. For example, in the Bugs table, the application might label bugs using a string with a mnemonic for the project the bug belongs to, or other identifying information.

ID-Required/anti/id-redundant.sql
```
CREATE TABLE Bugs (
  id           SERIAL PRIMARY KEY,
  bug_id       VARCHAR(10) UNIQUE,
  description VARCHAR(1000),
  -- . . .
);

INSERT INTO Bugs (bug_id, description, ...)
  VALUES ('VIS-078', 'crashes on save', ...);
```

The bug_id column in the previous example has similar usage to the id, in that it serves to identify each row uniquely.

Allowing Duplicate Rows

A compound key consists of multiple columns. One typical use for a compound key is in an intersection table like BugsProducts. The primary key should ensure that a given combination of values for bug_id and product_id appears only once in the table, even though each value may appear many times in different pairings.

However, when you use the mandatory id column as the primary key, the constraint no longer applies to two columns that should be unique.

ID-Required/anti/superfluous.sql
```
CREATE TABLE BugsProducts (
  id           SERIAL PRIMARY KEY,
  bug_id       BIGINT UNSIGNED NOT NULL,
  product_id  BIGINT UNSIGNED NOT NULL,
  FOREIGN KEY (bug_id) REFERENCES Bugs(bug_id),
  FOREIGN KEY (product_id) REFERENCES Products(product_id)
);

INSERT INTO BugsProducts (bug_id, product_id)
  VALUES (1234, 1), (1234, 1), (1234, 1); -- duplicates are permitted
```

Duplicates in this intersection table cause unintended results when you use the table to match Bugs to Products. To prevent duplicates, you could declare a UNIQUE constraint over the two columns besides id:

ID-Required/anti/superfluous.sql
```
CREATE TABLE BugsProducts (
  id           SERIAL PRIMARY KEY,
  bug_id       BIGINT UNSIGNED NOT NULL,
  product_id  BIGINT UNSIGNED NOT NULL,
```

```
  UNIQUE KEY (bug_id, product_id),
  FOREIGN KEY (bug_id) REFERENCES Bugs(bug_id),
  FOREIGN KEY (product_id) REFERENCES Products(product_id)
);
```

If you need a unique constraint over those two columns anyway, the id column is superfluous.

Obscuring the Meaning of the Key

The word *code* has a number of definitions, one of which is a way to communicate a message with brevity or secrecy. In programming, we should have the opposite goal—to make meaning clearer.

The name id is so generic that it holds no meaning. This is especially important when you join two tables and they have the same primary key column name.

ID-Required/anti/ambiguous.sql
```
SELECT b.id, a.id
FROM Bugs b
JOIN Accounts a ON (b.assigned_to = a.id)
WHERE b.status = 'OPEN';
```

You can't tell the bug id from the account id in your application code, if you reference columns by name instead of by ordinal position. This is a problem especially when a query result is returned as an associative array, JSON document, or dynamic object, because the value of a column overwrites another with the same name. To avoid this, you must specify column aliases in your query.

ID-Required/anti/ambiguous.sql
```
SELECT b.id AS bug_id, a.id AS account_id
FROM Bugs b
JOIN Accounts a ON (b.assigned_to = a.id)
WHERE b.status = 'OPEN';
```

The name of the id column doesn't help make the query any clearer. The client would have an easier time reading the query results if the columns were named bug_id and account_id. A primary key addresses individual rows of a given table, so the column's name should give a clue about the type of entity in that table.

Using USING

You're probably familiar with the SQL syntax for a join: using the keywords JOIN and ON preceding an expression to evaluate matching rows in the two tables:

ID-Required/anti/join.sql
```
SELECT * FROM Bugs AS b JOIN BugsProducts AS bp ON (b.bug_id = bp.bug_id);
```

SQL also supports a more concise syntax for expressing a join between two tables. You can rewrite the previous query in the following way if the columns have the same name in both tables:

ID-Required/anti/join.sql
```
SELECT * FROM Bugs JOIN BugsProducts USING (bug_id);
```

However, if all tables are required to define a pseudokey primary key named id, then a foreign key column in a dependent table can never use the same name as the primary key it references. Instead, you must always use the more verbose ON syntax:

ID-Required/anti/join.sql
```
SELECT * FROM Bugs AS b JOIN BugsProducts AS bp ON (b.id = bp.bug_id);
```

Special Scope for Sequences

Some people allocate a value for a new row by taking the greatest value currently in use and adding one.

```
SELECT MAX(bug_id) + 1 AS next_bug_id FROM Bugs;
```

This isn't reliable when you have concurrent clients both querying for the next value to use. The same value could be used by both clients. This is called a *race condition*.

To avoid the race condition, you have to block concurrent inserts while you read the current maximum value and then use it in a new row. To do this, you have to lock the whole table—row-level locking isn't enough. Table locks create a bottleneck because they cause concurrent clients to queue up for access.

Sequences solve this by operating outside of transaction scope. They never allocate the same value to multiple clients and so never roll back allocation of a value, whether or not you commit that value in a row. Because sequences work this way, multiple clients can generate unique values concurrently and be assured they won't try to use the same value.

Most databases support some function to return the last value a sequence generated. For example, MySQL calls this function LAST_INSERT_ID(), Microsoft SQL Server uses SCOPE_IDENTITY(), and Oracle uses SequenceName.CURRVAL().

These functions return the value generated during the current session, even if other clients generate their own values concurrently. No race condition exists.

Compound Keys Are Hard

Some developers refuse to use compound keys because they say these keys are too hard to use. Any expression that compares a key to another must compare all columns. A foreign key that references a compound primary key must itself be a compound foreign key. It requires more typing to use compound keys.

This refusal is like a mathematician refusing to use two-dimensional or three-dimensional coordinates, instead performing all calculations as though objects exist within a one-dimensional, linear space. It's true that this would make a lot of geometry and trigonometry much simpler, but it fails to describe real-world objects that we need to work with.

Do I Really Need a Primary Key?

Some software developers claim that their table doesn't need a primary key. Sometimes these programmers want to avoid the imagined overhead of maintaining a unique index, or else they have tables with no columns they can use for this purpose.

A primary key constraint is important when you need to do the following:

- Prevent a table from containing duplicate rows
- Reference individual rows in queries
- Support foreign key references

Another reason to use a primary key that you might not think of: database replication. For example, in MySQL, as row-based updates are replayed on a replica database instance, the primary key is used to apply changes efficiently. If the table has no primary key, then every row updated must run a table-scan. This is very bad for performance.

If you don't use primary key constraints, you create a chore for yourself: checking for duplicate rows.

```
SELECT bug_id FROM Bugs GROUP BY bug_id HAVING COUNT(*) > 1;
```

You would have to run this check frequently, or else duplicates could cause problems. If you find a duplicate bug_id with the previous query, then you have to examine both rows with that bug_id, and choose which one to keep. What if the query finds thousands of duplicate bug_id's?

A table without a primary key is like organizing your music collection with no song titles. You can still listen to the music, but you can't find the one you want or keep duplicates out of your collection.

How to Recognize the Antipattern

The symptom of this antipattern is easy to recognize: tables use the overly generic name id for the primary key. There's virtually no reason to prefer this column name over one that is more descriptive.

The following can also be evidence of the antipattern:

- "I don't think I need a primary key in this table."

  The developer who says this is confusing the term *primary key* with *pseudokey*. Every table must have a primary key *constraint* to prevent duplicate rows and identify individual rows. They might want to use a natural key or a compound key instead.

- "How did I get duplicate many-to-many associations?"

  An intersection table for a many-to-many relationship should declare a primary key constraint, or at least a *unique key* constraint, over the set of foreign key columns.

- "I read that database theory says I should move values to a lookup table and refer to them by ID. I don't want to do that because I have to do a join every time I want the actual values."

  This is a common misunderstanding of database design theory called *normalization*, which has nothing to do with pseudokeys in reality. For more on this, see Appendix 1, Rules of Normalization, on page 321.

Legitimate Uses of the Antipattern

While there is nothing wrong with using a pseudokey, or assigning values from an auto-incrementing integer mechanism, not every table needs a pseudokey, and it's not necessary to name every pseudokey id.

Some object-relational frameworks simplify development by assuming *convention over configuration*. They expect every table to define its primary key in the same way: as an integer pseudokey column named id. If you use such a framework, you may want to conform to its conventions, because this gives you access to other desirable features of the framework.

A pseudokey is a good choice as a surrogate for a natural key that's too long to be practical. For example, for a table that records attributes of a file on the filesystem, the path of the file might be a good natural key, but it would be costly to index a string column that long.

Likewise, when creating tables for multivalued attributes, a subordinate table that references a long compound primary key of its parent must add another column for its own primary key. As table references form longer "chains" of tables, the length of the primary key can become too long. In these cases, a pseudokey is the only practical solution.

Solution: Tailored to Fit

A primary key is a constraint, not a data type. You can declare a primary key on any column or set of columns, as long as the data types support indexing. The columns of a primary key must also be declared NOT NULL, but many implementations do this for you automatically. You should also be able to define a column as an auto-incrementing integer without making it the primary key of the table. The two concepts are independent of each other.

Don't let inflexible conventions get in the way of good design.

Tell It Like It Is

Choose sensible names for your primary key. The name should convey the type of entity that the primary key identifies. For example, the primary key of the Bugs table should be bug_id.

Use the same column name in foreign keys where possible. This often means that the name of a primary key should be unique within your schema; no two tables should use the same name for their primary key, unless one is also a foreign key referencing the other. However, there are exceptions. Sometimes it is appropriate for a foreign key to be named differently from the primary key it references, for instance, to be descriptive of the nature of the association.

ID-Required/soln/foreignkey-name.sql
```
CREATE TABLE Bugs (
  -- . . .
  reported_by  BIGINT UNSIGNED NOT NULL,
  FOREIGN KEY (reported_by) REFERENCES Accounts(account_id)
);
```

An industry standard exists to describe naming conventions for metadata. The standard, called ISO/IEC 11179,[1] is a guideline for "managing classification schemes" in information technology systems. In other words, this is how you should name your tables and columns sensibly. Like most ISO standards, this document is nearly impenetrable, but Joe Celko applies it practically to SQL in his book *SQL Programming Style [Cel05]*.

---

1.   https://www.iso.org/standard/74570.html

Be Unconventional

Object-relational frameworks expect you to use a pseudokey named id, but they also allow you to override this and declare a different name instead. The following example uses Ruby on Rails:

ID-Required/soln/custom-primarykey.rb
```
class Bug < ActiveRecord::Base
  set_primary_key "bug_id"
end
```

Some developers think that specifying the primary key column is necessary only when supporting *legacy* databases where they can't use their preferred conventions. In fact, supporting sensible column names is also important in new projects.

Embrace Natural Keys and Compound Keys

If your table contains an attribute that's guaranteed to be unique, is non-null, and can serve to identify the row, don't feel obligated to add a pseudokey solely for the sake of tradition.

Practically speaking, it's not uncommon for every attribute in a table to be subject to change or to be nonunique. Databases tend to evolve during the lifetime of a project, and decision makers may not respect the sanctity of a natural key. Sometimes a column that at first seemed like it would be a good natural key turns out to have legitimate duplicates. In cases like these, a pseudokey is the only solution.

Use compound keys when they're appropriate. When a row is best identified by the combination of multiple attribute columns, as in the BugsProducts table, use those columns in a compound primary key.

ID-Required/soln/compound.sql
```
CREATE TABLE BugsProducts (
  bug_id      BIGINT UNSIGNED NOT NULL,
  product_id  BIGINT UNSIGNED NOT NULL,
  PRIMARY KEY (bug_id, product_id),
  FOREIGN KEY (bug_id) REFERENCES Bugs(bug_id),
  FOREIGN KEY (product_id) REFERENCES Products(product_id)
);

INSERT INTO BugsProducts (bug_id, product_id)
  VALUES (1234, 1), (1234, 2), (1234, 3);

INSERT INTO BugsProducts (bug_id, product_id)
  VALUES (1234, 1); -- error: duplicate entry
```

Note that a foreign key that references a compound primary key also needs to be compound. While it may seem clumsy to duplicate these columns in dependent tables, it can have advantages too: you might simplify a query that would have required a join to fetch attributes of the referenced row.

> Conventions are good only if they are helpful.

Mini-Antipattern: Is a BIGINT Big Enough?

"What if the auto-increment id reaches its maximum value?"

If an application is very busy and inserts a lot of data every day into a table with an auto-increment id as its primary key, this makes developers uncertain about what happens if they use all the integer values.

To relieve this uncertainty, you should do a little bit of math. Estimate the number of rows your application inserts into your table per minute on average. For example, suppose this is 10,000 rows per minute. Divide the maximum integer value by this estimated number of rows per minute.

The maximum value of a signed 32-bit integer is 2^{31}-1, or 2,147,483,647. At a rate of 10,000 rows per minute, assuming your id is incremented by 1 per row, this will run out in about 214,749 minutes, or 149 days, 3 hours, 9 minutes. That's less than half a year, so clearly a regular INT column isn't big enough.

Changing to an unsigned INT (assuming the column doesn't need to use negative values) uses the same storage size (32-bit) but only doubles the range of values. Instead of running out in 149 days, it will run out in 298 days— still less than a year, at the rate of growth you had estimated.

Is a BIGINT big enough?

BIGINT is big. Really big. The maximum value of a signed 64-bit number isn't merely twice as a large as a 32-bit number, it's the *square* of a 32-bit number. It's 2^{32} times as large.

The maximum value of a signed 64-bit integer is 9,223,372,036,854,775,807. Now recalculate the estimate for how long it will take to run out. Divide that maximum value by 10,000 id values per minute. Divide that by 60 minutes per hour, then divide by 24 hours per day, and then divide by 365 days per year. The result is 1,754,827,252 years.

Developers have asked me what to do if a BIGINT runs out of values. Provided their auto-increment column starts at 1 and increments by 1 per row, I tell them, "I guarantee that a BIGINT won't run out while your application is still in use. If I'm wrong and it happens, then you may call me for a refund of my consulting fee."

## CHAPTER 5

Keyless Entry

"Bill, it looks like two managers have reserved the same server in our lab for the same days—how can this happen?" the testing lab manager messaged me. "Can you take a look into this and get it fixed? They're screaming at me that they both need the equipment and that I'm holding up their project schedule."

I designed an equipment-tracking application some years ago using MySQL. The default storage engine for MySQL was MyISAM, which doesn't support foreign key constraints. The database had many logical relationships but could not enforce referential integrity.

As the project evolved and the application manipulated data in new ways, we developed a problem: when referential integrity wasn't satisfied, discrepancies showed up in reports, subtotals didn't add up, and schedules became double booked.

The project manager asked me to write quality control scripts that we could run periodically to let us know when discrepancies occurred. These scripts examined the state of the database, found mistakes such as orphaned rows in child tables, and sent an email to report them.

Every table relationship had to be checked by these scripts. As the volume of data grew larger and the number of tables increased, the number of quality control queries also grew, and the scripts took longer to run. The email reports became longer too.

The script solution worked, of course, but it was a costly reinvention of the wheel. What I needed was a way to make the application *fail early* whenever a user submitted invalid data. That's what foreign key constraints do.

Objective: Simplify Database Architecture

Relational database design is almost as much about relationships between tables as it is about the individual tables themselves. *Referential integrity* is an important part of proper database design and operation. When you declare a foreign key constraint for a column or set of columns, the values in these columns must exist in the primary key or unique key columns of the parent table. This seems simple enough.

However, some software developers recommend avoiding referential integrity constraints. The reasons you might hear to ignore foreign keys include the following:

- Your data updates can conflict with the constraints.

- You're using a database design that's so flexible it can't support referential integrity constraints (see Chapter 7, Polymorphic Associations, on page 77).

- You believe that the index the database creates for the foreign key will impact performance.

- You use a database brand that doesn't support foreign keys.

- You have to look up the syntax for declaring foreign keys.

Antipattern: Leave Out the Constraints

Even though it seems at first that skipping foreign key constraints makes your database design simpler, more flexible, or speedier, you pay for this in other ways. You create more work for yourself because it's your responsibility to write code to ensure referential integrity manually.

Assuming Flawless Code

Many people's solution for referential integrity is to write application code so that data relationships are always satisfied. Every time you insert a row, make sure that values in foreign key columns reference existing values in the referenced table. Every time you delete a row, make sure that any child tables are also updated appropriately. In other words, the popular answer is simply to *make no mistakes.*

To avoid making referential integrity mistakes when you have no foreign key constraints, you'd have to run extra SELECT queries before you apply changes to confirm the change won't result in broken references. For instance, to insert a new row, you'd check that the parent row exists:

Keyless-Entry/anti/insert.sql
```
SELECT account_id FROM Accounts WHERE account_id = 1;
```

Then you could add a bug that references it:

Keyless-Entry/anti/insert.sql
```
INSERT INTO Bugs (reported_by) VALUES (1);
```

To delete a row, you'd have to make sure no child rows exist:

Keyless-Entry/anti/delete.sql
```
SELECT bug_id FROM Bugs WHERE reported_by = 1;
```

Then you could delete the account:

Keyless-Entry/anti/delete.sql
```
DELETE FROM Accounts WHERE account_id = 1;
```

If the user with account_id 1 sneaks in and enters a new bug in the moment after your query and before you delete that account, then the delete is blocked. This may seem unlikely, but as Gordon Letwin, architect of DOS 4, famously said, "One in a million is next Tuesday." That still leaves a broken reference —a bug reported by an account that no longer exists.

The only remedy is for you to explicitly lock the Bugs table while you're checking it and unlock it after you have finished deleting the account. Any architecture that requires that kind of locking is never going to do well when high concurrency and scalability are required.

Checking for Mistakes

The antisolution described in the story in this chapter uses developer-written scripts to report corrupted data.

For example, in our bugs database, the Bugs.status column references the lookup table BugStatus. To find bugs with an invalid status value, you could use a query like the following:

Keyless-Entry/anti/find-orphans.sql
```
SELECT b.bug_id, b.status
FROM Bugs b LEFT OUTER JOIN BugStatus s
  ON (b.status = s.status)
WHERE s.status IS NULL;
```

You can imagine that you'd have to write a similar query for every referential relationship in your database.

If you find yourself in the habit of checking for broken references like this, you have to decide how often you need to run these checks. If you run them too frequently, it might impact performance of regular database queries. If you don't run them frequently enough, then data anomalies creep in and might affect other work before you notice and correct them.

When you do find a broken reference, it's your responsibility to correct it. For instance, you might change an invalid bug status value to a sensible default.

Keyless-Entry/anti/set-default.sql
```
UPDATE Bugs SET status = DEFAULT WHERE status = 'BANANA';
```

Inevitably, there are other cases where you can't synthesize data to correct these kinds of mistakes. For example, the Bugs.reported_by column should reference the account of the user who reported the given bug, but if this value is invalid, it might not be clear which user's account to choose as a replacement.

"It's Not My Fault!"

It's pretty unlikely that all your code touching the database is perfect. You could easily perform similar database updates in several functions in your application. When you have to change the code, it's not easy to be sure you've applied compatible changes to every case in your application.

You might have a database that is accessed by applications or scripts you didn't write. You can't be certain that all of these have made their changes correctly.

You may also have users applying changes directly to the database, using an SQL query tool or using private scripts. It's easy to introduce broken references through ad hoc SQL statements. You should assume this will happen at some point in the life of your application.

You need the database to be *consistent*—that is, you need to be able to depend on references in the database being correct after every update.

Catch-22 Updates

Many developers avoid foreign key constraints because the constraints make it inconvenient to update related columns in multiple tables. For instance, if you need to delete a row that other rows depend on, you have to delete the child rows first to avoid violating foreign key constraints:

Keyless-Entry/anti/delete-child.sql
```
DELETE FROM BugStatus WHERE status = 'BOGUS'; -- ERROR!
DELETE FROM Bugs WHERE status = 'BOGUS';
DELETE FROM BugStatus WHERE status = 'BOGUS'; -- retry succeeds
```

You have to execute multiple statements manually, one for each child table. If you add another child table to your database in the future, you have to fix your code to delete from the new table too. This problem is solvable.

The unsolvable problem is when you UPDATE a column that child rows depend on. You can't update the child rows before you update the parent, and you can't update the parent before you update the child values that reference it. You need to make both changes simultaneously, but that's impossible using two separate updates. It's a catch-22 scenario.

Keyless-Entry/anti/update-catch22.sql

```
UPDATE BugStatus SET status = 'INVALID' WHERE status = 'BOGUS'; -- ERROR!

UPDATE Bugs SET status = 'INVALID' WHERE status = 'BOGUS'; -- ERROR!
```

Some developers find these scenarios difficult to manage, so they decide not to use foreign keys at all. We'll see later how foreign keys address multitable updates and deletes in a simple and effective way.

How to Recognize the Antipattern

If you hear people use phrases like the following, they're probably practicing the Keyless Entry antipattern:

- "How do I query to check for a value that exists in one table and not the other table?"

  Usually this is to find orphan child rows whose parent has been updated or deleted.

- "Is there a quick way to check that a value exists in one table as part of my insert to a second table?"

  This is to ensure that the parent row exists. A foreign key does this for you automatically and uses any index on the parent table to make the check as efficient as possible.

- "Foreign keys? I was told not to use them because they slow down the database."

  Performance is often used as a justification for cutting corners, but it usually creates more problems than it solves—it can even cause performance problems.

Some database designs are incompatible with the use of foreign keys. It should be a strong clue that you're using another SQL antipattern if you can't use traditional referential integrity constraints. For more detail, you may want to look at Chapter 6, Entity-Attribute-Value, on page 61 and Chapter 7, Polymorphic Associations, on page 77.

Legitimate Uses of the Antipattern

Some SQL implementations require extra locks on a parent row when you update child rows that reference it. The purpose is to prevent a parent row from being updated or deleted while an update is in progress on a dependent row. This can surprise some software developers, and they may choose to drop the foreign key constraint to avoid this type of locking.

Even though foreign key constraints are an effective way to reduce data anomalies, they might be removed to help data cleanup projects. That is, there could be known orphaned rows in a table because managers are still researching the data needed for the reference.

Some other database operations can be simplified if foreign key constraints are not present. For example, a popular open source tool for automating MySQL table alterations, pt-online-schema-change,[1] renames tables instead of altering them. If the old format of the altered table is referenced by foreign keys in other tables, those references must be dropped and defined after the table renaming is done. This potentially results in many tables being altered, instead of just the one that needed the change. To avoid this step, some developers choose a policy to not use foreign key constraints.

You might be forced to use a database brand that doesn't support foreign key constraints (for example, MySQL's MyISAM storage engine or SQLite prior to version 3.6.19). If that's the case, then you have to find a way to compensate, like the quality control scripts described in this chapter's story.

Solution: Declare Constraints

The Japanese phrase *poka-yoke* means "mistake proofing." Poka-yoke was coined by industrial engineer Dr. Shigeo Shingo in his study of the Toyota Production System. This term refers to a manufacturing process that helps eliminate product defects by preventing, correcting, or drawing attention to errors as they occur. This practice improves quality and decreases the need for correction, which more than makes up for the cost of its use.

You can apply the poka-yoke principle to your database design by using foreign key constraints to enforce referential integrity. Instead of searching for and

---

1. https://www.percona.com/doc/percona-toolkit/LATEST/pt-online-schema-change.html

correcting data integrity mistakes, you can prevent these mistakes from entering your database in the first place.

```
Keyless-Entry/soln/foreign-keys.sql
CREATE TABLE Bugs (
  -- . . .
  reported_by        BIGINT UNSIGNED NOT NULL,
  status             VARCHAR(20) NOT NULL DEFAULT 'NEW',
  FOREIGN KEY (reported_by) REFERENCES Accounts(account_id),
  FOREIGN KEY (status) REFERENCES BugStatus(status)
);
```

Your existing code and ad hoc queries obey the same constraints, so there's no way for any forgotten code or back doors to bypass enforcement. The database rejects any improper change, no matter where the change comes from.

Using foreign keys saves you from writing unnecessary code and ensures that all your code works the same way if you change the database. This reduces the time to develop the code and also many hours of debugging and maintenance. The software industry average is 15 to 50 bugs per 1,000 lines of code. All else being equal, if you have fewer lines of code, you have fewer bugs.

Supporting Multitable Changes

Foreign keys have another feature you can't mimic using application code: *cascading updates.*

```
Keyless-Entry/soln/cascade.sql
CREATE TABLE Bugs (
  -- . . .
  reported_by        BIGINT UNSIGNED NOT NULL,
  status             VARCHAR(20) NOT NULL DEFAULT 'NEW',
  FOREIGN KEY (reported_by) REFERENCES Accounts(account_id)
    ON UPDATE CASCADE
    ON DELETE RESTRICT,
  FOREIGN KEY (status) REFERENCES BugStatus(status)
    ON UPDATE CASCADE
    ON DELETE SET DEFAULT
);
```

This solution allows you to update or delete the parent row and lets the database take care of any child rows that reference it. Updates to the parent tables BugStatus and Accounts propagate automatically to child rows in Bugs. There's no longer a catch-22 problem.

The way you declare the ON UPDATE or ON DELETE clauses in the foreign key constraint allow you to control the result of a cascading operation. For example, RESTRICT for the foreign key on reported_by means that you can't delete an account if some rows in Bugs reference it. The constraint blocks the delete and raises an error. Whereas if you delete a status value, any bugs with that status are automatically reset to the default status value.

In either case, the database changes both tables atomically. The foreign key references remain satisfied both before and after the changes.

If you add a new child table to the database, the foreign keys in the child table dictate the cascading behavior. You don't need to change your application code. Neither do you need to change anything about the parent table, no matter how many child tables reference it.

Overhead? Not Really

It's true that foreign key constraints have a bit of overhead. In spite of this, foreign keys prove to be a lot more efficient than the alternative.

- You don't need to run SELECT queries to check before you insert or update or delete.

- You don't need to lock tables to protect multitable changes.

- You don't need to run periodic quality control scripts to correct the inevitable orphans.

Foreign keys are easy to use, improve performance, and help you maintain consistent referential integrity during any data change, both simple and complex.

For more tips on avoiding common mistakes when defining foreign keys, see Chapter 26, Foreign Key Mistakes in Standard SQL, on page 301 and Chapter 27, Foreign Key Mistakes in MySQL, on page 313.

Make your database mistake proof with constraints.

If you try and take a cat apart to see how it works, the first thing you have in your hands is a non-working cat.

> Douglas Adams

## CHAPTER 6

Entity-Attribute-Value

"How do I count the number of rows by date?" This is an example of a simple task for a database programmer. This solution is covered in any introductory tutorial on SQL. It involves basic SQL syntax:

```
EAV/intro/count.sql
SELECT date_reported, COUNT(*)
FROM Bugs
GROUP BY date_reported;
```

The simple solution assumes two things:

- The bug date is stored only in the column named Bugs.date_reported on every row of the table.

- Values can be compared to one another so that GROUP BY can accurately group dates with equal values together.

You can't always rely on those assumptions. The date might be stored in the date_reported or report_date column or in any other column name. It might be different on each row, depending on what the software developers thought was the appropriate name for that attribute on different days. Dates might be stored in a variety of different formats, and then the computer can't easily compare two dates.

You may encounter these problems and others when you employ the antipattern known as Entity-Attribute-Value.

Objective: Support Variable Attributes

Extensibility is frequently a goal of software projects. You would like to design software that can adapt fluidly to future usage with little or no additional programming.

This is not a new problem; similar arguments against the inflexibility of relational database metadata have been made almost continuously since 1970, when the relational model was first proposed in *A Relational Model of Data for Large Shared Data Banks [Cod70]* by E. F. Codd.

A conventional table consists of attribute columns that are relevant for every row in the table, since every row represents an instance of a similar object. A different set of attributes represents a different type of object, so it belongs in a different table.

In modern object-oriented programming models, however, different object types can be related, for instance, by extending the same base type. In object-oriented design, these objects are considered instances of the same base type, as well as instances of their respective subtypes. You would like to store objects as rows in a single database table to simplify comparisons and calculations over multiple objects. You also need to allow objects of each subtype to store their respective attribute columns, which may not apply to the base type or to other subtypes.

Consider an example from the bugs database. A Bug and a Feature Request share some attributes in common, seen in the Issue base type in the following class diagram.

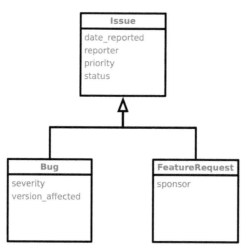

Every issue is associated with a person who reported it. It's also associated with a product, and it has a priority for completion. A Bug has some distinct attributes: the version of the product in which the bug occurs and the severity or impact of the bug. Likewise, a FeatureRequest may have its own attributes as well. For this example, suppose a feature is associated with a sponsor whose budget supports that feature's development.

Antipattern: Use a Generic Attribute Table

The solution that appeals to some programmers when they need to support variable attributes is to create a second table, storing attributes as rows. As you can see in the following figure, it looks simpler at first because you can use two tables instead of three (or more, if your data model has more variations).

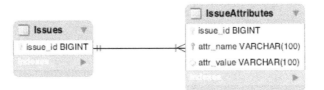

Each row in this attribute table has three columns:

- The *Entity*. Typically, this is a foreign key to a parent table that has one row per entity.

- The *Attribute*. This is simply the name of a column in a conventional table, but in this new design, you have to identify the attribute on each given row.

- The *Value*. Each entity has a value for each of its attributes.

  For example, a given bug is an entity you identify by its primary key value 1234. It has an attribute called status. The value of that attribute for bug 1234 is *NEW*.

This design is called Entity-Attribute-Value, or *EAV* for short. It's also sometimes called *open schema*, *schemaless*, or *name-value pairs*.

EAV/anti/create-eav-table.sql
```
CREATE TABLE Issues (
  issue_id    SERIAL PRIMARY KEY
);

INSERT INTO Issues (issue_id) VALUES (1234);

CREATE TABLE IssueAttributes (
  issue_id    BIGINT UNSIGNED NOT NULL,
  attr_name   VARCHAR(100) NOT NULL,
  attr_value  VARCHAR(100),
  PRIMARY KEY (issue_id, attr_name),
  FOREIGN KEY (issue_id) REFERENCES Issues(issue_id)
);

INSERT INTO IssueAttributes (issue_id, attr_name, attr_value)
  VALUES
```

```
(1234, 'product',          '1'),
(1234, 'date_reported',    '2009-06-01'),
(1234, 'status',           'NEW'),
(1234, 'description',      'Saving does not work'),
(1234, 'reported_by',      'Bill'),
(1234, 'version_affected', '1.0'),
(1234, 'severity',         'loss of functionality'),
(1234, 'priority',         'high');
```

By adding one additional table, you seem to gain the following benefits:

- Both tables have few columns.
- The number of columns doesn't need to grow to support new attributes.
- You avoid a clutter of columns that contain null in rows where the attribute is inapplicable.

This appears to be an improved design. However, the simple database structure doesn't make up for the difficulty of using it.

Querying an Attribute

Your boss needs to run a report of the bugs reported per day. In a conventional table design, the Issues table would have a simple attribute column such as date_reported. To query all bugs with their report dates, your boss could use a simple query like this:

EAV/anti/query-plain.sql
```
SELECT issue_id, date_reported FROM Issues;
```

To get the same information as the previous query using the EAV design, your boss needs to fetch rows from the IssueAttributes table that stores an attribute named by the string *date_reported*. This query is more verbose but less clear.

EAV/anti/query-eav.sql
```
SELECT issue_id, attr_value AS "date_reported"
FROM IssueAttributes
WHERE attr_name = 'date_reported';
```

Supporting Data Integrity

When you use EAV, you sacrifice many advantages that a conventional database design would have given you.

You Can't Make Mandatory Attributes

To help your boss generate accurate project reports, you should also require that the date_reported attribute has a value. In a conventional database design, it would be simple to enforce a mandatory column by declaring the column NOT NULL.

In the EAV design, each attribute corresponds to a row in the IssueAttributes table, not a column. You would need a constraint that checks that a row exists for each issue_id value, and the row must have the string *date_reported* in its attr_name column.

SQL doesn't support a constraint that can do this. So, you must write application code to enforce it. You also have to write code to check if the bug has the required reported date, every time it reads the entity, because some other client could have saved a bug with no date. If you do find a bug with no reported date, you should correct it (more code to write), but there's no way to know what the correct value was. If you make a guess or use some default value for a missing attribute, it could affect the accuracy of your boss's reports.

You Can't Use SQL Data Types

Your boss tells you he is having trouble running his report because people have entered dates in different formats or sometimes even a string that isn't a date. In a conventional database, you can prevent this if you declared the column with the DATE data type.

```
EAV/anti/insert-plain.sql
INSERT INTO Issues (date_reported) VALUES ('banana'); -- ERROR!
```

In the EAV design, the data type of the IssueAttributes.attr_value column is typically a string to accommodate all possible attributes in a single column. So, it has no way of rejecting invalid data.

```
EAV/anti/insert-eav.sql
INSERT INTO IssueAttributes (issue_id, attr_name, attr_value)
  VALUES (1234, 'date_reported', 'banana');  -- Not an error!
```

Some people try to extend the EAV design by defining a separate attr_value column for each SQL data type, leaving null in the unused columns. This allows you to use data types but makes queries even worse:

```
EAV/anti/data-types.sql
SELECT issue_id, COALESCE(attr_value_date, attr_value_datetime,
  attr_value_integer, attr_value_numeric, attr_value_float,
  attr_value_string, attr_value_text) AS "date_reported"
FROM IssueAttributes
WHERE attr_name = 'date_reported';
```

You would need to add even more columns to support user-defined data types or domains.

You Can't Enforce Referential Integrity

In a conventional database, you can restrict the range of some attributes by defining a foreign key to a lookup table. For example, the status attribute of a bug or issue should be one of a short list of values stored in the BugStatus table.

```
EAV/anti/foreign-key-plain.sql
CREATE TABLE Issues (
  issue_id          SERIAL PRIMARY KEY,
  -- other columns
  status            VARCHAR(20) NOT NULL DEFAULT 'NEW',
  FOREIGN KEY (status) REFERENCES BugStatus(status)
);
```

In the EAV design, you can't apply this kind of constraint on the attr_value column. A referential integrity constraint applies to every row in the table.

```
EAV/anti/foreign-key-eav.sql
CREATE TABLE IssueAttributes (
  issue_id          BIGINT UNSIGNED NOT NULL,
  attr_name         VARCHAR(100) NOT NULL,
  attr_value        VARCHAR(100),
  FOREIGN KEY (attr_value) REFERENCES BugStatus(status)
);
```

If you define this constraint, it would force *every* attribute to match a value in BugStatus, not just the status attribute.

You Can't Make Up Attribute Names

Your boss's reports are still not reliable. You find that attributes are not being named consistently. One bug uses an attribute named by the string *date_reported*, but another bug names the attribute by the string *report_date*. Both are clearly intended to represent the same information.

Here's how you could count bugs per date:

```
EAV/anti/count.sql
SELECT date_reported, COUNT(*) AS bugs_per_date
FROM (SELECT DISTINCT issue_id, attr_value AS date_reported
    FROM IssueAttributes
    WHERE attr_name IN ('date_reported', 'report_date'))
GROUP BY date_reported;
```

You have a risk that a given bug has stored an attribute by yet another name. The bug might even have stored a given attribute twice, by two different names. Now you have to write more code to check for this.

One remedy might be to declare a foreign key on the attr_name column to a lookup table that contains your approved attribute names. However, this doesn't support attributes you define on the fly for each entity. That's a common use of the EAV design.

Reconstructing a Row

It's natural to retrieve a row from the Issues table with all its attributes in columns. You want to fetch an issue in a single row as though it were stored in a conventional table.

issue_id	date_reported	status	priority	description
1234	2009-06-01	NEW	HIGH	Saving does not work

Because each attribute is stored on a separate row of the IssueAttributes table, retrieving them all as part of a single row requires a join for each attribute. You must know all attributes at the time you write this query. The following query reconstructs the row shown earlier, using joins.

```
EAV/anti/reconstruct.sql
SELECT i.issue_id,
  i1.attr_value AS "date_reported",
  i2.attr_value AS "status",
  i3.attr_value AS "priority",
  i4.attr_value AS "description"
FROM Issues AS i
  LEFT OUTER JOIN IssueAttributes AS i1
    ON i.issue_id = i1.issue_id AND i1.attr_name = 'date_reported'
  LEFT OUTER JOIN IssueAttributes AS i2
    ON i.issue_id = i2.issue_id AND i2.attr_name = 'status'
  LEFT OUTER JOIN IssueAttributes AS i3
    ON i.issue_id = i3.issue_id AND i3.attr_name = 'priority';
  LEFT OUTER JOIN IssueAttributes AS i4
    ON i.issue_id = i4.issue_id AND i4.attr_name = 'description';
WHERE i.issue_id = 1234;
```

As the number of attributes increases, so does the number of joins, and the cost of this query increases exponentially.

An alternative solution uses aggregation, grouping the rows with the same issue_id and picking each respective attribute out of the group using a CASE conditional expression.

```
EAV/anti/reconstruct-groupby.sql
SELECT issue_id,
  MAX(CASE attr_name WHEN 'date_reported'
      THEN attr_value END) AS "date_reported",
  MAX(CASE attr_name WHEN 'status'
      THEN attr_value END) AS "status",
  MAX(CASE attr_name WHEN 'priority'
      THEN attr_value END) AS "priority",
```

```
  MAX(CASE attr_name WHEN 'description'
      THEN attr_value END) AS "description"
FROM Issues
WHERE issue_id = 1234
GROUP BY issue_id;
```

The Inner-Platform Effect

EAV is a textbook example of a more general antipattern: designing a software application to be so customizable that it becomes a workalike of the platform used to create it.

It takes too much programming work to duplicate the platform fully. A mature platform represents many years of work, which is naturally more time than a given project can spend.

So the "inner-platform" code must cut corners, implementing limited forms of the platform's features. After spending a lot of time and effort, the result is not better than the platform the programmer started with, in fact it's inferior, buggy, and more difficult to use.

How to Recognize the Antipattern

If you hear phrases like the following spoken by your project team, it's a clue that someone is employing the EAV antipattern:

- "This database is totally extensible without metadata changes. You can define new attributes at runtime."

  Relational databases don't support that degree of flexibility. When someone claims to have designed an arbitrarily extensible database, they're probably using the EAV design.

- "What's the maximum number of joins I can do in a query?"

  If you need a query to support such a high number of joins that you're concerned about exceeding the database's limits, you may have a problem in your database design. It's common for an EAV design to lead to this problem.

- "I can't figure out how to write a report for our e-commerce platform. We need to hire a consultant to do it for us."

  It seems that many turnkey database-driven software packages designed for customizability use the EAV design. This makes most common reporting queries very complex or even impractical.

Legitimate Uses of the Antipattern

It's hard to justify using the EAV antipattern in a relational database. You have to compromise too many features that are strengths of the relational paradigm. But that doesn't address the legitimate need in some applications to support dynamic attributes.

Most applications that need schemaless data really need it for only a few tables or even just one table. The rest of your data requirements conform to standard table designs. If you account for the extra work and risk of EAV in your project plan, it may be the lesser evil to use it sparingly. Keep in mind that experienced database consultants report that systems using EAV become unwieldy within a year.

If you have nonrelational data management needs, the best answer is to use a *nonrelational* technology. This is a book about SQL, not about SQL alternatives, so the following list is only a sampling of these technologies:

- *Berkeley DB*[1] is a popular key-value store that's easy to embed in a variety of applications.

- *DynamoDB*[2] is a serverless key-value database offered as a cloud service at Amazon.com.

- *Elasticsearch*[3] is a distributed search and analytics engine.

- *Hadoop*[4] and *HBase* make up an open source DBMS inspired by Google's MapReduce algorithm for distributing queries against very large-scale semistructured data stores.

- *MongoDB*[5] is a document-oriented database.

- *Redis*[6] is a data structure server that stores data in memory by default.

Although these and other nonrelational projects are growing in popularity, the weaknesses of EAV relative to relational databases also apply to these alternatives. When metadata is fluid, it's harder to formulate simple queries. Applications spend a lot of energy discovering the structure of data and adapting to it.

---

1. https://www.oracle.com/database/technologies/related/berkeleydb.html
2. https://aws.amazon.com/dynamodb/
3. https://www.elastic.co/elasticsearch/
4. https://hadoop.apache.org/
5. https://www.mongodb.org/
6. https://redis.io/

Solution: Model the Subtypes

If EAV seems like the right design, you should take a second look before you implement it. If you do some good old-fashioned analysis, you will probably find that your project's data can be modeled in a traditional table design more easily and with greater assurance of data integrity.

There are several ways to store such data without using EAV. Most solutions work best when you have a finite number of subtypes and you know the attribute of each subtype. Which solution is best to use depends on how you intend to query the data, so you should decide on a design on a case-by-case basis.

Several of these designs comes from Martin Fowler's book *Patterns of Enterprise Application Architecture [Fow03]*.

Single Table Inheritance

The simplest design is to store all related types in one table, with distinct columns for every attribute that exists in any type. Use one attribute to define the subtype of a given row. In this example, this attribute is called issue_type. Some attributes are common to all subtypes. Many attributes are subtype-specific, and these columns must be given a null value on any row storing an object for which the attribute does not apply; the columns with non-null values become sparse.

```
EAV/soln/create-sti-table.sql
CREATE TABLE Issues (
  issue_id         SERIAL PRIMARY KEY,
  reported_by      BIGINT UNSIGNED NOT NULL,
  product_id       BIGINT UNSIGNED,
  priority         VARCHAR(20),
  version_resolved VARCHAR(20),
  status           VARCHAR(20),
  issue_type       VARCHAR(10),   -- BUG or FEATURE
  severity         VARCHAR(20),   -- only for bugs
  version_affected VARCHAR(20),   -- only for bugs
  sponsor          VARCHAR(50),   -- only for feature requests
  FOREIGN KEY (reported_by) REFERENCES Accounts(account_id)
  FOREIGN KEY (product_id) REFERENCES Products(product_id)
);
```

As new object types are introduced, the database must accommodate the attributes that describe these new object types. You must alter the table to add more columns as you add distinct attributes for the new object types. You may encounter a practical limit on the number of columns per table.

Another limitation of Single Table Inheritance is that there is no metadata to define which attributes belong to which subtypes. In your application, you can ignore some attributes if you know they don't apply to the object subtype on a given row. This takes some care, because it's your responsibility to track manually which attributes are applicable to each subtype. It would be better if you could use metadata to define this in the database.

Single Table Inheritance is best when you have few subtypes and few subtype-specific attributes, and you need to use a single-table database access pattern like Active Record.

Concrete Table Inheritance

Another solution is to create a separate table for each subtype. Every table contains the same attributes that are common to the base type, as well as the respective subtype-specific attribute.

EAV/soln/create-concrete-tables.sql
```
CREATE TABLE Bugs (
  issue_id         SERIAL PRIMARY KEY,
  reported_by      BIGINT UNSIGNED NOT NULL,
  product_id       BIGINT UNSIGNED,
  priority         VARCHAR(20),
  version_resolved VARCHAR(20),
  status           VARCHAR(20),
  severity         VARCHAR(20), -- only for bugs
  version_affected VARCHAR(20), -- only for bugs
  FOREIGN KEY (reported_by) REFERENCES Accounts(account_id),
  FOREIGN KEY (product_id) REFERENCES Products(product_id)
);

CREATE TABLE FeatureRequests (
  issue_id         SERIAL PRIMARY KEY,
  reported_by      BIGINT UNSIGNED NOT NULL,
  product_id       BIGINT UNSIGNED,
  priority         VARCHAR(20),
  version_resolved VARCHAR(20),
  status           VARCHAR(20),
  sponsor          VARCHAR(50),  -- only for feature requests
  FOREIGN KEY (reported_by) REFERENCES Accounts(account_id),
  FOREIGN KEY (product_id) REFERENCES Products(product_id)
);
```

An advantage of Concrete Table Inheritance over Single Table Inheritance is that you are prevented from storing a row containing values for attributes that don't apply to that row's subtype. If you reference an attribute column that doesn't exist in that table, the database informs you of the error automatically.

For example, the severity column does not appear in the FeatureRequests table:

EAV/soln/insert-concrete.sql
```
INSERT INTO FeatureRequests (issue_id, severity) VALUES ( ... ); -- ERROR!
```

Another advantage of Concrete Table Inheritance is that you don't need an extra attribute to define the subtype on each row, as you do in the Single Table Inheritance design.

On the other hand, there are disadvantages. It's hard to tell the common attributes from subtype-specific attributes. Also, if you add a new attribute to the set of common attributes, you must alter every subtype table.

No metadata shows that the data stored in these subtype tables belong to related objects. That is, if a programmer new to your project looks at the table definitions, he would see that some columns are common to all these subtype tables, but the metadata does not tell him whether any logical relationship exists or whether the tables have similarities merely by coincidence.

If you want to search all objects regardless of their subtypes, this is complicated if each subtype is stored in a separate table. To make this query easier, define a view that is the union of the tables, selecting only common attributes.

EAV/soln/view-concrete.sql
```
CREATE VIEW Issues AS
  SELECT b.issue_id, b.reported_by, ... 'bug' AS issue_type
  FROM Bugs AS b
   UNION ALL
  SELECT f.issue_id, f.reported_by, ... 'feature' AS issue_type
  FROM FeatureRequests AS f;
```

The Concrete Table Inheritance design is best used when you seldom need to query against all subtypes at once.

Class Table Inheritance

A third solution mimics inheritance, as though tables were object-oriented classes. Create a single table for the base type, containing attributes common to all subtypes. Then for each subtype, create another table, with a primary key that also serves as a foreign key to the base table.

EAV/soln/create-class-tables.sql
```
CREATE TABLE Issues (
  issue_id          SERIAL PRIMARY KEY,
  reported_by       BIGINT UNSIGNED NOT NULL,
  product_id        BIGINT UNSIGNED,
  priority          VARCHAR(20),
  version_resolved  VARCHAR(20),
```

```
    status          VARCHAR(20),
  FOREIGN KEY (reported_by) REFERENCES Accounts(account_id),
  FOREIGN KEY (product_id) REFERENCES Products(product_id)
);
CREATE TABLE Bugs (
  issue_id        BIGINT UNSIGNED PRIMARY KEY,
  severity        VARCHAR(20),
  version_affected VARCHAR(20),
  FOREIGN KEY (issue_id) REFERENCES Issues(issue_id)
);
CREATE TABLE FeatureRequests (
  issue_id        BIGINT UNSIGNED PRIMARY KEY,
  sponsor         VARCHAR(50),
  FOREIGN KEY (issue_id) REFERENCES Issues(issue_id)
);
```

The one-to-one relationship is enforced by the metadata, since the dependent table's foreign key is also a primary key and thus must be unique. This solution provides an efficient way to search against all subtypes, as long as your search references only the base type's attributes. Once you've found the entries that match your search, you can get the subtype-specific attributes by querying against the respective subtype tables.

You don't need the base table to hold the subtype attribute. As long as you have a small number of subtypes, you can write a join against all of them at once, producing a sparse result set like in the Single Table Inheritance table. Attributes are null where the attribute doesn't apply in the subtype for a given row.

EAV/soln/select-class.sql
```
SELECT i.*, b.*, f.*
FROM Issues AS i
  LEFT OUTER JOIN Bugs AS b USING (issue_id)
  LEFT OUTER JOIN FeatureRequests AS f USING (issue_id);
```

This is also a good candidate for defining a VIEW.

This design is best when you often need to query across all subtypes, referencing the columns they have in common.

A disadvantage of this design (as well as the Concrete Table Inheritence design) is that it's not possible to create a unique constraint across the tables. It's also hard to ensure a given entity is assigned only one subtype; it may appear in more than one of the subtype tables.

Semistructured Data

If you have many subtypes or if you must support new attributes frequently, you can add a column of type BLOB or related type to store data in a format such as XML or JSON, which encodes both the attribute names and their values. This pattern is also called the *Serialized LOB*. Many SQL databases now have a specialized JSON data type for this purpose.

EAV/soln/create-blob-tables.sql
```
CREATE TABLE Issues (
  issue_id          SERIAL PRIMARY KEY,
  reported_by       BIGINT UNSIGNED NOT NULL,
  product_id        BIGINT UNSIGNED,
  priority          VARCHAR(20),
  version_resolved  VARCHAR(20),
  status            VARCHAR(20),
  issue_type        VARCHAR(10),  -- BUG or FEATURE
  attributes        JSON NOT NULL, -- all dynamic attributes for the row
  FOREIGN KEY (reported_by) REFERENCES Accounts(account_id),
  FOREIGN KEY (product_id) REFERENCES Products(product_id)
);
```

The advantage of this design is that it's completely extensible, but the format is more or less standard, and tools exist for deriving the elements of data within. That's why it's called "semistructured." You can store new attributes in the semistructured column at any time. Every row may even potentially store a distinct set of attributes, so you can have as many subtypes as you have rows.

The disadvantage is that it's awkward to use SQL to access specific attributes in such a structure. Many SQL implementations have added built-in functions for searching or transforming XML or JSON, but these aren't as graceful or efficient as working with the more traditional data types. SQL expressions and operators were meant to treat each column as a discrete, scalar data value, not a complex, semistructured document.

Semistructured data is best used when you can't limit yourself to a finite set of subtypes and when you need complete flexibility to define new attributes at any time.

Post-Processing

Unfortunately, sometimes you're stuck with the EAV design, such as if you inherited a project and can't change it or if your company acquired a third-party software platform that uses EAV. If this is the case, familiarize yourself with the trouble areas in the "Antipattern" section so you can anticipate and plan for the extra work it takes to work with this design.

Above all, don't try to write queries that fetch entities as a single row as though data were stored in a conventional table. Instead, query the attributes associated with the entity and fetch them as a set of rows, the way that they are stored.

EAV/soln/post-process.sql
```sql
SELECT issue_id, attr_name, attr_value
FROM IssueAttributes
WHERE issue_id = 1234;
```

The result of this query might look like the following:

issue_id	attr_name	attr_value
1234	date_reported	2009-06-01
1234	description	Saving does not work
1234	priority	HIGH
1234	product	Open RoundFile
1234	reported_by	Bill
1234	severity	loss of functionality
1234	status	NEW

This query is easier for you to write, and it's easier for the database to process. It returns all the attributes associated with the issue, even if you don't know how many there are when you write the query.

To use a result in this format, you need to write application code to loop over the rows of the result set and set properties of an object in your application. See the following Python code for an example:

EAV/soln/post-process.py
```python
import mysql.connector

cnx = mysql.connector.connect(user='scott', database='test')
cursor = cnx.cursor()

issue_id = 1234
query = """
    SELECT attr_name, attr_value
    FROM IssueAttributes
    WHERE issue_id = %s"""
cursor.execute(query, (issue_id,))
issue = {}
for (row) in cursor:
    (field, value) = row
    issue[field] = value

cnx.commit()
```

This might seem like too much work, but it's the consequence of a system-within-a-system like EAV. SQL already offers a way to identify distinct attributes—in distinct columns. By using EAV, you have abandoned SQL's conventional way to manage metadata, so you shouldn't be surprised that you need to write more code to do the work that SQL would have done for you.

Use metadata for metadata.

When you come to a fork in the road, take it!

> Yogi Berra

## CHAPTER 7

Polymorphic Associations

Let's allow users to make *comments* on bugs. A given bug may have many comments, but any given comment must pertain to a single bug. So, there's a one-to-many relationship between Bugs and Comments. The entity-relationship diagram for this kind of simple association is shown in the following diagram.

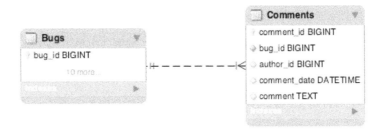

The following SQL shows how you would create this table:

Polymorphic/intro/comments.sql
```
CREATE TABLE Comments (
  comment_id    SERIAL PRIMARY KEY,
  bug_id        BIGINT UNSIGNED NOT NULL,
  author_id     BIGINT UNSIGNED NOT NULL,
  comment_date DATETIME NOT NULL,
  comment       TEXT NOT NULL,
  FOREIGN KEY (author_id) REFERENCES Accounts(account_id),
  FOREIGN KEY (bug_id) REFERENCES Bugs(bug_id)
);
```

However, you might have two tables you want to comment on. Bugs and FeatureRequests are similar entities, although you might store them as separate tables (see Concrete Table Inheritance, on page 71). You'd like to store Comments in a single table regardless of whether they pertain to either type of issue—a bug or a feature —but you can't declare a foreign key that references multiple parent tables. The following declaration is nonsense:

Polymorphic/intro/nonsense.sql

```
  ...
  FOREIGN KEY (issue_id)
      REFERENCES Bugs(issue_id) OR FeatureRequests(issue_id)
);
```

Developers also try to write invalid SQL to query multiple tables, such as the following:

Polymorphic/intro/nonsense.sql

```
SELECT c.*, i.summary, i.status
FROM Comments AS c
JOIN c.issue_type AS i USING (issue_id);
```

You can't join to a different table per row in SQL. SQL syntax requires that all the tables are named at the time you submit the query. The tables can't vary during the query. There's something wrong with this picture.

Objective: Reference Multiple Parents

At first, it seems like a natural and intuitive concept that the child table Comments can reference either of those parent tables. The foreign key on a given row is either a reference to Bugs, or a reference to FeatureRequests. Somehow the column must carry information about which table it references on a row-by-row basis.

Antipattern: Use Dual-Purpose Foreign Key

A solution for these cases has become popular enough to be given a name, *Polymorphic Associations.* This is also sometimes called a *promiscuous* association, because it references multiple tables.

Defining a Polymorphic Association

To make Polymorphic Associations work, you must add an extra string column alongside the foreign key on issue_id. The extra column contains the name of the parent table referenced by the current row.

In this example, the new column is called issue_type, and contains a string value, either *Bugs* or *FeatureRequests*, corresponding to the names of the two possible parent tables in this association.

Polymorphic/anti/comments.sql

```
CREATE TABLE Comments (
  comment_id   SERIAL PRIMARY KEY,
  issue_type   VARCHAR(20),    -- "Bugs" or "FeatureRequests"
  issue_id     BIGINT UNSIGNED NOT NULL,
  author       BIGINT UNSIGNED NOT NULL,
```

```
  comment_date DATETIME,
  comment      TEXT,
  FOREIGN KEY (author) REFERENCES Accounts(account_id)
);
```

You see one difference immediately: the foreign key declaration for issue_id is missing. In fact, since a legitimate foreign key constraint must specify exactly one table, a Polymorphic Association means that you can't declare this with SQL constraint syntax. As a result, there is no enforcement of data integrity to ensure that the value in Comments.issue_id matches a value in the parent table.

Likewise, no metadata ensures that the string in Comments.issue_type corresponds to a table that exists in this database.

Diagramming a Polymorphic Association

Entity-relationship diagrams don't have an official way to represent this relationship. Developers who want to use this design have to make up their own diagram style. You might see a diagram like the following:

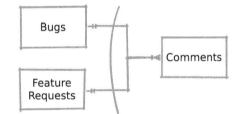

This diagram shows a foreign key that "forks," so a given row in the Comments table matches either one or the other parent table. The curved line that spans the fork is a convention that is sometimes used in these diagrams, but since this is an unofficial type of diagram, you shouldn't expect to see any style consistently.

Querying a Polymorphic Association

The issue_id value in the Comments table may occur in the primary key column of both parent tables, Bugs and FeatureRequests. Or the value may occur in one parent table but be missing in the other parent table. It's therefore crucial to use the issue_type correctly when joining the child table to the parent table. You must not match an issue_id value to the FeatureRequests table if it was intended to be matched to the Bugs table.

For example, this will retrieve comments for a given bug by its primary key value 1234:

Polymorphic/anti/select.sql

```
SELECT *
FROM Bugs AS b JOIN Comments AS c
  ON (b.issue_id = c.issue_id AND c.issue_type = 'Bugs')
WHERE b.issue_id = 1234;
```

Although the previous query works if bugs are stored in the single table Bugs, you run into a problem when Comments is associated with both tables Bugs and FeatureRequests. In SQL, you must specify all tables in a join; you can't join Comments to two separate tables, switching between them row by row, depending on the value in the Comments.issue_type column.

To retrieve either a bug or a feature given a specific comment, you need to run a query with an outer join to both parent tables. Only one of the parent tables will satisfy its join, since part of the join condition relies on the value in the Comment.issue_type column. Using an outer join means that fields from the table that does not match contain null in the result set.

Polymorphic/anti/select.sql

```
SELECT *
FROM Comments AS c
  LEFT OUTER JOIN Bugs AS b
    ON (b.issue_id = c.issue_id AND c.issue_type = 'Bugs')
  LEFT OUTER JOIN FeatureRequests AS f
    ON (f.issue_id = c.issue_id AND c.issue_type = 'FeatureRequests');
```

The result may look something like this:

c.comment_id	c.issue_type	c.issue_id	c.comment	b.issue_id	f.issue_id
6789	Bugs	1234	It crashes!	1234	NULL
9876	Feature...	2345	Great idea!	NULL	2345

Non-Object-Oriented Example

In the example of Bugs and FeatureRequests, these two parent tables are meant to model related subtypes. Polymorphic Associations may also be used when the parent tables are completely unrelated to each other. The following figure shows tables you might see in an ecommerce database. The two tables Users and Orders may be associated with Addresses. Again, the entity-relationship diagram must be improvised.

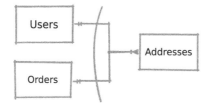

Polymorphic/anti/addresses.sql

```
CREATE TABLE Addresses (
  address_id    SERIAL PRIMARY KEY,
  parent        VARCHAR(20),       -- "Users" or "Orders"
  parent_id     BIGINT UNSIGNED NOT NULL,
  address       TEXT
);
```

In this case, the Addresses table contains a polymorphic column that names either *Users* or *Orders* as the parent table for a given address. Notice that you have to choose one or the other. You can't associate a given address with both a user and an order, even an order placed by that user, to ship merchandise to himself.

Also, if a user has a shipping address as well as a billing address, you need some way to make this distinction in the Addresses table; likewise, any other parents need to note the special usage of addresses in the Addresses table. These notes propagate like weeds.

Polymorphic/anti/addresses.sql

```
CREATE TABLE Addresses (
  address_id    SERIAL PRIMARY KEY,
  parent        VARCHAR(20),       -- "Users" or "Orders"
  parent_id     BIGINT UNSIGNED NOT NULL,
  users_usage   VARCHAR(20),       -- "billing" or "shipping"
  orders_usage  VARCHAR(20),       -- "billing" or "shipping"
  address       TEXT
);
```

How to Recognize the Antipattern

If you hear statements like the following, it's a clue that the Polymorphic Associations antipattern is being employed:

- "This tagging schema allows you to associate a tag (or other attribute) with *any* other resource in the database."

  As in EAV, you should be suspicious of any claims of unlimited flexibility, because it likely means that it breaks some rules.

- "You can't declare foreign keys in our database design."

  This is another red flag. Foreign keys are a fundamental feature of relational databases, and a design that can't work with proper referential integrity has a lot of problems.

- "What's the entity_type column for? Oh, that tells you which thing this other column points to."

  Any foreign key must reference the same table on all rows.

Chapter 7. Polymorphic Associations • 82

The Ruby on Rails framework supports Polymorphic Associations by declaring Active Record classes with the :polymorphic attribute.[1] For example, you could associate Comments to Bugs and FeatureRequests as follows:

Polymorphic/recog/commentable.rb
```
class Comment < ActiveRecord::Base
  belongs_to :commentable, :polymorphic => true
end

class Bug < ActiveRecord::Base
  has_many :comments, :as => :commentable
end

class FeatureRequest < ActiveRecord::Base
  has_many :comments, :as => :commentable
end
```

The Hibernate framework for Java supports inheritance relationships between entities using a variety of schema declarations.[2]

> ### Mixing Data with Metadata
>
> You might have noticed a similar characteristic between the Polymorphic Associations antipattern and the Entity-Attribute-Value antipattern described in the previous chapter. In both antipatterns, the name of a metadata object is stored as a string value. In EAV, the name of an attribute column is stored as a string in the attr_name column. In Polymorphic Associations, the names of the parent tables are stored in the issue_type column. This is sometimes called *mixing data with metadata*. This concept appears in another form in Chapter 8, Multicolumn Attributes, on page 89.

Legitimate Uses of the Antipattern

You should avoid the Polymorphic Associations antipattern—use constraints like foreign keys to ensure referential integrity. Polymorphic Associations often relies too much on application code instead of metadata.

You may find that this antipattern is unavoidable if you use an object-relational programming framework such as Hibernate. Such a framework may mitigate the risks introduced by Polymorphic Associations by encapsulating application logic to maintain referential integrity.

If you choose a mature and reputable framework, then you have some confidence that its designers have written the code to implement the association

---

1.   https://guides.rubyonrails.org/association_basics.html#polymorphic-associations
2.   https://docs.jboss.org/hibernate/orm/current/userguide/html_single/Hibernate_User_Guide.html#entity-inheritance

without error. However, if you are implementing Polymorphic Associations from scratch without the aid of a framework, you're reinventing the wheel.

Solution: Simplify the Relationship

It's better to redesign your database to avoid the weaknesses of Polymorphic Associations but still support the data modeling you need. The following sections describe a few solutions that accommodate the data relationship but make better use of metadata to enforce integrity.

Reverse the Reference

One solution to this antipattern is simple once you see the nature of the problem: *Polymorphic Associations are backward.*

Creating Intersection Tables

A foreign key in the child table Comments can't reference multiple parent tables, so instead, use multiple foreign keys to reference the Comments table. Create a separate intersection table for each parent table, and in each intersection table include a foreign key to Comments, as well as a foreign key to the respective parent table. This is shown in the following diagram.

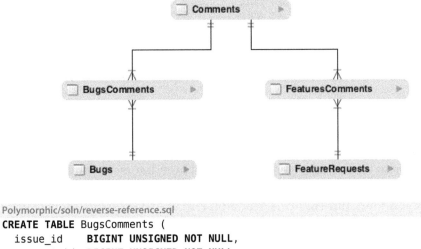

Polymorphic/soln/reverse-reference.sql
```sql
CREATE TABLE BugsComments (
  issue_id     BIGINT UNSIGNED NOT NULL,
  comment_id   BIGINT UNSIGNED NOT NULL,
  PRIMARY KEY (issue_id, comment_id),
  FOREIGN KEY (issue_id) REFERENCES Bugs(issue_id),
  FOREIGN KEY (comment_id) REFERENCES Comments(comment_id)
);
```

```
CREATE TABLE FeaturesComments (
  issue_id    BIGINT UNSIGNED NOT NULL,
  comment_id  BIGINT UNSIGNED NOT NULL,
  PRIMARY KEY (issue_id, comment_id),
  FOREIGN KEY (issue_id) REFERENCES FeatureRequests(issue_id),
  FOREIGN KEY (comment_id) REFERENCES Comments(comment_id)
);
```

This solution removes the need for the Comments.issue_type column. Now the metadata enforces data integrity, instead of relying on application code to manage the associations without error.

Putting Up Traffic Lights

A potential weakness of this solution is that it permits associations that you might not want to be permitted. Intersection tables usually model many-to-many associations, so this would allow a given comment to be associated with multiple bugs or multiple feature requests. However, you probably want each comment to pertain to only one bug or one feature request. Enforce at least part of this rule by declaring a UNIQUE constraint on the comment_id column of each intersection table.

Polymorphic/soln/reverse-unique.sql
```
CREATE TABLE BugsComments (
  issue_id    BIGINT UNSIGNED NOT NULL,
  comment_id  BIGINT UNSIGNED NOT NULL,
  UNIQUE KEY (comment_id),
  PRIMARY KEY (issue_id, comment_id),
  FOREIGN KEY (issue_id) REFERENCES Bugs(issue_id),
  FOREIGN KEY (comment_id) REFERENCES Comments(comment_id)
);
```

This ensures that a given comment can be referenced only once in the intersection table, which naturally prevents it from being associated with multiple bugs or multiple feature requests. However, the metadata doesn't prevent a given comment from being referenced once in both intersection tables, associating the comment with both a bug and a feature request. This is probably not what you want, but ensuring against it remains the responsibility of your application code.

Looking Both Ways

You can query the comments for a specific bug or feature request simply by using the intersection table.

Polymorphic/soln/reverse-join.sql

```
SELECT *
FROM BugsComments AS b
  JOIN Comments AS c USING (comment_id)
WHERE b.issue_id = 1234;
```

Query the matching bug or feature request based on an instance of a comment by using an outer join to both intersection tables. You have to name all the possible parent tables, but that's no more complex than the query you had to use in the Polymorphic Associations antipattern. Also, you can depend on referential integrity when using intersection tables, whereas with Polymorphic Associations you couldn't.

Polymorphic/soln/reverse-join.sql

```
SELECT *
FROM Comments AS c
  LEFT OUTER JOIN (
    BugsComments JOIN Bugs AS b USING (issue_id)
  ) USING (comment_id)
  LEFT OUTER JOIN (
    FeaturesComments JOIN FeatureRequests AS f USING (issue_id)
  ) USING (comment_id)
WHERE c.comment_id = 9876;
```

Merging Lanes

Sometimes you need to make the result of a query against multiple parent tables appear as if you had stored the parents in a single table (see Single Table Inheritance, on page 70). You can do this in either of two ways.

First look at the following query using UNION:

Polymorphic/soln/reverse-union.sql

```
SELECT b.issue_id, b.description, b.reporter, b.priority, b.status,
    b.severity, b.version_affected,
    NULL AS sponsor
  FROM Comments AS c
    JOIN (BugsComments JOIN Bugs AS b USING (issue_id))
      USING (comment_id)
  WHERE c.comment_id = 9876;

UNION
  SELECT f.issue_id, f.description, f.reporter, f.priority, f.status,
    NULL AS severity, NULL AS version_affected,
    f.sponsor
  FROM Comments AS c
    JOIN (FeaturesComments JOIN FeatureRequests AS f USING (issue_id))
      USING (comment_id)
  WHERE c.comment_id = 9876;
```

This query should be guaranteed to return a single row if your application has associated each comment with exactly one parent table. Since query results can be combined with UNION only if their columns are the same in number and data type, you must provide null placeholders for columns that are unique to each parent table. You must list the columns in the same order in both queries involved in the UNION.

Alternatively, look at the following query using the SQL COALESCE() function. This function returns its first non-null argument. Since you are using an outer join in the query, a comment that pertains to a feature request and has no matching row in Bugs would return all fields in b.* as null. Likewise, all fields in f.* would be null if the comment pertains to a bug instead of a feature request. List the fields specific to one parent table or the other in a simple manner; if they are irrelevant to the matching parent table, they are returned as null.

Polymorphic/soln/reverse-coalesce.sql

```sql
SELECT c.*,
  COALESCE(b.issue_id,    f.issue_id    ) AS issue_id,
  COALESCE(b.description, f.description) AS description,
  COALESCE(b.reporter,    f.reporter    ) AS reporter,
  COALESCE(b.priority,    f.priority    ) AS priority,
  COALESCE(b.status,      f.status      ) AS status,
  b.severity,
  b.version_affected,
  f.sponsor
FROM Comments AS c
  LEFT OUTER JOIN (BugsComments JOIN Bugs AS b USING (issue_id))
    USING (comment_id)
  LEFT OUTER JOIN (FeaturesComments JOIN FeatureRequests AS f USING (issue_id))
    USING (comment_id)
WHERE c.comment_id = 9876;
```

Both of these queries are pretty complex, so they're good candidates for a database view, and you can use them more simply in your application.

Create a Common Super-Table

In object-oriented polymorphism, two subtypes can be referenced similarly because they implicitly share a common supertype. In SQL, the Polymorphic Associations antipattern leaves out that crucial entity: the common supertype. Fix that by creating a base table that all of your parent tables extend (see Class Table Inheritance, on page 72). Add the foreign key in the child Comments table to reference the base table. You don't need an issue_type column. The diagram and code shown on page 87 shows how you can implement this.

```sql
CREATE TABLE Issues (
  issue_id     SERIAL PRIMARY KEY
);

CREATE TABLE Bugs (
  issue_id     BIGINT UNSIGNED PRIMARY KEY,
  FOREIGN KEY (issue_id) REFERENCES Issues(issue_id),
  . . .
);

CREATE TABLE FeatureRequests (
  issue_id     BIGINT UNSIGNED PRIMARY KEY,
  FOREIGN KEY (issue_id) REFERENCES Issues(issue_id),
  . . .
);

CREATE TABLE Comments (
  comment_id   SERIAL PRIMARY KEY,
  issue_id     BIGINT UNSIGNED NOT NULL,
  author       BIGINT UNSIGNED NOT NULL,
  comment_date DATETIME,
  comment      TEXT,
  FOREIGN KEY (issue_id) REFERENCES Issues(issue_id),
  FOREIGN KEY (author) REFERENCES Accounts(account_id),
);
```

Note that the primary keys of Bugs and FeatureRequests are also foreign keys. They reference the surrogate key value generated in the Issues table, instead of generating a new value for themselves.

Given a specific comment, you can retrieve the referenced bug or feature request using a relatively simple query. You don't have to include the Issues table in that query at all, unless you defined attribute columns in that table. Also, since the primary key value of the Bugs table and its ancestor Issues table are the same, you can join Bugs directly to Comments. You can join two tables even if there is no foreign key constraint linking them directly, as long as you use columns that represent comparable information in your database.

Polymorphic/soln/super-join.sql
```
SELECT *
FROM Comments AS c
  LEFT OUTER JOIN Bugs AS b USING (issue_id)
  LEFT OUTER JOIN FeatureRequests AS f USING (issue_id)
WHERE c.comment_id = 9876;
```

Given a specific bug, you can retrieve its comments just as easily.

Polymorphic/soln/super-join.sql
```
SELECT *
FROM Bugs AS b
  JOIN Comments AS c USING (issue_id)
WHERE b.issue_id = 1234;
```

The point is that if you use an ancestor table like Issues, you can rely on the enforcement of your database's data integrity by foreign keys.

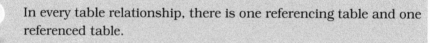

> In every table relationship, there is one referencing table and one referenced table.

*The sublime and the ridiculous are often so nearly related that
it is difficult to class them separately.*

> *Thomas Paine*

## CHAPTER 8

Multicolumn Attributes

I can't count the number of times I have created a table to store people's contact information. Always this kind of table has commonplace columns such as the person's name, salutation, address, and probably company name.

Phone numbers are a little trickier. People use multiple numbers: a home number, a work number, a fax number, and a mobile number are common. In the contact information table, it's easy to store these in four columns.

Users in this contact table are likely to have additional numbers. The person's assistant, second mobile phone, or field office have distinct phone numbers, and there could be other unforeseen categories. You could create more columns for the less common cases, but that seems clumsy because it adds seldom-used fields to data entry forms. It's unclear how many columns would be needed to store all potential variations.

Objective: Store Multivalue Attributes

This is the same objective as in Chapter 2, Jaywalking, on page 9: an attribute seems to belong in one table, but the attribute has multiple values. Previously, it was shown that combining multiple values into a comma-separated string makes it hard to validate the values, hard to read or change individual values, and hard to compute aggregate expressions such as counting the number of distinct values.

Let's use a new example to illustrate this antipattern. You want the bugs database to allow *tags* so you can categorize bugs. Some bugs may be categorized by the software subsystem that they affect, for instance *printing*, *reports*, or *email*. Other bugs may be categorized by the nature of the defect; for instance, a crash bug could be tagged *crash*, while you could tag a report of slowness with *performance*, and you could tag a bad color choice in the user interface with *cosmetic*.

The bug-tagging feature must support multiple tags, because tags are not necessarily mutually exclusive. A defect could affect multiple systems or could affect the performance of printing.

Antipattern: Create Multiple Columns

You still have to account for multiple values in the attribute, but the new solution must store only a single value in each column. It might seem natural to create multiple columns in this table, each containing a single tag.

Multi-Column/anti/create-table.sql
```
CREATE TABLE Bugs (
  bug_id       SERIAL PRIMARY KEY,
  description VARCHAR(1000),
  tag1         VARCHAR(20),
  tag2         VARCHAR(20),
  tag3         VARCHAR(20)
);
```

As you assign tags to a given bug, you'd put values in one of these three columns. Unused columns remain null.

Multi-Column/anti/update.sql
```
UPDATE Bugs SET tag2 = 'performance' WHERE bug_id = 3456;
```

bug_id	description	tag1	tag2	tag3
1234	Crashes while saving	crash	NULL	NULL
3456	Increase performance	printing	performance	NULL
5678	Support XML	NULL	NULL	NULL

Tasks you could do easily with a normal attribute are now more complex.

Searching for Values

When searching for bugs with a given tag, you must search all three columns, because the tag string could occupy any of these columns. For example, to retrieve bugs that reference *performance*, use a query like this one:

Multi-Column/anti/search.sql
```
SELECT * FROM Bugs
WHERE tag1 = 'performance'
   OR tag2 = 'performance'
   OR tag3 = 'performance';
```

You might need to search for bugs that reference both tags, *performance* and *printing*. To do this, use a query like the following one. Remember to use parentheses correctly, because OR has lower precedence than AND.

```
Multi-Column/anti/search-two-tags.sql
SELECT * FROM Bugs
WHERE (tag1 = 'performance' OR tag2 = 'performance' OR tag3 = 'performance')
  AND (tag1 = 'printing' OR tag2 = 'printing' OR tag3 = 'printing');
```

The syntax required to search for a single value over multiple columns is lengthy and tedious to write. You can make it more compact by using an IN predicate in a slightly untraditional manner:

```
Multi-Column/anti/search-two-tags.sql
SELECT * FROM Bugs
WHERE 'performance' IN (tag1, tag2, tag3)
  AND 'printing'    IN (tag1, tag2, tag3);
```

Adding and Removing Values

Adding and removing a value from the set of columns presents its own issues. Simply using UPDATE to change one of the columns isn't safe, since you can't be sure which column is unoccupied, if any. You might have to retrieve the row into your application to see.

```
Multi-Column/anti/add-tag-two-step.sql
SELECT * FROM Bugs WHERE bug_id = 3456;
```

In this case, for instance, the result shows you that tag2 is null. Then you can form the UPDATE statement.

```
Multi-Column/anti/add-tag-two-step.sql
UPDATE Bugs SET tag2 = 'performance' WHERE bug_id = 3456;
```

You face the risk that in the moment after you query the table and before you update it, another client has gone through the same steps of reading the row and updating it. Depending on who applied their update first, either you or he risks getting an update conflict error or having his changes overwritten by the other. You can avoid this two-step query by using complex SQL expressions.

The following statement uses the NULLIF() function to make each column null if it equals a specific value. NULLIF() is a standard SQL function that returns null if its two arguments are equal.

```
Multi-Column/anti/remove-tag.sql
UPDATE Bugs
SET tag1 = NULLIF(tag1, 'performance'),
    tag2 = NULLIF(tag2, 'performance'),
    tag3 = NULLIF(tag3, 'performance')
WHERE bug_id = 3456;
```

The following statement adds the new tag *performance* to the first column that is currently null. However, if none of the three columns is null, then the statement makes no change to the row, and the new tag value is not recorded at all. Also, constructing this statement is laborious. Notice you must repeat the string *performance* six times.

Multi-Column/anti/add-tag.sql
```sql
UPDATE Bugs
SET tag1 = CASE
      WHEN 'performance' IN (tag2, tag3) THEN tag1
      ELSE COALESCE(tag1, 'performance') END,
    tag2 = CASE
      WHEN 'performance' IN (tag1, tag3) THEN tag2
      ELSE COALESCE(tag2, 'performance') END,
    tag3 = CASE
      WHEN 'performance' IN (tag1, tag2) THEN tag3
      ELSE COALESCE(tag3, 'performance') END
WHERE bug_id = 3456;
```

Ensuring Uniqueness

You probably don't want the same value to appear in multiple columns, but when you use the Multicolumn Attributes antipattern, the database can't prevent this. In other words, it's hard to prevent the following statement:

Multi-Column/anti/insert-duplicate.sql
```sql
INSERT INTO Bugs (description, tag1, tag2, tag3)
  VALUES ('printing is slow', 'printing', 'performance', 'performance');
```

Handling Growing Sets of Values

Another weakness of this design is that three columns might not be enough. To keep the design of one value per column, you must define as many columns as the maximum number of tags a bug can have. How can you predict, at the time you define the table, what that greatest number will be?

One tactic is to guess at a moderate number of columns and expand later, if necessary, by adding more columns. Most databases allow you to restructure existing tables, so you can add Bugs.tag4, or even more columns, as you need them.

Multi-Column/anti/alter-table.sql
```sql
ALTER TABLE Bugs ADD COLUMN tag4 VARCHAR(20);
```

However, this change is costly in three ways:

- Restructuring a database table that already contains data may require locking the entire table, blocking access for other concurrent clients.

- Some databases implement this kind of table restructure by defining a new table to match the desired structure, copying the data from the old table, and then dropping the old table. If the table in question has a lot of data, this transfer can take a long time.

- When you add a column in the set for a multicolumn attribute, you must revisit every SQL statement in every application that uses this table, editing the statement to support new columns.

Multi-Column/anti/search-four-columns.sql
```
SELECT * FROM Bugs
WHERE tag1 = 'performance'
  OR tag2 = 'performance'
  OR tag3 = 'performance'
  OR tag4 = 'performance'; -- you must add this new term
```

This is a meticulous and time-consuming development task. If you forget to revise any of the queries that work with these tags columns, it will cause bugs that are difficult to detect.

How to Recognize the Antipattern

If the user interface or documentation for your project describes an attribute to which you can assign multiple values but is limited to a fixed maximum number of values, this might indicate that the Multicolumn Attributes antipattern is in use.

Admittedly, some attributes might have a limit on the number of selections on purpose, but it's more common that there's no such limit. If the limit seems arbitrary or unjustified, it might be because of this antipattern.

Another clue that the antipattern might be in use is if you hear statements such as the following:

- "How many is the greatest number of tags we need to support?"

  You need to decide how many columns to define in the table for a multi-value attribute like tag.

- "How can I search multiple columns at the same time in SQL?"

  If you're searching for a given value across multiple columns, this is a clue that the multiple columns should really be stored as a single logical attribute.

> ## Patterns Among Antipatterns
>
> The Jaywalking and Multicolumn Attributes antipatterns have a common thread: these two antipatterns are both solutions for the same objective: to store an attribute that may have multiple values.
>
> In the Jaywalking antipattern, the examples related to many-to-many relationships. In this chapter, a simpler one-to-many relationship is shown. Be aware that both antipatterns are sometimes used for both types of relationships.

Legitimate Uses of the Antipattern

In some cases, an attribute may have a fixed number of choices, and the position or order of these choices may be significant. For example, a given bug may be associated with several users' accounts, but the nature of each association is unique. One is the user who reported the bug, another is a programmer assigned to fix the bug, and another is the quality control engineer assigned to verify the fix. Even though the values in each of these columns are compatible, their significance and usage actually makes them logically different attributes.

It would be valid to define three ordinary columns in the Bugs table to store each of these three attributes. The drawbacks described in this chapter aren't as important, because you are more likely to use them separately. Sometimes you might still need to query over all three columns, for instance to report everyone involved with a given bug. You can accept this complexity for a few cases in exchange for greater simplicity in most other cases.

Another way to structure this is to create a dependent table for multiple associations from the Bugs table to the Accounts table and give this new table an extra column to note the role each account has relative to that bug. However, this structure might lead to some of the problems described in Chapter 6, Entity-Attribute-Value, on page 61.

Solution: Create Dependent Table

As in Chapter 2, Jaywalking, on page 9, the best solution is to create a dependent table with one column for the multivalue attribute. Store the multiple values in multiple rows instead of multiple columns. Also, define a foreign key in the dependent table to associate the values to its parent row in the Bugs table.

Multi-Column/soln/create-table.sql

```
CREATE TABLE Tags (
  bug_id        BIGINT UNSIGNED NOT NULL
  tag           VARCHAR(20),
  PRIMARY KEY (bug_id, tag),
  FOREIGN KEY (bug_id) REFERENCES Bugs(bug_id)
);

INSERT INTO Tags (bug_id, tag)
  VALUES (1234, 'crash'), (3456, 'printing'), (3456, 'performance');
```

When all the tags associated with a bug are in a single column, searching for bugs with a given tag is more straightforward.

Multi-Column/soln/search.sql

```
SELECT * FROM Bugs JOIN Tags USING (bug_id)
WHERE tag = 'performance';
```

Even more complex searches, such as a bug that relates to two specific tags, are easy to read.

Multi-Column/soln/search-two-tags.sql

```
SELECT * FROM Bugs
  JOIN Tags AS t1 USING (bug_id)
  JOIN Tags AS t2 USING (bug_id)
WHERE t1.tag = 'printing' AND t2.tag = 'performance';
```

You can add or remove an association more easily than with the Multicolumn Attributes antipattern—just insert or delete a row from the dependent table. There's no need to inspect multiple columns to see where you can add a value.

Multi-Column/soln/insert-delete.sql

```
INSERT INTO Tags (bug_id, tag) VALUES (1234, 'save');

DELETE FROM Tags WHERE bug_id = 1234 AND tag = 'crash';
```

The PRIMARY KEY constraint ensures that no duplication is allowed. A given tag can be applied to a given bug only once. If you attempt to insert a duplicate, SQL returns a duplicate key error.

You're not limited to three tags per bug, as you were when the Bugs table had three tagN columns. Now you can apply as many tags per bug as you need.

> Use a single column, over multiple rows, to store values with the same meaning.

Mini-Antipattern: Storing Prices

Usually, relational database design discourages storing redundant data. It's better to follow rules of normalization (see Appendix 1, Rules of Normalization, on page 321), and these rules guide us to store a column in only one table. A given fact is represented by a row of data, and should be stored only once. If the same fact is represented in more than one place in a database, there's a risk that the two instances will disagree, and then it's not clear which is really the correct information. Is there any exception to this rule?

Take for example a table Orders that stores a record of a customer buying a product in a commerce database. This example includes a column price, which is the result of multiplying the unit price times the quantity the customer bought.

Multi-Column/mini/orders.sql
```
CREATE TABLE Orders (
  order_id SERIAL PRIMARY KEY
  order_date DATE NOT NULL,
  customer_id INT NOT NULL,
  merchandise_id INT NOT NULL,
  quantity INT NOT NULL
  price NUMERIC(9,2) NOT NULL
);
```

We can assume the unit price of that product is already stored in another table, Merchandise. Is it then redundant to store the total order price in the Orders table? They should be the same.

Consider that prices can change. The price the customer paid on one day might not be the price for the same merchandise the next month, or even the next day. Besides that, the merchandise might have been on sale the day the customer bought it, so the price was lower. Or the customer may have qualified for a discount as a senior, or a veteran, or through some membership with the store. There are many legitimate reasons why a price in the Orders table isn't the same as the current price for the same item in the Merchandise table.

It's not really a violation of the rule that each fact must be stored only once. The column in the Orders table represents a different fact than the column in the Merchandise table: the price in Orders is the price that customer paid on the date they bought it and after all discounts were calculated.

This example is about prices, but the same principle could apply in other scenarios. The members of a sports team change every year, and you need to know who was on the team every year or even every game to analyze their past performance. An actor might change their name, so they are credited differently in some of their films.

These scenarios have something in common: they are all intersection tables for a many-to-many relationship (Orders is between customers and merchandise; Lineup is between sports players and games; Cast is between actors and films). The fact stored in the intersection table is about a given association between two (or more) entities. If one of the attributes had a different value on that occasion than it does today, it's necessary to store the value it had at that time, and it's appropriate to make that an attribute in the association table.

Why then, can one desire too much of a good thing?
> *William Shakespeare, As You Like It*

## CHAPTER 9

Metadata Tribbles

My wife worked for years as a programmer in Oracle PL/SQL and Java. She described a case that showed how a database design that was intended to simplify work instead created more work.

A table, Customers, used by the Sales division at her company kept data such as customers' contact information, their business type, and how much revenue had been received from that customer:

Metadata-Tribbles/intro/create-table.sql
```
CREATE TABLE Customers (
  customer_id   NUMBER(9) PRIMARY KEY,
  contact_info  VARCHAR(255),
  business_type VARCHAR(20),
  revenue       NUMBER(9,2)
);
```

The Sales division needed to break down the revenue by year so they could track recently active customers. They decided to add a series of new columns, each column's name indicating the year it covered:

Metadata-Tribbles/intro/alter-table.sql
```
ALTER TABLE Customers ADD (revenue2002 NUMBER(9,2));
ALTER TABLE Customers ADD (revenue2003 NUMBER(9,2));
ALTER TABLE Customers ADD (revenue2004 NUMBER(9,2));
```

Then they entered incomplete data, only for customers they thought were interesting to track. On most rows, they left null in those revenue columns. The programmers started wondering whether they could store other information in these mostly unused columns.

Each year, they needed to add one more column. A database administrator was responsible for managing Oracle's tablespaces. So each year, they had a series of meetings, scheduled a data migration to restructure the tablespace, and added the new column. Ultimately they wasted a lot of time and money.

Objective: Support Scalability

Performance degrades for any database query as the volume of data goes up. Even if a query returns results promptly with a few thousand rows, the tables naturally accumulate data to the point where the same query may not have acceptable performance. Using indexes intelligently helps, but nevertheless the tables grow, and this affects the speed of queries against them.

The objective is to structure a database to improve the performance of queries and support tables that grow steadily.

Antipattern: Clone Tables or Columns

In the television series *Star Trek* ("Star Trek" and related marks are trademarks of CBS Studios Inc.), "tribbles" are small furry animals kept as pets. Tribbles are very appealing at first, but soon they reveal their tendency to reproduce out of control, and managing the overpopulation of tribbles becomes a serious problem.

The tribble population outgrows every space, and no one wants to take responsibility for them. Eventually, Captain Kirk discovers that his ship and crew can't function, and he has to order his crew to make it top priority to remove the tribbles.

Database tables or columns can become like the tribbles, multiplying out of control, if your database design is to create new tables or columns for each successive data value.

We know from experience that querying a table with few rows is quicker than querying a table with many rows, all other things being equal. This leads to a common fallacy that we must make every table contain fewer rows, no matter what we have to do. This leads to two forms of the antipattern:

- Split a single long table into multiple smaller tables, using table names based on distinct data values in one of the table's attributes.

- Split a single column into multiple columns, using column names based on distinct values in another attribute.

You can't get something for nothing; to meet the goal of having few rows in every table, you have to either create tables that have too many columns or else create a greater number of tables. In both cases, you find that the number of tables or columns continues to grow, since new data values can make you create new schema objects.

Spawning Tables

To split data into separate tables, you'd need some policy for which rows belong in which tables. For example, you could split them up by the year in the date_reported column:

Metadata-Tribbles/anti/create-tables.sql
```
CREATE TABLE Bugs_2019 ( . . . );
CREATE TABLE Bugs_2020 ( . . . );
CREATE TABLE Bugs_2021 ( . . . );
```

As you insert rows into the database, it's your responsibility to use the correct table, depending on the values you insert:

Metadata-Tribbles/anti/insert.sql
```
INSERT INTO Bugs_2021 (..., date_reported, ...)
VALUES (..., '2021-06-01', ...);
```

Fast forward to January 1 of the next year. Your application starts getting an error from all new bug reports, because you didn't remember to create the Bugs_2023 table.

Metadata-Tribbles/anti/insert.sql
```
INSERT INTO Bugs_2022 (..., date_reported, ...)
VALUES (..., '2022-02-20', ...);
```

This means that introducing a new *data* value can cause a need for a new *metadata* object. This is not usually the relationship between data and metadata in SQL.

Managing Data Integrity

Suppose your boss is trying to count bugs reported during the year, but his numbers don't add up. After investigating, you discover that some 2022 bugs were entered in the Bugs_2021 table by mistake. The following query should always return an empty result, so if it doesn't, you have a problem:

Metadata-Tribbles/anti/data-integrity.sql
```
SELECT * FROM Bugs_2021
WHERE date_reported NOT BETWEEN '2021-01-01' AND '2021-12-31';
```

There's no way to limit the data relative to the name of its table automatically, but you can declare a CHECK constraint in each of your tables:

Metadata-Tribbles/anti/check-constraint.sql
```
CREATE TABLE Bugs_2021 (
  -- other columns
  date_reported DATE CHECK (EXTRACT(YEAR FROM date_reported) = 2021)
);
```

```
CREATE TABLE Bugs_2022 (
  -- other columns
  date_reported DATE CHECK (EXTRACT(YEAR FROM date_reported) = 2022)
);
```

Remember to adjust the value in the CHECK constraint when you create Bugs_2023. If you make a mistake, you could create a table that rejects the rows it's supposed to accept.

Synchronizing Data

One day, your customer support analyst asks to change a bug report date. It's in the database as reported on 2022-01-03, but the customer who reported it actually sent it a week earlier, on 2021-12-27.

You could change the date with a simple UPDATE:

Metadata-Tribbles/anti/anomaly.sql
```
UPDATE Bugs_2012
SET date_reported = '2021-12-27'
WHERE bug_id = 1234;
```

Unfortunately, this correction makes the row an invalid entry in the Bugs_2022 table. You would need to remove the row from one table and insert it into the other table, in the infrequent case that a simple UPDATE would cause this anomaly.

Metadata-Tribbles/anti/synchronize.sql
```
INSERT INTO Bugs_2021 (bug_id, date_reported, ...)
  SELECT bug_id, date_reported, ...
  FROM Bugs_2022
  WHERE bug_id = 1234;

DELETE FROM Bugs_2022 WHERE bug_id = 1234;
```

Ensuring Uniqueness

You should make sure that the primary key values are unique across all the split tables. If you need to move a row from one table to another, you need some assurance that the primary key value doesn't conflict with another row.

If you use a database that supports sequence objects, you can use a single sequence to generate values for all the split tables. For databases that support only per-table ID uniqueness, this may be more awkward. You have to define one extra table solely to produce primary key values:

Metadata-Tribbles/anti/id-generator.sql
```
CREATE TABLE BugsIdGenerator (bug_id SERIAL PRIMARY KEY);

INSERT INTO BugsIdGenerator (bug_id) VALUES (DEFAULT);
ROLLBACK;

INSERT INTO Bugs_2022 (bug_id, . . .)
  VALUES (LAST_INSERT_ID(), . . .);
```

Querying Across Tables

Inevitably, your boss needs a query that references multiple tables. For example, he may ask for a count of all open bugs regardless of the year they were created. You can reconstruct the full set of bugs using a UNION of all the split tables and query that as a derived table:

Metadata-Tribbles/anti/union.sql
```
SELECT b.status, COUNT(*) AS count_per_status FROM (
  SELECT * FROM Bugs_2020
    UNION
  SELECT * FROM Bugs_2021
    UNION
  SELECT * FROM Bugs_2022 ) AS b
GROUP BY b.status;
```

As the years go on and you create more tables such as Bugs_2023, you need to keep your application code up-to-date to reference the newly created tables.

Synchronizing Metadata

Your boss tells you to add a column to track the hours of work required to resolve each bug.

Metadata-Tribbles/anti/alter-table.sql
```
ALTER TABLE Bugs_2021 ADD COLUMN hours NUMERIC(9,2);
```

If you've split the table, then the new column applies only to the one table you alter. None of the other tables contains the new column.

If you use a UNION query across your split tables as in the previous section, you stumble upon a new problem: you can combine tables using UNION if they have the same columns. If they differ, then you have to name only the columns that all tables have in common, without using the * wildcard.

Managing Referential Integrity

If a dependent table like Comments references Bugs, the dependent table cannot declare a foreign key. A foreign key must specify a single table, but in this case the parent table is split into many.

Metadata-Tribbles/anti/foreign-key.sql
```
CREATE TABLE Comments (
  comment_id        SERIAL PRIMARY KEY,
  bug_id            BIGINT UNSIGNED NOT NULL,
  FOREIGN KEY (bug_id) REFERENCES Bugs_????(bug_id)
);
```

The split table may also have problems being a dependent instead of a parent. For example, Bugs.reported_by references the Accounts table. If you want to query all bugs reported by a given person regardless of year, use a query like this:

Metadata-Tribbles/anti/join-union.sql
```
SELECT * FROM Accounts a
JOIN (
    SELECT * FROM Bugs_2019
    UNION ALL
    SELECT * FROM Bugs_2020
    UNION ALL
    SELECT * FROM Bugs_2021
  ) t ON (a.account_id = t.reported_by)
```

Identifying Metadata Tribbles Columns

Columns can be Metadata Tribbles, too. You can create a table containing columns that are bound to propagate by their nature, as we saw in the story at the beginning of this chapter.

Another example we might have in our bugs database is a table that records summary data for project metrics, where individual columns store subtotals. For instance, in the following table, it's only a matter of time before you need to add the column bugs_fixed_2022:

Metadata-Tribbles/anti/multi-column.sql
```
CREATE TABLE ProjectHistory (
  bugs_fixed_2019  INT,
  bugs_fixed_2020  INT,
  bugs_fixed_2021  INT
);
```

How to Recognize the Antipattern

The following phrases may indicate that the Metadata Tribbles antipattern is growing in your database:

- "Then we need to create a table (or column) per..."

  When you describe your database with phrases using *per* in this way, you're splitting tables by distinct values in one of the columns.

> ### Mixing Metadata with Data
>
> Notice that by appending the year onto the base table name, we've combined a data value with a metadata identifier.
>
> This is the reverse of *mixing data with metadata* that we saw earlier in the Entity-Attribute-Value and Polymorphic Associations antipatterns. In those cases, we stored metadata identifiers (a column name and table name) as string data.
>
> In Multicolumn Attributes and Metadata Tribbles, we're making a data value into a column name or a table name. If you use any of these antipatterns, you create more problems than you solve.

- "What's the maximum number of tables (or columns) that the database supports?"

  Most brands of database can handle many more tables and columns than you would need, if you used a sensible database design. If you think you might exceed the maximum, it's a strong sign that you need to rethink your design.

- "We found out why the application failed to add new data this morning: we forgot to create a new table for the new year."

  This is a common consequence of Metadata Tribbles. When new data demands new database objects, you need to define those objects proactively or else risk unforeseen failures.

- "How do I run a query to search many tables at once? All the tables have the same columns."

  If you need to search many tables with identical structure, you should have stored them together in a single table, with one extra attribute column to distinguish the rows.

- "How do I pass a parameter for a table name? I need to query a table name appended with the year number dynamically."

  You wouldn't need to do this if your data were in one table.

Legitimate Uses of the Antipattern

One good use of manually splitting tables is for *archiving*—removing historical data from day-to-day use. Often the need to run queries against historical data is greatly reduced after the data is no longer current. If you have no need to query current data and historical data together, it's appropriate to copy the older data to another location and delete it from the active tables. Archiving keeps the data in a compatible table structure for occasional analysis but allows queries against current data to run with greater performance.

Sharding Databases at WordPress.com

At a MySQL Conference & Expo, I had lunch with Barry Abrahamson, database architect for WordPress.com, a popular hosting service for blogging software.

Barry said when he started out hosting blogs, he hosted all his customers together in a single database. The content of a single blog site really wasn't that much, after all. It stood to reason that a single database is more manageable.

This did work well for the site initially, but it soon grew to very large-scale operations. Now it hosts 7 million blogs on 300 database servers. Each server hosts a subset of their customers.

When Barry adds a server, it would be very hard to separate data within a single database that belongs to an individual customer's blog. By splitting the data into a separate database per customer, he made it much easier to move any individual blog from one server to another. As customers come and go and some customers' blogs are busy while others go stale, his job to rebalance the load over multiple servers becomes even more important.

It's easier to back up and restore individual databases of moderate size than a single database containing terabytes of data. For example, if a customer calls and says their data got SNAFU'd because of bad data entry, how would Barry restore one customer's data if all the customers share a single, monolithic database backup?

Although it seems like the right thing to do from a data modeling perspective to keep everything in a single database, splitting the database sensibly makes database administration tasks easier after the database size passes a certain threshold.

Solution: Partition and Normalize

There are better ways to improve performance if a table gets too large, instead of splitting the table manually. These include horizontal partitioning, vertical partitioning, and using dependent tables.

Using Horizontal Partitioning

You can gain the benefits of splitting a large table without the drawbacks by using a feature that is called either *horizontal partitioning* or *sharding*. You define a logical table with some rule for separating rows into individual partitions, and the database manages the rest. Physically, the table is split, but you can still execute SQL statements against the table as though it were whole.

You have flexibility in that you can define the way each individual table splits its rows into separate storage. For example, using the partitioning support in MySQL, you can specify partitions as an optional part of a CREATE TABLE statement.

```
Metadata-Tribbles/soln/horiz-partition.sql
CREATE TABLE Bugs (
  bug_id SERIAL PRIMARY KEY,
  -- other columns
  date_reported DATE
) PARTITION BY HASH ( bug_id )
  PARTITIONS 4;
```

The previous example achieves a partitioning similar to that which we saw earlier in this chapter, separating rows based on the year in the date_reported column. However, its advantages over splitting the table manually are that rows are never placed in the wrong split table, even if the value of date_reported column is updated, and you can run queries against the Bugs table without the need to reference individual split tables.

The number of separate physical tables used to store the rows is fixed at four in this example. When you have rows spanning more than four years, one of the partitions will be used to store more than one year's worth of data. This will continue as the years go on. You don't need to add new partitions unless the volume of data becomes so great that you feel the need to split it further.

Partitioning is not defined in the SQL standard, so each brand of database implements it in their own nonstandard way. The terminology, syntax, and specific features of partitioning vary between brands. Nevertheless, some form of partitioning is now supported by every major brand of database.

Using Vertical Partitioning

Whereas horizontal partitioning splits a table by rows, vertical partitioning splits a table by columns. Splitting a table by columns can have advantages when some columns are bulky or seldom needed.

BLOB and TEXT columns have variable size, and they may be very large. For efficiency of both storage and retrieval, many database brands automatically store columns with these data types separately from the other columns of a given row. If you run a query without referencing any BLOB or TEXT columns of a table, you can access the other columns more efficiently. If you use the column wildcard * in your query, the database retrieves all columns from that table, including any BLOB or TEXT columns.

For example, in the Products table of our bugs database, we might store a copy of the installation file for the respective product. This file is typically a self-extracting archive with an extension such as .exe on Windows or .dmg on a

Mac. The files are usually very large, but a BLOB column can store binary data of enormous size.

Logically, the installer file should be an attribute of the Products table. But in most queries against that table, you wouldn't need the installer. Storing such a large volume of data in the Products table, which you use infrequently, could lead to inadvertent performance problems if you're in the habit of retrieving all columns using the * wildcard.

The remedy is to store the BLOB column in another table, separate from but dependent on the Products table. Make its primary key also serve as a foreign key to the Products table to ensure there is at most one row per product row.

Metadata-Tribbles/soln/vert-partition.sql
```
CREATE TABLE ProductInstallers (
  product_id       BIGINT UNSIGNED PRIMARY KEY,
  installer_image BLOB,
  FOREIGN KEY (product_id) REFERENCES Products(product_id)
);
```

The previous example is extreme to make the point, but it shows the benefit of storing some columns in a separate table. For example, in MySQL's MyISAM storage engine, querying a table is most efficient when the rows are of fixed size. VARCHAR is a variable-length data type, so the presence of a single column with that data type in a table prevents the table from gaining that advantage. If you store all variable-length columns in a separate table, then queries against the primary table can benefit (if even a little bit).

Metadata-Tribbles/soln/separate-fixed-length.sql
```
CREATE TABLE Bugs (
  bug_id         SERIAL PRIMARY KEY, -- fixed length data type
  summary        CHAR(80),           -- fixed length data type
  date_reported DATE,                -- fixed length data type
  reported_by    BIGINT UNSIGNED,    -- fixed length data type
  FOREIGN KEY  (reported_by) REFERENCES Accounts(account_id)
);

CREATE TABLE BugDescriptions (
  bug_id         BIGINT UNSIGNED PRIMARY KEY,
  description    VARCHAR(1000),      -- variable length data type
  resolution     VARCHAR(1000),      -- variable length data type
  FOREIGN KEY (bug_id) REFERENCES Bugs(bug_id)
);
```

Fixing Metadata Tribbles Columns

Similar to the solution we saw in Chapter 8, Multicolumn Attributes, on page 89, the best remedy for Metadata Tribbles columns is to create a dependent table.

Metadata-Tribbles/soln/create-history-table.sql
```
CREATE TABLE ProjectHistory (
  project_id  BIGINT,
  year        SMALLINT,
  bugs_fixed  INT,
  PRIMARY KEY (project_id, year),
  FOREIGN KEY (project_id) REFERENCES Projects(project_id)
);
```

Instead of one row per project with multiple columns for each year, use multiple rows, with one column for bugs fixed. If you define the table in this way, you don't need to add new columns to support subsequent years. You can store any number of rows per project in this table as time goes on, and your queries won't need to be changed each year.

> Don't let data spawn metadata.

Part II

Physical Database Design Antipatterns

After you know what data you need to store, you implement the data management as efficiently as you can using the features of your RDBMS technology. This includes defining tables and indexes and choosing data types. You use SQL's data definition language—statements such as CREATE TABLE.

10.0 times 0.1 is hardly ever 1.0.

> Brian Kernighan

## CHAPTER 10

Rounding Errors

Your boss asks you to produce a report of the cost of programmer time for the project, based on the total work to fix each bug. Each programmer in the Accounts table has a different hourly rate, so you record the number of hours required to fix each bug in the Bugs table, and you multiply it by the hourly_rate of the programmer assigned to do the work.

Rounding-Errors/intro/cost-per-bug.sql

```
SELECT b.bug_id, b.hours * a.hourly_rate AS cost_per_bug
FROM Bugs AS b
  JOIN Accounts AS a ON (b.assigned_to = a.account_id);
```

To support this query, you need to create new columns in the Bugs and Accounts tables. Both columns should support fractional values, because you need to track the costs precisely. You decide to define the new columns as FLOAT, because this data type supports fractional values.

Rounding-Errors/intro/float-columns.sql

```
ALTER TABLE Bugs ADD COLUMN hours FLOAT;

ALTER TABLE Accounts ADD COLUMN hourly_rate FLOAT;
```

You update the columns with information from the bug work logs and the programmers' rates, test the report, and call it a day.

The next day, your boss shows up in your office with a copy of the project cost report. "These numbers don't add up," he tells you through gritted teeth. "I did the calculation by hand for comparison, and your report is inaccurate —slightly, by only a few dollars." You start to perspire with worry about how you will explain what went wrong with such a simple calculation.

Objective: Use Fractional Numbers Instead of Integers

The integer is a useful data type, but it stores only whole numbers like 1 or 327 or -19. It can't represent fractional values like 2.5. You need a different data type if you need numbers with more precision than an integer. For example, sums of money are usually represented by numbers with two decimal places, like $19.95.

So, the objective is to store numeric values that aren't whole numbers and to use them in arithmetic computations. There is an additional objective, although it ought to go without saying: the results of arithmetic computations must be *correct*.

Antipattern: Use FLOAT Data Type

Most programming languages support a data type for real numbers, called float or double. SQL supports a similar data type of the same name. Many programmers naturally use the SQL FLOAT data type everywhere they need fractional numeric data, because they are accustomed to programming with the float data type.

The FLOAT data type in SQL, like float in most programming languages, encodes a real number in a binary format according to the IEEE 754 standard. You need to understand some characteristics of floating-point numbers in this format to use them effectively.

Rounding by Necessity

Many programmers are not aware of a characteristic of this floating-point format: not all values you can describe in decimal can be stored in binary. Out of necessity, some numbers must be rounded to a value that is very close.

To give some context for this rounding behavior, compare with rational numbers such as one-third, represented by a repeating decimal number like 0.333.... The true value cannot be represented in decimal, because you would need to write an infinite number of digits. The number of digits is the precision of the number, so a repeating decimal number would require *infinite precision*.

The compromise is to use *finite precision*, choosing a numeric value as close as possible to the original value, for example 0.333. However, this means that the value isn't exactly the same number we intended.

$$\frac{1}{3} + \frac{1}{3} + \frac{1}{3} \qquad = 1.000$$
$$0.333 + 0.333 + 0.333 \quad = 0.999$$

Even if we increase the precision, we still can't add three of these approximations of one-third to get a true value of 1.0. This is the necessary compromise of using finite precision to represent numbers that may have repeating decimals.

$$\tfrac{1}{3} + \tfrac{1}{3} + \tfrac{1}{3} \qquad\qquad = 1.000000$$
$$0.333333 + 0.333333 + 0.333333 \quad = 0.999999$$

This means some legitimate numbers that you can imagine cannot be represented with finite precision. You might think this is OK, because you can't really type a number with infinite digits anyway, so naturally you assume any number you can type has finite precision and should be stored precisely. Unfortunately, this is not the case.

IEEE 754 represents floating-point numbers in a base-2 format. The values that require infinite precision in binary are different values from those that behave this way in decimal. Some values that only need finite precision in decimal, for instance 59.95, require infinite precision to be represented exactly in binary. The FLOAT data type can't do this, so it uses the closest value in base-2 it can store, which is equal to 59.950000762939 in base-10.

Coincidentally, some values can be represented with finite precision in both formats. In theory, if you understand the details of storing numbers in the IEEE 754 format, you can predict how a given decimal value is represented in binary. In practice, most people won't do this computation for every floating-point value they use. You can't guarantee that a FLOAT column in the database will be given only values that are cooperative, so your application should assume that any value in this column may have been rounded.

Some databases support related data types called DOUBLE PRECISION and REAL. The precision that these data types and FLOAT support varies by database implementation, but they all represent floating-point values with a finite number of binary digits, so they all have similar rounding behavior.

Using FLOAT in SQL

Some databases can compensate for the inexactness and display the intended value.

Rounding-Errors/anti/select-rate.sql
```
SELECT hourly_rate FROM Accounts WHERE account_id = 123;
```

Returns: 59.95

The actual value stored in the FLOAT column may not be exactly this value. If you magnify the value by a billion, you see the discrepancy:

Rounding-Errors/anti/magnify-rate.sql

```
SELECT hourly_rate * 1000000000 FROM Accounts WHERE account_id = 123;
```

Returns: 59950000762.939

You might expect the magnified value returned by the previous query to be 59950000000.000. This shows that the value 59.95 has been rounded to a value that can be represented in the finite precision offered by the IEEE 754 binary format. In this case, the value is within 1 ten-millionth, which is close enough for many calculations.

However, it's not close enough for some other kinds of calculations to be accurate. One example is using a FLOAT in an equality comparison.

Rounding-Errors/anti/inexact.sql

```
SELECT * FROM Accounts WHERE hourly_rate = 59.95;
```

Result: empty set; no rows match.

We saw before that the value stored in hourly_rate is actually slightly more than 59.95. So even though you assigned the value 59.95 to this column for account_id 123, now the row fails to match the previous query.

One common workaround for this issue is to treat floating-point values as "effectively equal" if they are close within a small threshold. Subtract one value from the other, and use SQL's absolute value function ABS() to strip the sign from the difference. If the result is zero, then the two values were exactly equal. If the result is small enough, then the two values can be treated as effectively equal. The following query succeeds in finding the row:

Rounding-Errors/anti/threshold.sql

```
SELECT * FROM Accounts WHERE ABS(hourly_rate - 59.95) < 0.000001;
```

However, the difference is still large enough that a comparison of finer precision fails:

Rounding-Errors/anti/threshold.sql

```
SELECT * FROM Accounts WHERE ABS(hourly_rate - 59.95) < 0.0000001;
```

The appropriate threshold varies, because the absolute difference between the base-10 value and the rounded base-2 value varies.

Another example of the inexact nature of FLOAT causing accuracy problems is when you calculate aggregates of many values. For example, if you use SUM() to add up the floating-point values in a column, the sum accumulates the discrepancy caused by rounding all the values.

Rounding-Errors/anti/cumulative.sql

```
SELECT SUM( b.hours * a.hourly_rate ) AS project_cost
FROM Bugs AS b
JOIN Accounts AS a ON (b.assigned_to = a.account_id);
```

The cumulative impact of inexact floating-point numbers is even more severe when calculating the aggregate product of a set of numbers instead of the sum. The difference seems small, but it compounds. For example, if you multiply the value 1 by a factor of exactly 1.0, the result is always 1. It doesn't matter how many times you apply this factor. However, if the factor is actually 0.999, this has a different result. If you multiply a value of one by 0.999 a thousand times in succession, you get a result of about 0.3677. The more times you multiply, the more the discrepancy grows.

A good example of applying a multiplication many times in succession is to calculate compounding interest in a financial application. Using inexact floating-point numbers introduces an error that seems tiny but grows as it compounds on itself. So, using exact values in financial applications is important.

Meet the IEEE 754 Format

The proposals for a standard binary format for floating-point numbers dates back to 1979. It was formally made a standard in 1985, and it is now widely implemented in software, most programming languages, and microprocessors.

The format has three fields to encode a floating-point value: a field for a *fraction* portion of the value, a field for the *exponent* to which to raise the fraction, and a single-bit *sign* field.

One advantage of IEEE 754 is that by using the exponent, it can represent fractional values that are both very small and very large. The format not only supports real numbers, but the range of values it supports is greater than integers in fixed-point format. The double-precision format supports an even greater range of values. So, these formats are useful for scientific applications.

The most common use of fractional numeric values is probably to represent quantities of money. There's no need to use IEEE 754 for money, because the scaled decimal format described in this chapter can handle money values just as easily and more accurately.

Good references for learning more about this format are the Wikipedia article on IEEE 754[a] or David Goldberg's article, *What Every Computer Scientist Should Know About Floating-Point Arithmetic.* [Gol91]

a.   https://en.wikipedia.org/wiki/IEEE_754

How to Recognize the Antipattern

Virtually any use of FLOAT, REAL, or DOUBLE PRECISION data types is suspect. Most applications that use floating-point numbers don't require the range of values supported by IEEE 754 formats.

It seems natural to use FLOAT data types in SQL, because it shares its name with a data type found in most programming languages. However, there's a better choice for the data type.

Legitimate Uses of the Antipattern

FLOAT is a good data type when you need real number values with a greater range than INTEGER or NUMERIC data types support. Scientific applications are often the best use of a FLOAT. For example, if you store daily temperature data in a database, the fractional values will vary, and will seldom be a whole degree. It's okay to store a temperature value with a billionth of a degree, because the common use of those data is to make aggregate calculations, like MIN(), MAX(), or AVG(). You might also search for rows where the temperature is in a range of values, and a query using inequality or BETWEEN will work fine with inexact numerics. But you're not likely to search for the row where the temperature is exactly equal to some specific value. Oracle uses the FLOAT data type to mean an exact scaled numeric, whereas the BINARY_FLOAT data type is an inexact numeric, using the IEEE 754 encoding.

Solution: Use NUMERIC Data Type

Instead of FLOAT or its siblings, use the NUMERIC or DECIMAL SQL data types for fixed-precision fractional numbers.

```
Rounding-Errors/soln/numeric-columns.sql
ALTER TABLE Bugs ADD COLUMN hours NUMERIC(9,2);
ALTER TABLE Accounts ADD COLUMN hourly_rate NUMERIC(9,2);
```

These data types store numeric values exactly, up to the *precision* you specify in the column definition. Specify precision as an argument to the data type, similar to the syntax you would use for the length of a VARCHAR data type. The precision is the total number of decimal digits you can use in a value in this column. A precision of 9 means that you can store a value like 123456789, but you may not be able to store 1234567890.

You may also specify a *scale* in a second argument to the data type. The scale is the number of digits to the right of the decimal point. These digits are included in the precision digits, so a precision of 9 with a scale of 2 means you can store a value like 1234567.89, but not 12345678.91 or 123456.789.

The precision and scale you specify applies to the column on all rows in the table. In other words, you can't store values with scale 2 on some rows and scale 4 on other rows. It's ordinary in SQL that a column's data type applies uniformly on all rows (just as a column defined as VARCHAR(20) would allow a string of that length on every row).

The advantage of NUMERIC and DECIMAL are that they store rational numbers without rounding. After you set a value to 59.95, you can depend on that value being stored exactly. When you compare it for equality to a literal value 59.95, the comparison succeeds.

Rounding-Errors/soln/exact.sql
```
SELECT hourly_rate FROM Accounts WHERE hourly_rate = 59.95;
```

Returns: 59.95

Likewise, if you scale up the value by a billion, you get the expected value:

Rounding-Errors/soln/magnify-rate-exact.sql
```
SELECT hourly_rate * 1000000000 FROM Accounts WHERE hourly_rate = 59.95;
```

Returns: 59950000000

The data types NUMERIC and DECIMAL behave identically; there should be no difference between them. DEC is also a synonym for DECIMAL.

You still can't store values that require infinite precision, such as one-third. At least we're more familiar with values that have this restriction in decimal format.

If you need exact decimal values, use the NUMERIC data type. The FLOAT data type is unable to represent many decimal rational numbers, so they should be treated as inexact values.

> If I had a dime for every time I've seen someone use FLOAT to store currency, I'd have $1000.0000000001588.

Science is feasible when the variables are few and can be enumerated; when their combinations are distinct and clear.

> Paul Valéry

## CHAPTER 11

31 Flavors

In a personal contact information table, the *salutation* is a good example of a column that can have only a few values. Once you support *Mr.*, *Mrs.*, *Ms.*, *Dr.*, and *Rev.*, you've accounted for virtually everyone. You could specify this list in the column definition, using a data type or a constraint, so that no one can accidentally enter an invalid string into the salutation column.

31-Flavors/intro/create-table.sql
```sql
CREATE TABLE PersonalContacts (
  -- other columns
  salutation VARCHAR(4)
    CHECK (salutation IN ('Mr.', 'Mrs.', 'Ms.', 'Dr.', 'Rev.')),
);
```

That should settle it—you assume there are no other salutations to support.

Unfortunately, your boss tells you that your company is opening a subsidiary in France. You need to support the salutations *M.*, *Mme.*, and *Mlle.* Your mission is to alter your contact table to permit these values. This is a delicate job and may not be possible without interrupting availability of that table.

You also thought your boss mentioned that the company is trying to open an office next month in Brazil.

Objective: Restrict a Column to Specific Values

Restricting a column's values to a fixed set of values is very useful. If we can ensure that the column never contains an invalid entry, it can simplify use of that column. For example, in the Bugs table of our example database, the status column indicates whether a given bug is *NEW*, *IN PROGRESS*, *FIXED*, and so on. The significance of each of these status values depends on how we manage bugs in our project, but the point is that the data in the column must be one of these values.

Ideally, we need the database to reject invalid data:

```
31-Flavors/obj/insert-invalid.sql
INSERT INTO Bugs (status) VALUES ('NEW'); -- OK

INSERT INTO Bugs (status) VALUES ('BANANA'); -- Error!
```

Antipattern: Specify Values in the Column Definition

Many people choose to specify the valid data values when they define the column. The column definition is part of the *metadata*—the definition of the table structure itself.

For example, you could define a *check constraint* on the column. This constraint disallows any insert or update that would make the constraint false.

```
31-Flavors/anti/create-table-check.sql
CREATE TABLE Bugs (
  -- other columns
  status   VARCHAR(20) CHECK (status IN ('NEW', 'IN PROGRESS', 'FIXED'))
);
```

MySQL supports a nonstandard data type called ENUM that restricts the column to a specific set of values.

```
31-Flavors/anti/create-table-enum.sql
CREATE TABLE Bugs (
  -- other columns
  status ENUM('NEW', 'IN PROGRESS', 'FIXED'),
);
```

In MySQL's implementation, you declare the values as strings, but internally the column is stored as the ordinal number of the string in the enumerated list. The storage is thus compact, but when you sort a query by this column, the default order of the result is by the ordinal value, not alphabetically by the string value. You may not expect this behavior.

Other solutions include *domains* and *user-defined types* (UDTs). You can use these to restrict a column to a specific set of values and conveniently apply the same domain or data type to several columns within your database. Unfortunately, these features are not supported in a standard way among brands of RDBMSs yet.

Finally, you could write a trigger that contains the set of permitted values and raises an error unless the status matches one of these values.

All of these solutions share some disadvantages. The following sections describe some of these problems.

> ## Baskin-Robbins "31 Flavors" Ice Cream
>
> In 1953, this famous chain of ice cream parlors offered one flavor for each day of the month. The chain used the slogan *31 Flavors* for many years.
>
> Today, more than sixty years later, Baskin-Robbins offers twenty-one classic flavors, twelve seasonal flavors, sixteen regional flavors, as well as a variety of Bright Choices and Flavors of the Month. Even though its ice cream flavors were once an immutable set that defined its brand, Baskin-Robbins expanded its choices and made them configurable and variable.
>
> The same thing could happen in the project for which you're designing a database—in fact, you should count on it.

What Was the Middle One?

Suppose you're developing a user interface so a user can edit bug reports. To make it guide the user to pick one of the valid status values, you choose to fill a drop-down menu control with these values. You need to query the database for an enumerated list of values that are currently allowed in the status column.

Your first instinct might be to query all the values currently in use, with a simple query like the following one:

31-Flavors/anti/distinct.sql
```
SELECT DISTINCT status FROM Bugs;
```

However, if all the bugs are new, the previous query returns only *NEW*. If you use this result to populate a user interface control for the status of bugs, you could create a chicken-and-egg situation; you can't change a bug to any status other than those currently in use.

To get the complete list of permitted status values, you need to query the definition of that column's metadata. Most SQL databases support *system views* for these kinds of queries, but using them can be complex. For example, if you used MySQL's ENUM data type, you can use the following query to query the INFORMATION_SCHEMA system views:

31-Flavors/anti/information-schema.sql
```
SELECT column_type
FROM information_schema.columns
WHERE table_schema = 'bugtracker_schema'
  AND table_name = 'bugs'
  AND column_name = 'status';
```

You can't simply get the discrete enumeration values from the INFORMATION_SCHEMA in a conventional result set. Instead, you get a string containing the definition of the check constraint or ENUM data type. For example, the previous query in MySQL returns a column of type LONGTEXT, with the value *ENUM('NEW', 'IN PROGRESS', 'FIXED')*, including the parentheses, commas, and single quotes. You must write application code to parse this string and extract the individual quoted values before you can use them to populate a user interface control.

The queries needed to report check constraints, domains, or UDTs are progressively more complex. Most people choose the better part of valor and manually maintain a parallel list of values in application code. This is an easy way for bugs to affect your project as application data becomes out of sync with the database metadata.

Adding a New Flavor

The most common alterations are to add or remove one of the permitted values. There's no syntax to add or remove a value from an ENUM or check constraint; you can only redefine the column with a new set of values. The following is an example of adding *DUPLICATE* as one new status value in the MySQL ENUM:

31-Flavors/anti/add-enum-value.sql
```
ALTER TABLE Bugs MODIFY COLUMN status
  ENUM('NEW', 'IN PROGRESS', 'FIXED', 'DUPLICATE');
```

You need to know that the previous definition of the column allowed *NEW*, *IN PROGRESS*, and *FIXED*. This leads you back to the difficulty of querying the current set of values as described earlier.

Some database brands can't change the definition of a column unless the table is empty. You might need to dump the contents of the table, redefine the table, and then import your saved data, making the table inaccessible in the meantime. This work is common enough that it has a name: *ETL* for "extract, transform, and load." Other brands of database support restructuring a populated table with ALTER TABLE commands, but it can still be complex and expensive to perform these changes.

As a matter of policy, changing metadata—that is, changing the definition of tables and columns—should be infrequent and with attention to testing and quality assurance. If you need to change metadata to add or remove a value from an ENUM, then you either have to skip the appropriate testing or spend a lot of software engineering effort on short notice to make the change. Either way, these changes introduce risk and destabilize your project.

Old Flavors Never Die

If you make a value obsolete, you could upset historical data. For example, you change your quality control process to replace *FIXED* with two stages, *CODE COMPLETE* and *VERIFIED*:

```
31-Flavors/anti/remove-enum-value.sql
ALTER TABLE Bugs MODIFY COLUMN status
  ENUM('NEW', 'IN PROGRESS', 'CODE COMPLETE', 'VERIFIED');
```

If you remove *FIXED* from the enumeration, you need to decide what to do with bugs whose status was *FIXED*. One possible change is to update all *FIXED* bugs to *VERIFIED*. Another option is set obsolete values to null or a default value. Unfortunately, ALTER TABLE can't guess which one of these changes you want.

You may have to keep an obsolete value that old rows reference. You can't know only from the column definition which values are obsolete, so you exclude them from your user interface. Someone could still choose one of those values.

Portability Is Hard

Check constraints, domains, and UDTs are not supported uniformly among brands of SQL databases. The ENUM data type is a proprietary feature in MySQL. Each brand of database may have a different limit on the length of the list you can give in a column definition. Trigger languages vary as well. These variations make it hard to choose a solution if you need to support multiple brands of database.

How to Recognize the Antipattern

The problems with using ENUM or a check constraint arise when the set of values is not fixed. If you're considering using ENUM, first ask yourself whether the set of values are expected to change or even whether they *might* change. If so, it's probably not a good time to employ an ENUM.

- "We have to take the database offline so we can add a new choice in one of our application's menus. It should take no more than thirty minutes, if all goes well."

  This is a sign that a set of values is baked into the definition of a column. You should never need to interrupt service for a change like this.

- "The status column can have one of the following values. We shouldn't need to revise this list."

> *Shouldn't need to* are weasel words, and this says something quite different from *can't*.

- "The list of values in the application code got out of sync with the business rules in the database—again."

This is a risk of maintaining information in two different places.

Legitimate Uses of the Antipattern

As we discussed, ENUM may cause fewer problems if the set of values is unchanging. It's still difficult to query the metadata for the set of values, but you can maintain a matching list of values in application code without getting out of sync.

ENUM is most likely to succeed when it would make no sense to alter the set of permitted values, such as when a column represents an either/or choice with two mutually exclusive values: *LEFT/RIGHT*, *ACTIVE/IN-ACTIVE*, *ON/OFF*, *INTERNAL/EXTERNAL*, and so on.

Check constraints can be used in many ways other than simply to implement an ENUM-like mechanism, such as checking that a time interval's start is less than its end.

Solution: Specify Values in Data

There's a better solution to restrict values in a column: create a *lookup table* with one row for each value you allow in the Bugs.status column. Then declare a foreign key constraint on Bugs.status referencing the new table.

31-Flavors/soln/create-lookup-table.sql
```sql
CREATE TABLE BugStatus (
  status  VARCHAR(20) PRIMARY KEY
);

INSERT INTO BugStatus (status) VALUES ('NEW'), ('IN PROGRESS'), ('FIXED');

CREATE TABLE Bugs (
  -- other columns
  status  VARCHAR(20),
  FOREIGN KEY (status) REFERENCES BugStatus(status)
    ON UPDATE CASCADE
);
```

When you insert or update a row in the Bugs table, you must use a status value that exists in the BugStatus table. This enforces the status values like the ENUM or a check constraint, but there are several ways this solution offers more flexibility.

Querying the Set of Values

The set of permitted values is now stored in data, not metadata as it was with the ENUM data type. You can query data values from a lookup table with SELECT, just like any other table. This makes it much easier to retrieve the set of values as a data set to present in your user interface. You can even sort the set of values the user can choose from.

31-Flavors/soln/query-canonical-values.sql
```
SELECT status FROM BugStatus ORDER BY status;
```

Updating the Values in the Lookup Table

When you use a lookup table, you can add a value to the set with an ordinary INSERT statement. You can make a change like this without interrupting access to the table. You don't need to redefine any columns, schedule downtime, or perform an ETL operation. You also don't need to know the current set of values in the lookup table to add or remove a value.

31-Flavors/soln/insert-value.sql
```
INSERT INTO BugStatus (status) VALUES ('DUPLICATE');
```

You can also rename a value easily. If you declared the foreign key with the ON UPDATE CASCADE option, then updating the name in the lookup table BugStatus automatically updates any foreign key references to it in other tables.

31-Flavors/soln/update-value.sql
```
UPDATE BugStatus SET status = 'INVALID' WHERE status = 'BOGUS';
```

Supporting Obsolete Values

You can't DELETE a row from the lookup table if it's referenced by a row in Bugs. The foreign key on the status column enforces referential integrity, so the value must exist in the lookup table.

However, you can add another attribute column to the lookup table to designate some values as obsolete. This allows you to maintain historical data in the Bugs.status column, while distinguishing between the obsolete values and values that are eligible to appear in your user interface.

31-Flavors/soln/inactive.sql
```
ALTER TABLE BugStatus ADD COLUMN active
  ENUM('INACTIVE', 'ACTIVE') NOT NULL DEFAULT 'ACTIVE';
```

Use UPDATE instead of DELETE to make a value obsolete:

31-Flavors/soln/update-inactive.sql
```
UPDATE BugStatus SET active = 'INACTIVE' WHERE status = 'DUPLICATE';
```

When you retrieve the set of values to show in a user interface for users to pick, restrict the query to status values that are *ACTIVE*:

31-Flavors/soln/select-active.sql
```
SELECT status FROM BugStatus WHERE active = 'ACTIVE';
```

This gives you more flexibility than an ENUM or a check constraint, because those solutions don't support extra attributes per value.

Portability Is Easy

Unlike the ENUM data type, check constraints, or domains or UDTs, the lookup table solution relies only on the standard SQL feature of declarative referential integrity using foreign key constraints. This makes the solution more portable.

You can also keep a virtually unlimited number of values in your lookup table, since you store each value on a separate row.

> Use metadata when validating against a fixed set of values. Use data when validating against a fluid set of values.

Mini-Antipattern: Reserved Words

"What does this error mean? I've checked my syntax against the reference documentation and I'm sure it's correct. I've used a similar query on other tables with no error."

> ERROR 1064: You have an error in your SQL syntax; check the manual that corresponds to your MySQL server version for the right syntax to use near 'order'.

The query that resulted in this error is following:

31-Flavors/mini/query-order.sql
```
SELECT * FROM Bugs WHERE order = 123;
```

It's true there is nothing wrong with the syntax, if order is a column identifier. But it's not—ORDER has meaning as an SQL reserved keyword, introducing an ORDER BY clause. SQL is case-insensitive by default, so order and ORDER are treated as the same keyword.

SQL must treat some keywords differently from identifiers, because if a word can be either an identifier or a keyword, then some queries might be ambiguous, and this would confuse the parser.

It's normal for programming languages to have reserved keywords. For example, in Java you aren't allowed to use class or while or try, or a few dozen other words as the name of your methods, variables, constants, or other identifiers. Other languages have their own lists of reserved keywords, and SQL does too.

Some languages, such as PHP or Perl, use a *sigil* character, such as $, before a variable name, to distinguish it from the reserved keywords. You can't name a function while(), but you can name a variable $while.

SQL doesn't use sigils, but it does allow you to use delimiters around any word to make it clear it is an identifier. The standard SQL identifier delimiters are double quotes:

31-Flavors/mini/query-order-doublequotes.sql
```
SELECT * FROM Bugs WHERE "order" = 123;
```

MySQL uses backticks by default as the identifier delimiter:

31-Flavors/mini/query-order-backticks.sql
```
SELECT * FROM Bugs WHERE `order` = 123;
```

Microsoft SQL Server uses square brackets by default for the same purpose:

31-Flavors/mini/query-order-brackets.sql
```
SELECT * FROM Bugs WHERE [order] = 123;
```

SQLite recognizes all three styles of delimited identifiers, for the convenience of programmers who are used to other brands of SQL database.

Delimited identifiers also allow you to do some things that you can't do in most other languages: spell identifiers with whitespace or punctuation characters.

31-Flavors/mini/query-special.sql
```
SELECT * FROM Bugs WHERE "the order" = 123;

SELECT * FROM Bugs WHERE "the-order" = 123;
```

You can use reserved keywords as identifiers, but it's your responsibility to help the SQL parser by making it clear that you mean them to be an identifier.

In the preceding examples, order is the keyword. This may be the most common keyword that software developers accidentally choose, not realizing they are reserved. Other keywords that typically cause confusion include: by, default, from, rows, row_number, table, to, or year_month. It's not hard to imagine someone trying to use these words or other reserved keywords for a table name or a column name.

Finally, be careful when you upgrade the version of your RDBMS software. As new software often includes new features with new SQL syntax, new words need to be added to the list of reserved keywords. You may find that an identifier that you had used in your database for years needs to be delimited before you can upgrade the database.

CHAPTER 12

Phantom Files

Catastrophe strikes your database server. While relocating a rack full of hard
drives, the rack tipped over and crashed. Fortunately, no one was hurt, but
the massive hard drives shattered. Even the raised floor was broken where
they fell. Fortunately, the IT department is prepared: they make good backups
of every important system every day, and they quickly deploy a new server
and restore your database.

It doesn't take long during smoke testing to notice a problem: your application
associates graphic images with many database entities, but all the images
are missing! You call the IT technician immediately.

"We restored the database and verified it's complete as of the last backup,"
the technician says. "Where were the images stored?"

You remember now that in this application, images are stored outside the
database, and ordinary files are stored on the filesystem. The database stores
the path to the image, and the application opens each image file at that path.
"The images were stored as files. They were on the /var filesystem, same as
the databases."

The technician shakes his head. "We don't back up files on the /var filesystem
unless you specifically told us which ones. We back up any databases, of
course, but other files on /var are usually just logs, cache data, or other temporary files. By default, they don't get backed up."

Your heart sinks. There were more than 11,000 images used in your product
catalog database. Most of them probably exist in other places, but tracking
them all down, reformatting them, and generating thumbnail versions for
web searches will take weeks.

Objective: Store Images or Other Bulky Media

Images and other media are used in most applications these days. Sometimes media are associated with entities stored in the database. For example, you may allow a user to have a portrait or avatar that is displayed when he posts a comment. In our bugs database, bugs often need a screenshot to illustrate the circumstances of the defect.

The objective described in this chapter is to store images and associate them with database entities, such as user accounts or bugs. When we query these entities from the database, we need the capability to retrieve the associated images in the application.

Antipattern: Assume You Must Use Files

Conceptually, an image is an attribute in a table. For example, the Accounts table may have a portrait_image column.

Phantom-Files/anti/create-accounts.sql

```
CREATE TABLE Accounts (
  account_id       SERIAL PRIMARY KEY,
  account_name     VARCHAR(20),
  portrait_image   BLOB
);
```

Likewise, you can store multiple images of the same type in a dependent table. For example, a bug may have multiple screenshots that illustrate it.

Phantom-Files/anti/create-screenshots.sql

```
CREATE TABLE Screenshots (
  image_id           SERIAL NOT NULL,
  bug_id             BIGINT UNSIGNED NOT NULL,
  screenshot_image   BLOB,
  caption            VARCHAR(100),
  PRIMARY KEY        (image_id, bug_id),
  FOREIGN KEY (bug_id) REFERENCES Bugs(bug_id)
);
```

That much is straightforward, but choosing the data type for an image is a subject of controversy. Raw binary data for an image can be stored in a BLOB data type, as shown previously. However, many people instead store the image as a file on the filesystem and store only the path to this file as a VARCHAR.

Phantom-Files/anti/create-screenshots-path.sql

```
CREATE TABLE Screenshots (
  image_id           SERIAL NOT NULL,
  bug_id             BIGINT UNSIGNED NOT NULL,
  screenshot_path    VARCHAR(100),
```

```
   caption              VARCHAR(100),
   PRIMARY KEY          (image_id, bug_id),
   FOREIGN KEY (bug_id) REFERENCES Bugs(bug_id)
);
```

Software developers argue passionately about this issue. There are good reasons for both solutions, but some programmers are opinionated that images must always be stored external to the database. However, there are several real risks to this design, described in the following sections.

Files Don't Obey DELETE

The first problem is one of garbage collection. If your images are outside the database and you delete the row that contains the path, there is no way for the file named by that path to be removed automatically.

Phantom-Files/anti/delete.sql
```
DELETE FROM Screenshots WHERE bug_id = 1234 and image_id = 1;
```

Unless you design your application to remove these "orphaned" image files as you delete the database row that references them, they will accumulate.

Files Don't Obey Transaction Isolation

Normally, when you update or delete data, these changes aren't visible to other clients until you finish your transaction with COMMIT.

However, any change you make to files outside the database don't work this way. If you remove a file, it is immediately inaccessible to other clients. And if you change the contents of the file, other clients see those changes immediately, instead of seeing the previous content of the file while your transaction is still uncommitted.

Phantom-Files/anti/transaction.py
```python
import mysql.connector
import os

cnx = mysql.connector.connect(user='scott', database='test')

cursor = cnx.cursor()

query = "DELETE FROM Screenshots WHERE bug_id = %s AND image_id = %s"
cursor.execute(query, (1234, 1,))

os.unlink('screenshot1234-1.jpg');

# At this time, other clients still see the row in the database,
# but not the image file.

cnx.commit()
```

In practice, these kinds of anomalies may be infrequent. Also, the impact is minor in this example; a missing image is hardly rare in a web application. In other scenarios, the consequences could be unfortunate.

Files Don't Obey ROLLBACK

It's normal to roll back transactions in case of errors, or even if the logic of your application requires that changes be canceled.

For example, suppose you remove a screenshot file as you execute a DELETE statement to remove the corresponding row in the database. If you roll back this change, the deletion of the row in the database is reversed, but the file is still gone.

```
Phantom-Files/anti/rollback.py
import mysql.connector
import os

cnx = mysql.connector.connect(user='scott', database='test')

cursor = cnx.cursor()

query = "DELETE FROM Screenshots WHERE bug_id = %s AND image_id = %s"
cursor.execute(query, (1234, 1,))

os.unlink('screenshot1234-1.jpg');

cnx.rollback()
```

The row in the database is restored but not the image file.

Files Don't Obey Database Backup Tools

Most database brands provide a client tool to assist in backing up a database that is in use. For example, MySQL provides mysqldump, Oracle provides rman, PostgreSQL provides pg_dump, SQLite provides the .dump command, and so on. Using a backup tool is important because if other clients are making changes concurrently, your backup could contain partial changes, potentially breaking referential integrity or even making the backup corrupt and useless for recovery.

A backup tool doesn't know how to include files referenced by pathname in a VARCHAR column of a table. So when you back up a database, you need to remember a two-step process: use the database backup tool, and then use a filesystem backup tool for the collection of external image files.

Even if you include the external files with the backup, it's hard to ensure that copies of these files are in sync with the transaction you used to back up the database. Applications may add or change image files at any time, perhaps only a moment after you began your database backup.

Files Don't Obey SQL Access Privileges

External files circumvent any privileges that you assign with the GRANT and REVOKE SQL statements. SQL privileges manage access to tables and columns, but they don't apply to external files named by strings in the database.

Files Are Not SQL Data Types

The path stored in screenshot_path is merely a string. The database doesn't verify that the string is a valid pathname, nor can the database verify that the file exists at the path you name. If the file is renamed, moved, or deleted, the database doesn't update the string in the database automatically. Any logic that treats this string as a pathname depends on code you write in your application.

```
Phantom-Files/anti/file-get.py
import mysql.connector
import os

cnx = mysql.connector.connect(user='scott', database='test')

cursor = cnx.cursor()

query = "SELECT image_path FROM Screenshots WHERE bug_id = %s AND image_id = %s"
cursor.execute(query, (1234, 1,))
row = cursor.fetchone()
cursor.close()

if row:
    image_path = row[0]
    with open(image_path) as image_file:
        image_content = image_file.read()
```

One advantage of using a database is that it helps us preserve data integrity. When you put some of your data in external files, you circumvent this advantage, and you have to write application code to perform checks that should be handled by the database.

How to Recognize the Antipattern

The signs of this antipattern require a little investigation. If the project has any documentation to guide software administrators or if you have the opportunity to interview the programmers who designed it (even if that's you), look for explanations of how the system handles tasks like the following:

• Backing up and restoring data, including the images and file attachments

- Verifying the data after restoring it on a different server than where the backup was made

- Removing images once they are no longer referenced by any rows in the database

- Granting the users of the application access to view images, as well as the reverse: preventing users from viewing images they don't have privileges to view

- Editing or replacing images, including canceling such a change. Restoring the original image after canceling a change

Projects that are guilty of the antipattern typically fail to think through some or all of these questions. Not every application needs robust transaction management or SQL access control for image files. You might find that taking a database offline during backups is a fair trade-off. If these answers are unclear or not forthcoming, it could indicate that the project designed their use of external files carelessly.

Legitimate Uses of the Antipattern

There are good reasons to store images or other large objects in files outside the database:

- The database is much leaner without images, because images tend to be large compared to simple datatypes like integers and strings.

- Backing up the database is faster and the result is smaller if images are not included. You must copy images from the filesystem as a separate backup step, but this can be more manageable than a huge database backup.

- If images are in files external to the database, it's easier to do ad hoc image previewing or editing. For example, if you need to apply a batch edit to all your images, it's especially good to keep images external to the database.

If these advantages of storing images in files are important and the issues described earlier are not deal-breakers, you may decide that it's the right thing to do in this project.

Some database brands support special SQL data types that do reference external files more or less transparently. Oracle calls this data type BFILE, while SQL Server 2008 calls it FILESTREAM.

Don't Rule Out Either Design

I designed an application that stored images outside a database for a contract project. My employer was hired to develop a registration application for a technical conference. As conference attendees arrived, a video camera took their picture, added it to their registration record, and printed it on their conference badge.

My application was fairly simple. Each image could be inserted and updated only by one client application (if the person blinked or didn't like their photo, we could replace it during registration). There was no requirement for sophisticated transaction handling, concurrent access from multiple clients, or rollback. We were not using SQL access privileges. Previewing the images was simpler without having to fetch them from the database.

I worked on this project at a time when the practical limits of applications and databases were much lower than what today's technology can handle. It made sense given these constraints to store images in a collection of directories and manage them with application code.

You need to plan how your application uses images to know whether the issues described in the "Antipattern" section would affect you. Make an informed decision, instead of listening to generalizations from programmers who believe that storing images in external files is always the best solution.

Solution: Use BLOB Data Types As Needed

If any of the issues described in the "Antipattern" section of this chapter apply to you, you should consider storing images inside the database instead of in external files. All database brands support the BLOB data type, which you can use to store any binary data.

Phantom-Files/soln/create-screenshots.sql
```sql
CREATE TABLE Screenshots (
  bug_id              BIGINT UNSIGNED NOT NULL,
  image_id            BIGINT UNSIGNED NOT NULL,
  screenshot_image    BLOB,
  caption             VARCHAR(100),
  PRIMARY KEY         (bug_id, image_id),
  FOREIGN KEY (bug_id) REFERENCES Bugs(bug_id)
);
```

If you store an image in this way in a BLOB column, all the issues are solved:

- The image data is stored in the database. There is no extra step to load it. There's no risk that the file's pathname is incorrect.

- Deleting a row deletes the image automatically.

- Changes to an image are not visible to other clients until you commit the change.

- Rolling back a transaction restores the previous state of the image.

- Updating a row creates a lock, so no other client can update the same image concurrently.

- Database backups include all the images.

- SQL privileges control access to the image as well as the row.

The maximum size for a BLOB varies by database brand, but it's enough to store most images. All databases should support BLOB or something akin to it. MySQL, for example, provides data types MEDIUMBLOB and LONGBLOB that store up to 16 megabytes or 4 gigabytes, respectively. Oracle supports data types called LONG RAW or BLOB, with capacity up to 2 or 4 gigabytes, respectively. Similar data types are available in other database brands.

Images usually exist in a file to begin with, so you need some way to load them into a BLOB column in the database. Some databases provide functions to load external files. For example, MySQL has a function called LOAD_FILE() you can use to read a file, typically to store the content in a BLOB column.

Phantom-Files/soln/load-file.sql
```
UPDATE Screenshots
SET screenshot_image = LOAD_FILE('images/screenshot1234-1.jpg')
WHERE bug_id = 1234 AND image_id = 1;
```

You can also save the contents of a BLOB column to a file. For example, MySQL has an optional clause of the SELECT statement to store the result of a query verbatim, without any formatting to denote column or row termination.

Phantom-Files/soln/dumpfile.sql
```
SELECT screenshot_image
INTO DUMPFILE 'images/screenshot1234-1.jpg'
FROM Screenshots
WHERE bug_id = 1234 AND image_id =1;
```

You can also fetch the image data from the BLOB and output it directly. The response of a web request can be binary content such as an image, if you set the content type appropriately. Following is an example Python Flask web application that returns the screenshot image.

Phantom-Files/soln/binary-content.py
```
import mysql.connector
from flask import Flask, Response

app = Flask(__name__)

@app.route('/')
def screenshot():
    cnx = mysql.connector.connect(user='scott', database='test')

    cursor = cnx.cursor()
```

```
    query = """
      SELECT screenshot_image FROM Screenshots
      WHERE bug_id = %s AND image_id = %s"""
    cursor.execute(query, (1234, 1,))
    row = cursor.fetchone()
    cursor.close()

    if row:
        screenshot_image = row[0]
        return Response(screenshot_image, mimetype='image/jpeg')
    else:
        return Response(status=404)

if __name__ == '__main__':
    app.run()
```

Before following a convention that images or other content belong in files outside the database, think about whether it would make your code simpler and more mistake proof to use a BLOB column to store that data.

> If you break the relationship between the data and the database, then you take on the burden of managing that data yourself.

Whenever any result is sought by its aid, the question will then arise—
By what course of calculation can these results be arrived at by the
machine in the shortest time?

   Charles Babbage, Passages from the Life of a Philosopher
   (1864)

CHAPTER 13

Index Shotgun

"Hey! You got a minute? I could use your help," the Oklahoman accent on the phone is shouting over the data center ventilation. It's the lead database administrator for your company.

"Sure," you answer, a little unsure what he could want.

"The thing is, you've got a database here that's pretty much taken over the server," the DBA continues. "I got in there to take a look, and I see the problem. You've got no indexes on some tables and every index in the world on some other tables. We've got to get this worked out or give you a server all to yerself, because nobody else can get any time!"

"I'm sorry—actually, I don't know that much about databases," you reply, trying to calm down the DBA. "We did our best to guess at the optimization, but obviously that's what an expert like you can do. Isn't there some database tuning you can do?"

"Son, I tuned everything I can; that's why we're still running down here at all," the DBA answers. "The only option left is to throttle your app, and I don't think you want that. We've got to stop guessing and start getting some answers on what your app needs the database to do."

You can tell this is getting over your head. Warily you ask, "What do you have in mind? I told you, we don't have expert database knowledge in our team."

"That's no problem," the DBA laughs. "You do know your application, right? That's the part that counts—and the part I *can't* help with. I'll get one of my team to set you up with the right tools, and then we'll fix your bottleneck. You just need a little mentoring. You'll see."

Objective: Optimize Performance

Performance is the single most common concern from database developers. Just look at the talks scheduled at any technical conference: they're full of tools and techniques to squeeze more work out of your database. When I give a talk about a way to structure a database or write SQL to give better reliability, security, or correctness, I'm not surprised when the first question (or perhaps the only question) from the audience is, "OK, but how does that affect performance?"

The best technique for improving performance in your database is to use indexes well. An index is a data structure that the database uses to correlate values to the rows where these values occur in a given column. An index provides an easy way for the database to find values more quickly than the brute-force method of searching the whole table from top to bottom.

Software developers typically don't understand how or when to use an index. Documentation and books about databases rarely or never contain a clear guide for when to use an index. Developers can only guess at how to use indexes effectively.

Antipattern: Using Indexes Without a Plan

When we choose our indexes by guessing, we inevitably make some wrong choices. Misunderstandings about when to use indexes leads to mistakes in one of these three categories:

- Defining no indexes or not enough indexes
- Defining too many indexes or indexes that don't help
- Running queries that no index can help

No Indexes

We commonly read that a database incurs overhead as it keeps an index up-to-date. Each time we use INSERT, UPDATE, or DELETE, the database has to update the index data structures for that table to be consistent so that our subsequent searches use these indexes to find the right set of rows reliably.

We're trained to think that overhead means waste. So when we read that the database incurs overhead to keep an index updated, we want to eliminate that overhead. Some developers conclude that the remedy is to eliminate the indexes. This advice is common, but it ignores the fact that indexes have benefits that justify their overhead.

Not all overhead is waste. Does your company employ administrative staff, legal professionals, accountants, and pay for facilities, even though those expenses don't directly contribute to generating revenue? Yes, because those people contribute to the success of your company in important ways.

In a typical application, you'll run hundreds of queries against a table for every one update. Every time you run a query that uses an index, you win back the overhead that went into maintaining that index.

An index can also help an UPDATE or DELETE statement by finding the desired rows quickly. The index on the bug_id primary key helps the following statement:

Index-Shotgun/anti/update.sql
```
UPDATE Bugs SET status = 'FIXED' WHERE bug_id = 1234;
```

A statement that searches an unindexed column has to perform a full table scan to find matching rows.

Index-Shotgun/anti/update-unindexed.sql
```
UPDATE Bugs SET status = 'OBSOLETE' WHERE date_reported < '2000-01-01';
```

Indexes Aren't Standard

Did you know that the ANSI/ISO SQL standard says nothing about indexes? The implementation and optimization of data storage is not specified by the SQL language, so every brand of database is free to implement indexes differently.

Most brands have similar CREATE INDEX syntax, but each brand has flexibility to innovate and add their own proprietary technology. There's no standard for index capabilities. Likewise, there is no standard for index maintenance, automatic query optimization, query plan reporting, or commands like EXPLAIN.

To get the most out of indexes, you have to study the documentation for your brand of database. The specific syntax and features of indexes vary greatly, but the logical concepts apply across the board.

Too Many Indexes

You benefit from an index only if you run queries that use that index. There's no benefit to creating indexes that you don't use. Here are some examples:

Index-Shotgun/anti/create-table.sql
```
CREATE TABLE Bugs (
  bug_id          SERIAL PRIMARY KEY,
  date_reported   DATE NOT NULL,
  summary         VARCHAR(80) NOT NULL,
  status          VARCHAR(10) NOT NULL,
  hours           NUMERIC(9,2),
```

```
   INDEX (bug_id),
   INDEX (summary),
   INDEX (hours),
   INDEX (bug_id, date_reported, status)
);
```

In the previous example, there are several useless indexes:

① bug_id: Most databases create an index automatically for a primary key, so it's redundant to define another index. There's no benefit to it, and it could just be extra overhead. Each database brand has its own rules for when to create an index automatically. You need to read the documentation for the database you use.

② summary: An index for a long string datatype like VARCHAR(80) is larger than an index for a more compact data type. Also, you're not likely to run queries that search or sort by the full summary column.

③ hours: This is another example of a column in which you're probably not going to search for specific values.

④ bug_id, date_reported, status: There are good reasons to use compound indexes, but many people create compound indexes that are redundant or seldom used. Also, the order of columns in a compound index is important; you should use the columns left-to-right in search criteria, join criteria, or sorting order.

When No Index Can Help

The next type of mistake is to run a query that can't use any index. Developers create more and more indexes, trying to find some magical combination of columns or index options to make their query run faster.

Think of a database index using an analogy to a telephone book. If you're asked to look up everyone in the telephone book whose last name is Charles, it's an easy task. All the people with the same last name are listed together, because that's how the telephone book is ordered.

Index-Shotgun/anti/indexable.sql
```
CREATE INDEX LastNameFirstName ON TelephoneBook(last_name, first_name);

SELECT * FROM TelephoneBook WHERE last_name = 'Charles'; -- OK
```

However, if you're asked to look up everyone in the telephone book whose *first name* is Charles, this doesn't benefit from the order of names in the book. Anyone can have that first name, regardless of their last name, so you have to search through the entire book line by line.

Index-Shotgun/anti/not-indexable.sql
```
SELECT * FROM TelephoneBook WHERE first_name = 'Charles'; -- NOT indexable
```

The telephone book is ordered by last name and then by first name, just like a compound database index on last_name, first_name. This index doesn't help you search by first name.

The following examples show more index definitions and queries that can't use the indexes shown:

Index-Shotgun/anti/not-indexable.sql
```
CREATE INDEX LastNameFirstName ON Accounts(last_name, first_name);

SELECT * FROM Accounts ORDER BY first_name, last_name;
```

This query shows the telephone book scenario. If you create a compound index for the columns last_name followed by first_name (as in a telephone book), the index doesn't help you sort primarily by first_name.

Index-Shotgun/anti/not-indexable.sql
```
CREATE INDEX DateReported ON Bugs(date_reported);

SELECT * FROM Bugs WHERE MONTH(date_reported) = 4;
```

Even if you create an index for the date_reported column, the order of the index doesn't help you search by month. The order of this index is based on the entire date, starting with the year. Each year has a fourth month, so the rows where the month is equal to 4 are scattered through the index.

Some databases support indexes on expressions, or indexes on generated columns, as well as indexes on plain columns. You have to define the index prior to using it, and that index helps only for the expression you specify in its definition.

Index-Shotgun/anti/not-indexable.sql
```
CREATE INDEX LastNameFirstName ON Accounts(last_name, first_name);

SELECT * FROM Accounts WHERE last_name = 'Charles' OR first_name = 'Charles';
```

We're back to the problem that rows with that specific first name are scattered unpredictably with respect to the order of the index we defined. The result of the previous query is the same as the result of the following:

Index-Shotgun/anti/not-indexable.sql
```
SELECT * FROM Accounts WHERE last_name = 'Charles'
UNION
SELECT * FROM Accounts WHERE first_name = 'Charles';
```

The index shown in the example helps to find that last name, but it doesn't help find that first name.

Index-Shotgun/anti/not-indexable.sql

```
CREATE INDEX Description ON Bugs(description);

SELECT * FROM Bugs WHERE description LIKE '%crash%';
```

Because the pattern in this search predicate could occur anywhere in the string, there's no way the sorted index data structure can help.

> ### Low-Selectivity Indexes
>
> *Selectivity* is a statistic about a database index. It's the ratio of the number of distinct values in the index to the total number of rows in the table:
>
> ```
> SELECT COUNT(DISTINCT status) / COUNT(status) AS selectivity FROM Bugs;
> ```
>
> The lower the selectivity ratio, the less effective an index is. Why is this? Consider an analogy.
>
> This book has an index of a different type: each entry in a book's index lists the pages where the entry's words appear. If a word appears frequently in the book, it may list many page numbers. To find the part of the book you're looking for, you have to turn to each page in the list one by one.
>
> Indexes don't bother to list words that appear on too many pages. If you have to flip back and forth from the index to the pages of the book too much, then you might as well just read the whole book cover to cover.
>
> Likewise in a database index, if a given value appears on many rows in the table, it's more trouble to read the index than simply to scan the entire table. In fact, in these cases it can actually be more expensive to use that index.
>
> Ideally your database tracks the selectivity of indexes and shouldn't use an index that gives no benefit.

How to Recognize the Antipattern

The following are symptoms of the Index Shotgun antipattern:

- "Here's my query; how can I make it faster?"

  This is probably the single most common SQL question, but it's missing details about table description, indexes, data volume, and measurements of performance and optimization. Without this context, any answer is just guesswork.

- "I defined an index on every field; why isn't it faster?"

  This is the classic Index Shotgun antisolution. You've tried every possible index—but you're shooting in the dark.

- "I read that indexes make the database slow, so I don't use them."

Like many developers, you're looking for a one-size-fits-all strategy for performance improvement. No such blanket rule exists.

Legitimate Uses of the Antipattern

If you need to design a database for general use, without knowing what queries are important to optimize, you can't be sure of which indexes are best. You have to make an educated guess. It's likely that you'll miss some indexes that could have given benefit. It's also likely that you'll create some indexes that turn out to be unneeded. You have to make the best guess you can.

The Database Isn't Always the Bottleneck

Common wisdom in software developer communities is that the database is always the slowest part of your application and the source of performance issues. However, this isn't true.

For example, in one application I worked on, my manager asked me to find out why it was so slow, and he insisted it was the fault of the database. After I used a profiling tool to measure the application code, I found that it spent 80 percent of its time parsing its own HTML output to find form fields so it could populate values into forms. The performance issue had nothing to do with the database queries.

Before making an assumption about the cause of the performance problem, try to use software measuring tools to identify the code that is taking too long. Otherwise, you could be practicing premature optimization.

Solution: MENTOR Your Indexes

The Index Shotgun antipattern is about creating or dropping indexes without reason, so you need a methodology to analyze a database and find good reasons to include indexes or omit them.

You can use the mnemonic *MENTOR* to describe a checklist for analyzing your database for good index choices: *Measure*, *Explain*, *Nominate*, *Test*, *Optimize*, and *Rebuild*.

Measure

You can't make informed decisions without information. Most databases provide some way to log the time to execute SQL queries so you can identify the operations with the greatest cost. For example:

- Microsoft SQL Server and Oracle both have *SQL Trace* facilities and tools to report and analyze trace results. Microsoft calls this tool the *SQL Server Profiler*, and Oracle calls it *TKProf*.

- MySQL and PostgreSQL can log queries that take longer to execute than a specified threshold of time. MySQL calls this the *slow query log*, and its long_query_time configuration parameter defaults to 10 seconds. PostgreSQL has a similar configuration variable, log_min_duration_statement.

Once you know which queries account for the most time in your application, you know where you should focus your optimizing attention for the greatest benefit. You might even find that all queries are working efficiently except for one single bottleneck query. This is the query you should start optimizing.

The area of greatest cost in your application isn't necessarily the most time-consuming query, if that query is run only rarely. Other simpler queries might be run frequently, more often than you would expect, so they account for more total time. Giving attention to optimizing these queries gives you more bang for your buck.

Disable any query result caching while you're measuring query performance. This type of cache is designed to bypass query execution and index usage, so it won't give an accurate measurement.

You can get more accurate information by profiling your application after you deploy it. Collect aggregate data of where the code spends its time when real users are using it, and against the real database. You should monitor profiling data from time to time to be sure you haven't acquired a new bottleneck.

Remember to disable or reduce the reporting rate of profilers after you're done measuring, because these tools cause some overhead.

Explain

Having identified the query that has the greatest cost, your next step is to find out *why* it's so slow. Every database uses an optimizer to pick indexes for your query. You can get the database to give you a report of its analysis, called the *query execution plan* (QEP).

The syntax to request a QEP varies by database brand, as you can see in the table shown on page 149.

There's no standard for what information a QEP report includes or the format of the report. In general, the QEP shows you which tables are involved in a query, how the optimizer chooses to use indexes, and what order it will access

Database Brand	QEP Reporting Solution
IBM DB2	EXPLAIN, db2expln command, or Visual Explain
Microsoft SQL Server	SET SHOWPLAN_XML, or Display Execution Plan
MySQL	EXPLAIN
Oracle	EXPLAIN PLAN
PostgreSQL	EXPLAIN
SQLite	EXPLAIN

the tables. The report may also include statistics, such as the number of rows generated by each stage of the query.

Look at a sample SQL query and request a QEP report:

Index-Shotgun/soln/explain.sql
```
EXPLAIN SELECT Bugs.*
FROM Bugs
JOIN (BugsProducts JOIN Products USING (product_id))
  USING (bug_id)
WHERE summary LIKE '%crash%'
  AND product_name = 'Open RoundFile'
ORDER BY date_reported DESC;
```

Take a look at this MySQL QEP report:

table	type	possible_keys	key	key_len	ref	rows	filtered	extra
Bugs	ALL	PRIMARY,bug_id	NULL	NULL	NULL	4650	100	Using where; Using temporary; Using filesort
BugsProducts	ref	PRIMARY,product_id	PRIMARY	8	Bugs.bug_id	1	100	Using index
Products	ALL	PRIMARY,product_id	NULL	NULL	NULL	3	100	Using where; Using join buffer

The key column shows that this query makes use of only the primary key index BugsProducts. Also, the extra notes in the last column indicate that the query will sort the result in a temporary table, without the benefit of an index.

The LIKE expression forces a full table scan in Bugs, and there is no index on Products.product_name. We can improve this query if we create a new index on product_name and also use a full-text search solution (see Chapter 17, Poor Man's Search Engine, on page 191).

The information in a QEP report is vendor-specific. In this example, you should read the MySQL manual page "Optimizing Queries with EXPLAIN" to understand how to interpret the report.[1]

---

1. https://dev.mysql.com/doc/refman/en/using-explain.html

Nominate

Now that you have the optimizer's QEP for your query, you should look for cases where the query accesses a table without using an index.

Some databases have tools to do this for you, collecting query trace statistics and proposing a number of changes, including creating new indexes that you're missing but would benefit your query.

For example:

- IBM DB2 Design Advisor
- Microsoft SQL Server Database Engine Tuning Advisor
- MySQL Enterprise Query Analyzer
- Oracle Automatic SQL Tuning Advisor

Even without automatic advisors, you can learn how to recognize when an index could benefit a query. You need to study your database's documentation to interpret the QEP report.

Covering Indexes

If an index provides all the columns we need, then the query doesn't need to read data from the table at all.

Imagine if telephone book entries contained only a page number; after you looked up a name, you would then have to turn to the page it referenced to get the actual phone number. It makes more sense to look up the information in one step. Looking up a name is quick because the book is ordered, and it would be best to get other attributes you need from that entry, such as the phone number and perhaps also an address.

This is how a *covering index* works. You can define the index to include extra columns, even though they're not otherwise necessary for searching or sorting.

```
CREATE INDEX BugCovering ON Bugs
  (status, bug_id, date_reported, reported_by, summary);
```

If your query references only the columns included in the index data structure, the database generates your query results by reading only the index.

```
SELECT status, bug_id, date_reported, summary
FROM Bugs WHERE status = 'OPEN';
```

You can't use covering indexes for every query, but when you can, it's usually a great win for performance.

Test

This step is important: after creating indexes, profile your queries again. It's important to confirm that your change made a difference so you know that your work is done.

You can also use this step to impress your boss and justify the work you put into this optimization. You don't want your weekly status to be like this: "I've tried everything I can think of to fix our performance issues, and we'll just have to wait and see...." Instead, you should have the opportunity to report this: "I determined we could create one new index on a high-activity table, and I improved the performance of our critical queries by 38 percent."

Optimize

Indexes are compact, frequently used data structures, which makes them good candidates for keeping in cache memory. Reading indexes in memory improves performance an order of magnitude greater than reading indexes via disk I/O.

Database servers allow you to configure the amount of system memory to allocate for caching. The specific options are different in each brand of database product. For example, in MySQL the most important option for this purpose is innodb_buffer_pool_size.

Most database products set the default cache buffer size pretty low to ensure that the database works even on a low-powered laptop computer. When you deploy your database to a real server, you should probably increase the size of the cache.

How much memory should you allocate to cache? There's no universal answer to this, because it depends on the size of your database, the types of queries you run, and how much system memory you have available. A common recommendation is to monitor the rate of disk I/O requests; increasing the cache size slightly each day while doing that results in lower I/O activity. Don't allocate more memory than the system is equipped with, and leave some free for other processes and uses of the memory.

Rebuild

Indexes provide the most efficiency when they are *balanced*. Over time, as you update and delete rows, the indexes may become progressively imbalanced, similar to how filesystems become fragmented over time. In practice, you may not see a large difference between an index that is optimal vs. one that has some imbalance. You want to get the most out of indexes, so it's worthwhile to perform maintenance on a regular schedule.

Like most features related to indexes, each database brand uses vendor-specific terminology, syntax, and capabilities.

Database Brand	Index Maintenance Command
IBM DB2	REORG INDEX
Microsoft SQL Server	ALTER INDEX ... REORGANIZE, ALTER INDEX ... REBUILD, or DBCC DBREINDEX
MySQL	OPTIMIZE TABLE
Oracle	ALTER INDEX ... REBUILD
PostgreSQL	VACUUM or ANALYZE
SQLite	VACUUM

How frequently should you rebuild an index? You might hear generic answers such as "once a week," but in truth there's no single answer that fits all applications. It depends on how frequently you commit changes to a given table that could introduce imbalance. It also depends on how large the table is and how important it is to get optimal benefit from indexes for this table. Is it worth spending hours rebuilding indexes for a large but seldom-used table if you can expect to gain only an extra 1 percent performance? You're the best judge of this, because you know your data and your operation requirements better than anyone else does.

A lot of the knowledge about getting the most out of indexes is vendor specific, so you'll need to research the brand of database you use. Your resources include the database manual, books and magazines, blogs and mailing lists, and also lots of experimentation on your own. The most important rule is that guessing blindly at indexing isn't a good strategy.

> Know your data, know your queries, and MENTOR your indexes.

Mini-Antipattern: Indexing Every Column

Some people create indexes on every column—and every combination of columns—when they don't know which indexes will benefit their queries. In Too Many Indexes, on page 143, you saw an example.

In fact, creating every index that potentially could be used is much harder than creating an index on every column. It isn't just an index on every column that might be useful to some queries. Queries might need compound indexes, to optimize searches on multiple columns, or ORDER BY or GROUP BY, or even extra columns to make it a covering index. The order of columns in an index is also important. So, to make all potential indexes, you must make as many indexes as the number of *permutation* of columns in the table.

Index-Shotgun/mini/permutations.sql
```
CREATE TABLE Bugs (
  bug_id        SERIAL PRIMARY KEY,
  date_reported DATE NOT NULL,
  summary       VARCHAR(80) NOT NULL,
  status        VARCHAR(10) NOT NULL,
  INDEX (bug_id, date_reported, summary, status),
  INDEX (date_reported, bug_id, summary, status),
  INDEX (summary, date_reported, bug_id, status),
  INDEX (bug_id, date_reported, summary, status),
  INDEX (summary, bug_id, date_reported, status),
  INDEX (bug_id, summary, date_reported, status),
  INDEX (date_reported, bug_id, summary, status),
  INDEX (summary, date_reported, bug_id, status),
  INDEX (status, date_reported, bug_id, summary),
  INDEX (date_reported, status, bug_id, summary),
  ...
);
```

The number of indexes needed to form all permutations is actually the factorial of the number of columns in the table. That is, for four columns, the number of indexes would be four times three times two, or 24. If you had five columns, it would require 120 indexes to make all permutations. Some SQL database implementations don't allow that many indexes in a given table.

Each index increases the storage required for the table, and the cost of updates. If you create a database table with too many indexes, you incur a lot of overhead with no assurance of payoff.

Create only the indexes needed to support queries you currently execute. If you need a different query in the future, then you should analyze the queries at that time to determine if you need to add a new index.

Part III

Query Antipatterns

You need to add data to your database and then retrieve data. SQL queries are made with data manipulation language—statements such as SELECT, UPDATE, and DELETE.

As we know, there are known knowns; there are things we know we
know. We also know there are known unknowns; that is to say we know
there are some things we do not know. But there are also unknown
unknowns—the ones we don't know we don't know.

> *Donald Rumsfeld*

## CHAPTER 14

Fear of the Unknown

In the example bugs database, the Accounts table has columns first_name and last_name. You can use an expression to format the user's full name as a single column using the string concatenation operator:

Fear-Unknown/intro/full-name.sql
```
SELECT first_name || ' ' || last_name AS full_name FROM Accounts;
```

Suppose your boss asks you to modify the database to add the user's middle initial to the table (perhaps two users have the same first name and last name, and the middle initial is a good way to avoid confusion). This is a pretty simple alteration. You also manually add the middle initials for a few users.

Fear-Unknown/intro/middle-name.sql
```
ALTER TABLE Accounts ADD COLUMN middle_initial CHAR(2);

UPDATE Accounts SET middle_initial = 'J.' WHERE account_id = 123;
UPDATE Accounts SET middle_initial = 'C.' WHERE account_id = 321;

SELECT first_name || ' ' || middle_initial || ' ' || last_name AS full_name
FROM Accounts;
```

Suddenly, the application ceases to show any names. Actually, on a second look, you notice it isn't universal. Only the names of users who have specified their middle initial appear normally; every else's name is now blank.

What happened to everyone else's names? Can you fix this before your boss notices and starts to panic, thinking you've lost data in the database?

Objective: Distinguish Missing Values

It's inevitable that some data in your database has no value. Either you need to insert a row before you have discovered the values for all the columns, or else some columns have no meaningful value in some legitimate circumstances. SQL supports a special null value, corresponding to the NULL keyword.

There are many ways you can use a null value productively in SQL tables and queries:

- You can use null in place of a value that is not available at the time the row is created, such as the date of termination for an employee who is still working.

- A given column can use a null value when it has no applicable value on a given row, such as the fuel efficiency rating for a car that is fully electric.

- A function can return a null value when given invalid inputs, as in DAY('2021-12-32').

- An outer join uses null values as placeholders for the columns of an unmatched table in an outer join.

The objective is to write queries against columns that contain null.

Antipattern: Use Null as an Ordinary Value, or Vice Versa

Many software developers are caught off-guard by the behavior of null in SQL. Unlike in most programming languages, SQL treats null as a special value, different from zero, false, or an empty string. This is true in standard SQL and most brands of database. However, in Oracle and Sybase, null is exactly the same as a string of zero length. The null value follows some special behavior, too.

Using Null in Expressions

One case that surprises some people is when you perform arithmetic on a column or expression that is null. For example, many programmers would expect the result to be 10 for bugs that have been given no estimate in the hours column, but instead the query returns null.

Fear-Unknown/anti/expression.sql
```
SELECT hours + 10 FROM Bugs;
```

Null is not the same as zero. A number ten greater than an unknown is still an unknown.

Null is not the same as a string of zero length. Combining any string with null in standard SQL returns null (despite the behavior in Oracle and Sybase).

Null is not the same as false. Boolean expressions with AND, OR, and NOT also produce results that some people find confusing.

Searching Nullable Columns

The following query returns only rows where assigned_to has the value 123, not rows with other values or rows where the column is null:

Fear-Unknown/anti/search.sql
```
SELECT * FROM Bugs WHERE assigned_to = 123;
```

You might think that the next query returns the complementary set of rows, that is, all rows *not* returned by the previous query:

Fear-Unknown/anti/search-not.sql
```
SELECT * FROM Bugs WHERE NOT (assigned_to = 123);
```

However, neither query result includes rows where assigned_to is null. Any comparison to null returns *unknown*, not true or false. Even the negation of null is still null.

It's common to make the following mistakes searching for null values or non-null values:

Fear-Unknown/anti/equals-null.sql
```
SELECT * FROM Bugs WHERE assigned_to = NULL;

SELECT * FROM Bugs WHERE assigned_to <> NULL;
```

The condition in a WHERE clause is satisfied only when the expression is true, but a comparison to NULL is never true; it's unknown. It doesn't matter whether the comparison is for equality or inequality; it's still unknown, which is certainly not true. Neither of the previous queries return rows where assigned_to is null.

Using Null in Query Parameters

It's also difficult to use null in a parameterized SQL expression as if the null were an ordinary value.

Fear-Unknown/anti/parameter.sql
```
SELECT * FROM Bugs WHERE assigned_to = ?;
```

The previous query returns predictable results when you send an ordinary integer value for the parameter, but you can't use a literal NULL as the parameter.

Avoiding the Issue

If handling null makes queries more complex, many software developers choose to disallow nulls in the database. Instead, they choose an ordinary value to signify "unknown" or "inapplicable."

"We Hate Nulls!"

Jack, a software developer, described to me his client's request that he avoid using any null values in their database. Their explanation was simply, "we hate nulls," and that the presence of nulls would lead to errors in their application code. Jack asked me what other value he should use to represent a missing value.

I told Jack that representing a missing value is the exact purpose of null. No matter what other value he chose to signify a missing value, he would have needed to modify the application code to treat that value as special.

Jack's client's attitude about null was wrong; similarly, a client could have said that they don't like writing code to prevent division by zero errors, but that wouldn't make it a good choice to prohibit all instances of the value zero.

What exactly is wrong with using a non-null value in place of NULL? In the following example, declare the previously nullable columns assigned_to and hours as NOT NULL:

Fear-Unknown/anti/special-create-table.sql
```sql
CREATE TABLE Bugs (
  bug_id              SERIAL PRIMARY KEY,
  -- other columns
  assigned_to         BIGINT UNSIGNED NOT NULL,
  hours               NUMERIC(9,2) NOT NULL,
  FOREIGN KEY (assigned_to) REFERENCES Accounts(account_id)
);
```

You might try to use -1 to represent an unknown value.

Fear-Unknown/anti/special-insert.sql
```sql
INSERT INTO Bugs (assigned_to, hours) VALUES (-1, -1);
```

The hours column is numeric, so you're restricted to a numeric value to mean "unspecified." It has to have no meaning in that column, so you chose a negative value. Unfortunately, the value -1 would throw off calculations such as SUM() or AVG(). You have to exclude rows with this value, using special-case expressions, which is what you were trying to avoid by prohibiting null.

Fear-Unknown/anti/special-select.sql
```sql
SELECT AVG( hours ) AS average_hours_per_bug FROM Bugs
WHERE hours <> -1;
```

In another column, the value -1 might be significant, so you have to choose a different value on a case-by-case basis for each column. You also have to remember or document the special values used by each column. This adds a lot of meticulous and unnecessary work to a project.

Now look at the assigned_to column. It's a foreign key to the Accounts table. When a bug has been reported but not assigned yet, what non-null value can you use? Any non-null value must reference a row in Accounts, so you need to create a placeholder row in Accounts, meaning "no one" or "unassigned." It seems ironic to create an account to reference, so you can represent the absence of a reference to a real user's account.

When you declare a column as NOT NULL, it should be because it would make no sense for the row to exist without a value in that column. For example, the Bugs.reported_by column must have a value, because every bug was reported by someone. However, it's okay for a bug to exist without having been assigned yet. Missing values should be null.

How to Recognize the Antipattern

If you find yourself or another member of your team describing issues like the following, it could be because of improper handling of nulls:

- "How do I find rows where no value has been set in the assigned_to (or other) column?"

  You can't use the equality operator for null. We'll see how to use the IS NULL predicate later in this chapter.

- "The full names of some users appear blank in the application presentation, but I can see them in the database."

  The problem might be that you're concatenating strings with null, which produces null.

- "The report of total hours spent working on this project includes only a few of the bugs that we completed! Only those for which we assigned a priority are included."

  Your aggregate query to sum the hours probably includes an expression in the WHERE clause that fails to be true when priority is null. Watch out for unexpected results when you use *not equals* expressions. For example, on rows where priority is null, the expression priority <> 1 will fail.

- "It turns out we can't use the string we've been using to represent *unknown* in the Bugs table, so we need to have a meeting to discuss what new special value we can use and estimate the development time to migrate our data and convert our code to use that value."

  This is a likely consequence of assigning a special flag value that could be a legitimate value in your column's domain. Eventually, you may find you need to use that value for its literal meaning instead of its flag meaning.

Recognizing problems with your handling of nulls can be elusive. Problems may not occur during application testing, especially if you overlooked some edge cases while designing sample data for tests. However, when your application is used in production, data can take many unanticipated forms. If a null can creep into the data, you can count on it happening.

Are Nulls Relational?

There is some controversy about null in SQL. E. F. Codd, the computer scientist who developed relational theory, recognized the need for null to signify missing data. However, C. J. Date has shown that the behavior of null as defined in the SQL standard has some edge cases that conflict with relational logic.

The fact is that most programming languages are not perfect implementations of computer science theories. The SQL language supports null, for better or for worse. We've seen some of the hazards, but you can learn how to account for these cases and use null productively.

Legitimate Uses of the Antipattern

Using null is not the antipattern; the antipattern is using null like an ordinary value or using an ordinary value like null.

One situation where you need to treat null as an ordinary value is when you import or export external data. In a text file with comma-separated fields, all values must be represented by text. For example, in MySQL's mysqlimport tool for loading data from a text file, \N represents a null.

Similarly, user input cannot represent a null directly. An application that accepts user input may provide a way to map some special input sequence to null. For example, Microsoft .NET 2.0 and newer supports a property called ConvertEmptyStringToNull for web user interfaces. Parameters and bound fields with this property automatically convert an empty string value ("") to null.

Finally, null won't work if you need to support several distinct missing-value cases. Suppose you want to distinguish between a bug that has never been assigned and a bug that was previously assigned to a person who has left the project—you have to use a distinct value for each state.

Solution: Use Null as a Unique Value

Most problems with null values are based on a common misunderstanding of the behavior of SQL's three-valued logic. For programmers accustomed to the conventional true/false logic implemented in most other languages, this can be a challenge. You can handle null values in SQL queries with a little study of how they work.

Null in Scalar Expressions

Suppose Stan is thirty years old, while Oliver's age is unknown. If you ask whether Stan is older than Oliver, the only possible answer is "I don't know." If you ask whether Stan is the same age as Oliver, the answer is also "I don't know." If you ask what is the sum of Stan's age and Oliver's age, the answer is the same.

Charlie's age is also unknown. If you ask whether Oliver's age is equal to Charlie's age, the answer is still "I don't know." This shows why the result of a comparison like NULL = NULL is also null.

The following table describes some cases where programmers expect one result but get something different.

Expression	Expected	Actual	Because
NULL = 0	TRUE	NULL	Null is not zero.
NULL = 12345	FALSE	NULL	Unknown if the unspecified value is equal to a given value.
NULL <> 12345	TRUE	NULL	Also unknown if it's unequal.
NULL + 12345	12345	NULL	Null is not zero.
NULL || 'string'	'string'	NULL	Null is not an empty string.
NULL = NULL	TRUE	NULL	Unknown if one unspecified value is the same as another.
NULL <> NULL	FALSE	NULL	Also unknown if they're different.

Of course, these examples apply not only when using the NULL keyword but also to any column or expression whose value is null.

Null in Boolean Expressions

Null is neither true nor false. A null value certainly isn't true, but it isn't the same as false. If it were, then applying NOT to a null value would result in true. However, that's not the way it works; NOT (NULL) results in another null. This confuses some people who try to use boolean expressions with null.

The following table shows some some additional cases where programmers expect one result but get something different.

Expression	Expected	Actual	Because
NULL AND TRUE	FALSE	NULL	Null is not false.
NULL AND FALSE	FALSE	FALSE	Any truth value AND FALSE is false.
NULL OR FALSE	FALSE	NULL	Null is not false.
NULL OR TRUE	TRUE	TRUE	Any truth value OR TRUE is true.
NOT (NULL)	TRUE	NULL	Null is not false.

The Right Result for the Wrong Reason

Consider the following case, where a nullable column may behave in a more intuitive way by serendipity.

```
SELECT * FROM Bugs WHERE assigned_to <> 'NULL';
```

Here the nullable column assigned_to is compared to the string value 'NULL' (notice the quotes), instead of the actual NULL keyword.

Where assigned_to is null, comparing it to the string 'NULL' is not true. The row is excluded from the query result, which is the programmer's intent.

The other case is that the column is an integer compared to the string 'NULL'. The integer value of a string like 'NULL' is zero in most brands of database. The integer value of assigned_to is almost certainly greater than zero. It's unequal to the string, so the row is included in the query result.

Thus, by making another common mistake, that of putting quotes around the NULL keyword, some programmers may unwittingly get the result they wanted. Unfortunately, this coincidence doesn't hold in other searches, such as WHERE assigned_to = 'NULL'.

Searching for Null

Since neither equality nor inequality return true when comparing one value to a null value, you need some other operation if you are searching for a null. Older SQL standards define the IS NULL predicate, which returns true if its single operand is null. The opposite, IS NOT NULL, returns false if its operand is null.

Fear-Unknown/soln/search.sql
```
SELECT * FROM Bugs WHERE assigned_to IS NULL;
SELECT * FROM Bugs WHERE assigned_to IS NOT NULL;
```

In addition, the SQL-99 standard defines another comparison predicate, IS DISTINCT FROM. This works like an ordinary inequality operator <>, except that it always returns true or false, even when its operands are null. This relieves you from writing tedious expressions that must test IS NULL before comparing to a value. The following two queries are equivalent:

Fear-Unknown/soln/is-distinct-from.sql

```
SELECT * FROM Bugs WHERE assigned_to IS NULL OR assigned_to <> 1;

SELECT * FROM Bugs WHERE assigned_to IS DISTINCT FROM 1;
```

You can use this predicate with query parameters to which you want to send either a literal value or NULL:

Fear-Unknown/soln/is-distinct-from-parameter.sql

```
SELECT * FROM Bugs WHERE assigned_to IS DISTINCT FROM ?;
```

Support for IS DISTINCT FROM is inconsistent among database brands. PostgreSQL, IBM DB2, and Firebird do support it, whereas Oracle and Microsoft SQL Server don't support it yet. MySQL offers a proprietary operator <=> that works like IS NOT DISTINCT FROM.

Declare Columns NOT NULL

It's recommended to declare a NOT NULL constraint on a column for which a null would break a policy in your application or otherwise be nonsensical. It's better to allow the database to enforce constraints uniformly rather than rely on application code.

For example, it's reasonable that any entry in the Bugs table should have a non-null value for the date_reported, reported_by, and status columns. Likewise, rows in child tables like Comments must include a non-null bug_id, referencing an existing bug. You should declare these columns with the NOT NULL option.

Some people recommend that you define a DEFAULT for every column, so that if you omit the column in an INSERT statement, the column gets some value instead of null. That's good advice for some columns but not for other columns. For example, Bugs.reported_by should not be null. It should be the account id of the user who reported it, but it's not possible to declare this as a default. It's valid and common for a column to need a NOT NULL constraint yet have no logical default value.

Dynamic Defaults

In some query results, you may need to force a column or expression to be non-null for the sake of simplifying the query logic, but you don't want that value to be stored in the table. You need a way to set a non-null value to be used if a given expression would return a null result. For this you should use the COALESCE() function. This function accepts a variable number of arguments and returns its first non-null argument.

In the story about concatenating users' names in the opening of this chapter, you could use COALESCE() to make an expression that uses a single space in place of the middle initial, so a null-valued middle initial doesn't make the whole expression become null.

Fear-Unknown/soln/coalesce.sql
```
SELECT first_name || COALESCE(' ' || middle_initial || ' ', ' ') || last_name
  AS full_name
FROM Accounts;
```

COALESCE() is a standard SQL function. Some database brands support a similar function by another name, such as NVL() or ISNULL().

> Use null to signify a missing value for any data type.

Mini-Antipattern: NOT IN (NULL)

If the logic of null isn't confusing enough, there are edge cases where it's even harder to avoid getting lost in the boolean rules.

You may have mastered the logic enough to understand that the following two queries are equivalent:

Fear-Unknown/mini/in-null.sql
```
SELECT * FROM Bugs WHERE status IN (NULL, 'NEW');

SELECT * FROM Bugs WHERE status = NULL OR status = 'NEW';
```

You know that comparing a value equals null is unknown, and that's not true, so the first term of that comparison will never be satisfied. That's okay, because the query still matches rows with "NEW".

This gets really interesting when the search is negated.

Fear-Unknown/mini/not-in-null.sql
```
SELECT * FROM Bugs WHERE status NOT IN (NULL, 'NEW');
```

You might think this simply matches the complement of the set of rows matched by the previous query. That is, all rows except those with status "NEW". In fact, *none* of the rows match. Why?

The query with the NOT IN predicate can be rewritten as either of the following:

Fear-Unknown/mini/not-in-null.sql
```
SELECT * FROM Bugs WHERE NOT (status = NULL OR status = 'NEW');

SELECT * FROM Bugs WHERE NOT (status = NULL) AND NOT (status = 'NEW');
```

The first rewrite looks familiar, as an IN predicate is equivalent to equality comparisons to each respective value, as terms of OR operations. Then the negation NOT is applied to the expression. You know by now that comparing a column equal to null is unknown, and the negation of unknown is still unknown.

The second rewrite is an application of *DeMorgan's law*, a boolean algebra transformation. The negation of an expression negates each term in the expression, as it converts OR to AND or vice versa.

Now you should see that NOT (status = NULL) will still be unknown, and using AND to combine that with the other term makes the whole expression unknown for any row evaluated. So, the SQL query always fails to match any rows, regardless of any value in the status column.

CHAPTER 15

Ambiguous Groups

Suppose your boss needs to know which projects in the bugs database are still active and which projects have been abandoned. One report he asks you to generate is the latest bug reported per product. You write a query using the MySQL database to calculate the greatest value in the date_reported column per group of bugs sharing a given product_id. The report looks like this:

product_name	latest	bug_id
Open RoundFile	2010-06-01	1234
Visual TurboBuilder	2010-02-16	3456
ReConsider	2010-01-01	5678

Your boss is a detail-oriented person, and he spends some time looking up each bug listed in the report. He notices that the row listed as the most recent for "Open RoundFile" shows a bug_id that isn't the latest bug. The full data shows the discrepancy:

product_name	date_reported	bug_id	
Open RoundFile	2009-12-19	1234	*This bug_id…*
Open RoundFile	2010-06-01	2248	*doesn't match this date*
Visual TurboBuilder	2010-02-16	3456	
Visual TurboBuilder	2010-02-10	4077	
Visual TurboBuilder	2010-02-16	5150	
ReConsider	2010-01-01	5678	
ReConsider	2009-11-09	8063	

How can you explain this problem? Why does it affect one product but not the others? How can you get the desired report?

Objective: Get Row with Greatest Value per Group

Most programmers who learn SQL get to the stage of using GROUP BY in a query, applying some aggregate function to groups of rows, and getting a result with one row per group. This is a powerful feature that makes it easy to get a wide variety of complex reports using relatively little code.

For example, a query to get the latest bug reported for each product in the bugs database looks like this:

Groups/anti/groupbyproduct.sql

```sql
SELECT product_id, MAX(date_reported) AS latest
FROM Bugs JOIN BugsProducts USING (bug_id)
GROUP BY product_id;
```

A natural extension to this query is to request the ID of the specific bug with the latest date reported:

Groups/anti/groupbyproduct.sql

```sql
SELECT product_id, MAX(date_reported) AS latest, bug_id
FROM Bugs JOIN BugsProducts USING (bug_id)
GROUP BY product_id;
```

However, this query results in either an error or an unreliable answer. This is a common source of confusion for programmers using SQL.

The objective is to run a query that not only reports the greatest value in a group (or the least value or the average value) but also includes other attributes of the row where that value is found.

Antipattern: Reference Nongrouped Columns

The root cause of this antipattern is simple, and it reveals a common misconception that many programmers have about how grouping queries work in SQL.

The Single-Value Rule

The rows in each group are those rows with the same value in the column or columns you name after GROUP BY. For example, in the following query, there is one row group for each distinct value in product_id.

Groups/anti/groupbyproduct.sql

```sql
SELECT product_id, MAX(date_reported) AS latest
FROM Bugs JOIN BugsProducts USING (bug_id)
GROUP BY product_id;
```

Every column in the select-list of a query must have a single value row per row group. This is called the *Single-Value Rule*. Columns named in the GROUP BY clause are guaranteed to be exactly one value per group, no matter how many rows the group matches.

The MAX() expression is also guaranteed to result in a single value for each group: the highest value found in the argument of MAX() over all the rows in the group.

However, the database server can't be so sure about any other column named in the select-list. It can't always guarantee that the same value occurs on every row in a group for those other columns.

Groups/anti/groupbyproduct.sql
```
SELECT product_id, MAX(date_reported) AS latest, bug_id
FROM Bugs JOIN BugsProducts USING (bug_id)
GROUP BY product_id;
```

In this example, there are many distinct values for bug_id for a given product_id, because the BugsProducts table associates multiple bugs to a given product. In a grouping query that reduces to a single row per product, there's no way to represent all the values of bug_id.

Since there is no guarantee of a single value per group in the "extra" columns, the database assumes that they violate the Single-Value Rule. Most brands of database report an error if you try to run any query that tries to return a column other than those columns named in the GROUP BY clause or as arguments to aggregate functions.

MySQL and SQLite have different behavior from other brands of database, which we'll explore in Legitimate Uses of the Antipattern, on page 173.

Do-What-I-Mean Queries

The common misconception that programmers have is that SQL can guess which bug_id you want in the report, based on the fact that MAX() is used in another column. Most people assume that if the query fetches the greatest value, then other columns named will naturally take their value from the same row where that greatest value occurs.

Unfortunately, SQL can't make this inference in several cases:

- If two bugs have the exact same value for date_reported and that is the greatest value in the group, which value of bug_id should the query report?

- If you query for two different aggregate functions, for example MAX() and MIN(), these probably correspond to two different rows in the group. Which bug_id should the query return for this group?

Groups/anti/maxandmin.sql

```
SELECT product_id, MAX(date_reported) AS latest,
  MIN(date_reported) AS earliest, bug_id
FROM Bugs JOIN BugsProducts USING (bug_id)
GROUP BY product_id;
```

- If none of the rows in the table matches the value returned by the aggregate function, what is the value of bug_id? This is commonly true for the functions AVG(), COUNT(), and SUM().

Groups/anti/sumbyproduct.sql

```
SELECT product_id, SUM(hours) AS total_project_estimate, bug_id
FROM Bugs JOIN BugsProducts USING (bug_id)
GROUP BY product_id;
```

These are examples of why the Single-Value Rule is important. Not every query that fails to follow this rule would produce an ambiguous result, but many do. It would be clever if the database could tell an ambiguous query from an unambiguous one and produce an error only when the data contains ambiguity. That's not good for application reliability; it would mean that the same query might be valid or invalid, depending on the state of data.

GROUP BY and DISTINCT

SQL supports a query modifier called DISTINCT that reduces the rows of the query result so that every row is unique. For example, the following query reports who reported bugs and which days they reported bugs, but only one row per date and person:

```
SELECT DISTINCT date_reported, reported_by FROM Bugs;
```

A grouping query can achieve the same result by omitting any aggregate function. The query result is reduced to one row for each distinct pair of values in the column named in the GROUP BY clause:

```
SELECT date_reported, reported_by FROM Bugs
GROUP BY date_reported, reported_by;
```

Both queries produce the same result and should be optimized and executed similarly. In this example, it's more appropriate to use DISTINCT because the query has no aggregate functions.

How to Recognize the Antipattern

In most brands of database, writing a query that violates the Single-Value Rule should elicit an error immediately as you prepare the query. The following are examples of error messages given by some brands of database:

- IBM DB2:

  ```
  An expression starting with "BUG_ID" specified in a SELECT clause,
  HAVING clause, or ORDER BY clause is not specified in the GROUP BY
  clause or it is in a SELECT clause, HAVING clause, or ORDER BY clause
  with a column function and no GROUP BY clause is specified.
  ```

- Microsoft SQL Server:

  ```
  Column 'Bugs.bug_id' is invalid in the select list because it is not
  contained in either an aggregate function or the GROUP BY clause.
  ```

- MySQL, since version 5.7, enables the ONLY_FULL_GROUP_BY SQL mode by default, to prevent ambiguous queries.

  ```
  ERROR 1055 (42000): Expression #3 of SELECT list is not in GROUP BY
  clause and contains nonaggregated column 'test.Bugs.bug_id'
  which is not functionally dependent on columns in GROUP BY clause;
  this is incompatible with sql_mode=only_full_group_by
  ```

- Oracle:

  ```
  not a GROUP BY expression
  ```

- PostgreSQL:

  ```
  column "bp.bug_id" must appear in the GROUP BY clause or be
  used in an aggregate function
  ```

In SQLite, and in MySQL if the ONLY_FULL_GROUP_BY SQL mode is not enabled, ambiguous columns may contain unexpected and unreliable values. In MySQL, the value returned is from the first row in the group, where *first* corresponds to physical storage. SQLite gives the opposite result: the value is from the *last* row in the group. In both cases, the behavior is not documented, and these databases aren't obligated to work the same in future versions. It's your responsibility to notice these cases and to design your queries to avoid ambiguity.

Legitimate Uses of the Antipattern

As we've seen, MySQL and SQLite can't guarantee a reliable result for a column that doesn't fit the Single-Value Rule. There are cases when you can take advantage of the fact that these databases enforce the rule less strictly than other brands.

Groups/legit/functional.sql

```
SELECT b.reported_by, a.account_name
FROM Bugs b JOIN Accounts a ON (b.reported_by = a.account_id)
GROUP BY b.reported_by;
```

In the previous query, the account_name column technically violates the Single-Value Rule, since it's named neither in the GROUP BY clause nor in an aggregate function. Nevertheless, there is only one value possible for account_name in each group; the groups are based on Bugs.reported_by, which is a foreign key to the Accounts table. So, the groups correspond one-to-one with rows in the Accounts table.

In other words, if you know the value of reported_by, then you know the value of account_name unambiguously, like if you had queried by the primary key of the Accounts table.

This kind of unambiguous relationship is called a *functional dependency*. The most common example of this is between the primary key of a table and the table's attributes: account_name is a functional dependency of its primary key, account_id. If you group a query by a table's primary key column(s), then the groups correspond to a single row of that table, and so all other columns of the same table must have a single value per group.

Bugs.reported_by has a similar relationship with the dependent attributes of the Accounts table, because it references the primary key of the Accounts table. When the query groups by the reported_by column, which is a foreign key, the attributes of the Accounts table are functionally dependent, and the query result contains no ambiguity.

However, most brands of database still return an error. Not only is this the behavior required by the SQL standard, but it's difficult for software to detect functional dependencies in all cases. If you use MySQL or SQLite and you're careful to query only functionally dependent columns, you can use this kind of grouping query and still avoid problems of ambiguity.

Solution: Use Columns Unambiguously

The sections that follow describe several ways you can resolve this antipattern and write unambiguous queries.

Query Only Functionally Dependent Columns

The most straightforward solution is to eliminate ambiguous columns from the query.

```
Groups/anti/groupbyproduct.sql
SELECT product_id, MAX(date_reported) AS latest
FROM Bugs JOIN BugsProducts USING (bug_id)
GROUP BY product_id;
```

The query reveals the date of the latest bug per product, even though it doesn't report the bug_id corresponding to that latest bug. Sometimes this is enough, so don't overlook a simple solution.

Using a Window Function

Modern SQL products implement *window functions*, which you can use to filter for the first (or last) row in a group. Review the documentation for your database to make sure you use a version that supports these functions. For example, MySQL 8.0 is required to get support for these functions.

```
Groups/soln/window-function.sql
SELECT t.product_id, t.date_reported, t.bug_id
FROM (
  SELECT bp.product_id, b.date_reported, b.bug_id,
    ROW_NUMBER() OVER (PARTITION BY bp.product_id
      ORDER BY b.date_reported DESC) AS rownum
  FROM Bugs b JOIN BugsProducts bp USING (bug_id)
) AS t
WHERE t.rownum = 1;
```

The rownum column returned by the subquery starts numbering over at 1 for each partition, that is, each group of rows by product_id. The condition in the outer query ensures that only the first row of each partition is included in the result.

Using a Correlated Subquery

A correlated subquery contains a reference to the outer query and so produces different results for each row of the outer query. We can use this to find the latest bug per product by running a subquery to search for bugs with the same product and a greater date. When the subquery finds none, the bug in the outer query is the latest.

```
Groups/soln/notexists.sql
SELECT bp1.product_id, b1.date_reported AS latest, b1.bug_id
FROM Bugs b1 JOIN BugsProducts bp1 USING (bug_id)
WHERE NOT EXISTS
```

```
 (SELECT * FROM Bugs b2 JOIN BugsProducts bp2 USING (bug_id)
  WHERE bp1.product_id = bp2.product_id
    AND b1.date_reported < b2.date_reported);
```

This is a simple solution that is readable and easy to code. However, keep in mind that this solution isn't likely to be the best for performance, because correlated subqueries are executed once for each row of the outer query.

Using a Derived Table

You can use a subquery as a *derived table*, producing an interim result that contains only the product_id and the corresponding greatest bug report date for each product. Then use this result to join against the tables so that the query result contains only bugs with the latest date per product.

Groups/soln/derived-table.sql
```
SELECT m.product_id, m.latest, b1.bug_id
FROM Bugs b1 JOIN BugsProducts bp1 USING (bug_id)
  JOIN (SELECT bp2.product_id, MAX(b2.date_reported) AS latest
    FROM Bugs b2 JOIN BugsProducts bp2 USING (bug_id)
    GROUP BY bp2.product_id) m
  ON (bp1.product_id = m.product_id AND b1.date_reported = m.latest);
```

product_id	latest	bug_id
1	2010-06-01	2248
2	2010-02-16	3456
2	2010-02-16	5150
3	2010-01-01	5678

Notice that you can get multiple rows per product if the latest date returned by the subquery matches multiple rows. If you need to ensure a single row per product_id, you can use another grouping function in the outer query:

Groups/soln/derived-table-no-duplicates.sql
```
SELECT m.product_id, m.latest, MAX(b1.bug_id) AS latest_bug_id
FROM Bugs b1 JOIN
  (SELECT product_id, MAX(date_reported) AS latest
    FROM Bugs b2 JOIN BugsProducts USING (bug_id)
    GROUP BY product_id) m
  ON (b1.date_reported = m.latest)
GROUP BY m.product_id, m.latest;
```

product_id	latest	latest_bug_id
1	2010-06-01	2248
2	2010-02-16	5150
3	2010-01-01	5678

Use the derived table solution as a more scalable alternative to the correlated sub-query. The derived table is noncorrelated, so most database brands should be able to execute the subquery once. However, the database must store the interim result set in a temporary table, so this solution still isn't the best for performance.

Using a JOIN

You can create a join that tries to match against a set of rows that may not exist. This type of join is called an *outer join*. Where the matching rows don't exist, null is used for all columns in that nonexistent row. So, where the query finds null, we know no such row was found.

Groups/soln/outer-join.sql
```
SELECT bp1.product_id, b1.date_reported AS latest, b1.bug_id
FROM Bugs b1 JOIN BugsProducts bp1 ON (b1.bug_id = bp1.bug_id)
LEFT OUTER JOIN
  (Bugs AS b2 JOIN BugsProducts AS bp2 ON (b2.bug_id = bp2.bug_id))
  ON (bp1.product_id = bp2.product_id
    AND (b1.date_reported < b2.date_reported
    OR b1.date_reported = b2.date_reported AND b1.bug_id < b2.bug_id))
WHERE b2.bug_id IS NULL;
```

product_id	latest	bug_id
1	2010-06-01	2248
2	2010-02-16	5150
3	2010-01-01	5678

It takes a few minutes of gazing at this query, and perhaps some doodles on notepaper, for most people to see how it works. Once you do, this technique can be an important tool.

Use the JOIN solution when the scalability of the query over large sets of data is important. Although it's a tougher concept to grasp and thus more difficult to maintain, it often scales better than a subquery-based solution. Remember to measure the performance of several query forms, instead of assuming that one performs better than the other.

Using an Aggregate Function for Extra Columns

You can make the extra column comply with the Single-Value Rule by applying another aggregate function to it.

Groups/soln/extra-aggregate.sql
```
SELECT product_id, MAX(date_reported) AS latest,
  MAX(bug_id) AS latest_bug_id
FROM Bugs JOIN BugsProducts USING (bug_id)
GROUP BY product_id;
```

Use this solution only when you can rely on the latest bug_id being the bug with the latest date, in other words, if bugs are guaranteed to be reported in chronological order.

Concatenating All Values per Group

Finally, you can use another aggregate function on bug_id to avoid violating the Single-Value Rule. MySQL and SQLite support a function GROUP_CONCAT() that concatenates all the values in the group into one value. By default, this is a comma-separated string.

```
Groups/soln/group-concat-mysql.sql
SELECT product_id, MAX(date_reported) AS latest
  GROUP_CONCAT(bug_id) AS bug_id_list,
FROM Bugs JOIN BugsProducts USING (bug_id)
GROUP BY product_id;
```

product_id	latest	bug_id_list
1	2010-06-01	1234,2248
2	2010-02-16	3456,4077,5150
3	2010-01-01	5678,8063

This query doesn't reveal which bug_id corresponds to the latest date; the bug_id_list includes all bug_id values in each group.

Another disadvantage of this solution is that it isn't standard SQL, and other brands of database don't support this function. Some brands of database support custom functions and custom aggregate functions. For example, here's the solution for PostgreSQL:

```
Groups/soln/group-concat-pgsql.sql
CREATE AGGREGATE GROUP_ARRAY (
  BASETYPE = ANYELEMENT,
    SFUNC = ARRAY_APPEND,
    STYPE = ANYARRAY,
  INITCOND = '{}'
);

SELECT product_id, MAX(date_reported) AS latest,
  ARRAY_TO_STRING(GROUP_ARRAY(bug_id), ',') AS bug_id_list
FROM Bugs JOIN BugsProducts USING (bug_id)
GROUP BY product_id;
```

Some other brands of database don't support custom functions, so the solution may require writing a stored procedure to loop over a nongrouped query result, concatenating values manually.

Use this solution when you expect the extra column to have a single value per group but the column still violates the Single-Value Rule.

Using Proprietary Solutions

MySQL has another nonstandard function called ANY_VALUE(), which allows you to query a column that would violate the Single-Value Rule. This function suppresses the check for an ambiguous column, so it returns the column's value from an arbitrary row in the group.

Groups/soln/extra-aggregate-any.sql
```
SELECT product_id, MAX(date_reported) AS latest,
  ANY_VALUE(assigned_to) AS any_developer
FROM Bugs JOIN BugsProducts USING (bug_id)
GROUP BY product_id;
```

You can use this function if the column in fact has only one value per group, but MySQL can't infer the functional dependency. Another case when you might use this function is if you simply don't care which value it returns, as long as it's a value in the respective group.

It's best to write queries that are logically predictable and unambiguous, because query results that depend on arbitrary behavior might change unexpectedly.

> Follow the Single-Value Rule to avoid ambiguous query results.

Mini-Antipattern: Portable SQL

Not all brands of SQL databases implement SQL the same way. SQL is a standard language, described by a detailed technical specification, but the language specification allows "levels" of compliance. Any company that produces an SQL database product can choose to implement subsets of the features in the specification. Different companies choose different subsets of features described in the language.

Software developers try to write so-called "portable" SQL code, by restricting themselves to use only the features common to all implementations of SQL database software. They want to make sure that whatever SQL code they develop will work the same even if the database is changed.

This causes at least two problems:

First, you deny yourself the opportunity to use any proprietary features of any database product. In addition to standard SQL language features, all vendors add their own extended features that are their own inventions. Some of these are quite useful, even though they aren't strictly part of the standard SQL language. If you use only standard SQL syntax supported in all implementations, then you can't use extensions.

Second, it won't work. Vendors don't implement even the standard features of SQL the same way. They fib slightly about their compliance with the specification. Or they interpret the specification differently. The standard is detailed, but it's still written in English, which can't be as precise as a code implementation. The result is that even if you try to write queries using only standard SQL language features, you might still see your query work differently on another database product.

Years ago I developed a database class for a PHP framework, intending to make a single interface to support SQL code for six RDBMS products: MySQL, PostgreSQL, Microsoft SQL Server, IBM DB2, Oracle, and SQLite. I was surprised that even for a core SQL feature like standard data types, none of the data types was implemented exactly the same way in all six.

These issues make it difficult to adhere to portable SQL. Even if it were possible, you'd lose the opportunity to use the value-added features of any given implementation.

Instead, design your code to use the Adapter design pattern (see *Design Patterns: Elements of Reusable Object-Oriented Software [GHJV95]*) so you have alternative implementations for each of the brands of SQL databases you need to support.

The generation of random numbers is too important to be left to chance.

> ≫ *Robert R. Coveyou*

## CHAPTER 16

Random Selection

You're writing a web application that displays advertisements. You're supposed to choose a random ad on each viewing so that all your advertisers have an even chance of showing their ads and so that readers don't get bored seeing the same ad repeatedly.

Things go well for the first few days, but the application gradually becomes more sluggish. A few weeks later, people are complaining that your website is too slow. You discover it's not just psychological; you can measure a real difference in the page load time. Your readership is starting to lose interest, and traffic is declining.

Learning from past experiences, you first try to find the performance bottleneck using profiling tools and a test version of your database with a sample of the data. You measure the time to load a web page, but curiously, there are no problems with the performance in any of the SQL queries used to produce the page. Yet the production website is getting slower and slower.

Finally, you realize that the database on your production website is much greater than the sample in your tests. You repeat your tests with a database of similar size to the production data and find that it's the ad-selection query. With a greater number of ads to choose from, the performance of that query drops sharply. Identifying the culprit query is an important first step.

How can you redesign the query that chooses random ads before your website loses its audience and thus loses your sponsors?

Objective: Fetch a Sample Row

It's surprising how frequently we need an SQL query that returns a random result. This seems to go against the principles of repeatability and deterministic programming. However, it's ordinary to ask for a sample from a large data set. The following are some examples:

- Displaying rotating content, such as an advertisement or a news story
- Auditing a subset of records
- Assigning incoming calls to available operators
- Generating test data

It's better to query the database for this sample, as an alternative to fetching the entire data set into your application just so you can pick a sample.

The objective is to write an efficient SQL query that returns only a random sample of data. Mathematicians and computer scientists make a distinction between truly random and *pseudorandom*. In practice, computers can produce only pseudorandom values.

Antipattern: Sort Data Randomly

The most common SQL trick to pick a random row from a query is to sort the query randomly and pick the first row. This technique is easy to understand and easy to implement:

Random/anti/orderby-rand.sql
```
SELECT * FROM Bugs ORDER BY RAND() LIMIT 1;
```

Although this is a popular solution, it quickly shows its weakness. To understand this weakness, let's first compare it to conventional sorting, in which we compare values in a column and order the rows according to which row has a greater or lesser value in that column. This kind of sort is repeatable, in that it produces the same results when you run it more than once. It also benefits from an index, because an index is essentially a presorted set of the values from a given column.

Random/anti/indexed-sort.sql
```
SELECT * FROM Bugs ORDER BY date_reported;
```

If your sorting criteria is a function that returns a random value per row, this makes it random whether a given row is greater or less than another row. So, the order has no relationship to the values in each row. The order is also different each time you sort in this way. So far so good—this is the result we want.

Sorting by a nondeterministic expression (RAND()) means the sorting cannot benefit from an index. There is no index containing the values returned by the random function. That's the point of them being random: they are different and unpredictable each time they're selected.

This is a problem for the performance of the query, because using an index is one of the best ways of speeding up sorting. The consequence of not using an index is that the query result set has to be sorted by the database "manually." This is called a *table scan*, and it often involves saving the entire result as a temporary table and sorting it by physically swapping rows. A table scan sort is much slower than an index-assisted sort, and the performance difference grows with the size of the data set.

This problem is unnoticeable when you run the query against a small number of rows, so during development and testing it may appear to be a good solution. Unfortunately, as the volume in your database increases over time, the query fails to scale well.

How to Recognize the Antipattern

The technique shown in the antipattern is straightforward, and many programmers use it, either after reading it in an article or coming up with it on their own. Some of the following quotes are clues that your colleague is practicing the antipattern:

- "In SQL, returning a random row is really slow."

  The query to select a random sample worked well against trivial data during development and testing, but it gets progressively slower as the real data grows. No amount of database server tuning, indexing, or caching can improve the scalability.

- "How can I increase memory for my application? I need to fetch all the rows so I can randomly pick one."

  You shouldn't have to load all the rows into the application, and it's wildly wasteful to do this. Besides, the database tends to grow larger than your application memory can handle.

- "Does it seem to you like some entries come up more frequently than they should? This randomizer doesn't seem very random."

  Your random numbers are not synchronized with the gaps in primary key values in the database (see Choose Next Higher Key Value, on page 184).

Legitimate Uses of the Antipattern

The inefficiency of the sort-by-random solution is tolerable if your data set is bound to be small. For example, you could use a random method for assigning a programmer to fix a given bug. It's safe to assume that you'll never have so many programmers that you need to use a highly scalable method for choosing a random person.

Another example could be selecting a random US state from a list of the 50 states, which is a list of modest size and not likely to grow during our lifetimes.

Solution: In No Particular Order…

The sort-by-random technique is an example of a query that's bound to perform a table scan and an expensive manual sort. When you design solutions in SQL, you should be on the lookout for inefficient queries like this. Instead of searching fruitlessly for a way to optimize an unoptimizable query, rethink your approach. You can use one of the alternative techniques shown in the following sections to query a random row from a query result set.

Choose a Random Key Value Between MIN and MAX

One technique that avoids sorting the table is to choose a random value between the least primary key value and the greatest primary key value.

Random/soln/rand-min-to-max.sql
```
SELECT MIN(bug_id), MAX(bug_id) INTO @min_bug_id, @max_bug_id FROM Bugs;

SELECT * FROM Bugs
WHERE bug_id = ROUND(RAND() * (@max_bug_id - @min_bug_id)) + @min_bug_id;
```

This solution assumes that primary key values are contiguous. That is, there are no values unused between the least value and the greatest value. If there are gaps, a randomly chosen value may not match a row in the table.

Choose Next Higher Key Value

This is similar to the preceding solution, but if you have gaps of unused values between the least and the greatest key value, this query matches the first key value it finds that is greater than or equal to the random value.

Random/soln/rand-next-greater.sql
```
SELECT MIN(bug_id), MAX(bug_id) INTO @min_bug_id, @max_bug_id FROM Bugs;

SELECT * FROM Bugs
WHERE bug_id >= ROUND(RAND() * (@max_bug_id - @min_bug_id)) + @min_bug_id;
ORDER BY bug_id LIMIT 1;
```

This solves the problem of a random number that fails to match any key value, but it means that a key value that follows a gap of unused values is chosen more often. All the random values have a roughly equal chance of being chosen, but bug_id values aren't equally distributed. The larger the gap is preceding a given primary key value, the greater the number of randomly chosen values that map to it.

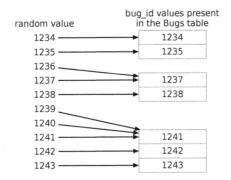

Use this solution if it's not important for key values to be chosen with equal frequency.

Get a List of All Key Values, Choose One at Random

You can use application code to pick one value from the primary keys in the result set. Then query the full row from the database using that primary key. This technique is shown in the following Python code:

Random/soln/rand-key-from-list.py
```
import mysql.connector
import random

cnx = mysql.connector.connect(user='scott', database='test')
cursor = cnx.cursor()

cursor.execute("SELECT bug_id FROM Bugs")
bug_ids = cursor.fetchall()
rand_bug_id = random.choice(bug_ids)[0]

cursor.execute("SELECT * FROM Bugs WHERE bug_id = %s", (rand_bug_id,))
for bug in cursor:
    print(bug)

cnx.commit()
```

This avoids sorting the table, and the chance of choosing each key value is approximately equal, but this solution has other costs:

• Fetching all the bug_id values from the database might return a list of impractical size. It can even exceed application memory resources.

- The query must be run twice: once to produce the list of primary keys and a second time to fetch the random row. If the query is too complex and costly, this is a problem.

Use this solution when you're selecting a random row from a simple query with a moderately sized result set. This solution is good for choosing from a list of noncontiguous values.

Choose a Random Row Using an Offset

Still another technique that avoids problems found in the preceding alternatives is to count the rows in the data set and return a random number between 0 and the count. Use this number as an offset.

Random/soln/rand-limit-offset.py
```python
import mysql.connector

cnx = mysql.connector.connect(user='scott', database='test')
cursor = cnx.cursor()

cursor.execute("SELECT ROUND(RAND() * (SELECT COUNT(*) FROM Bugs))")
for row in cursor:
    offset = int(row[0])
cursor.execute("SELECT * FROM Bugs LIMIT 1 OFFSET %s", (offset,))
for bug in cursor:
    print(bug)

cnx.commit()
```

The preceding solution relies on the nonstandard LIMIT clause, supported by MySQL, PostgreSQL, and SQLite. The following alternative uses the standard ROW_NUMBER() window function:

Random/soln/rand-row-number.py
```python
import mysql.connector

cnx = mysql.connector.connect(user='scott', database='test')
cursor = cnx.cursor()

cursor.execute("SELECT 1 + ROUND(RAND() * COUNT(*)) FROM Bugs")
for row in cursor:
    offset = row[0]

cursor.execute("""
    WITH NumberedBugs AS (
      SELECT *, ROW_NUMBER() OVER (ORDER BY bug_id) AS rownum FROM Bugs
    )
    SELECT * FROM NumberedBugs WHERE rownum = %s""", (offset,))
for bug in cursor:
    print(bug)

cnx.commit()
```

Use this solution when you can't assume contiguous key values and you need to make sure each row has an even chance of being selected.

Proprietary Solutions

Any given brand of database might implement its own solution for this kind of task. For example, Microsoft SQL Server 2005 added a TABLESAMPLE clause:

Random/soln/tablesample-sql2005.sql
```
SELECT * FROM Bugs TABLESAMPLE (1 ROWS);
```

Oracle uses a slightly different SAMPLE clause, for example, to return 1 percent of the rows in the table:

Random/soln/sample-oracle.sql
```
SELECT * FROM (SELECT * FROM Bugs SAMPLE (1)
ORDER BY dbms_random.value) WHERE ROWNUM = 1;
```

Read the documentation for the proprietary solution in your brand of database to learn about limitations or other options.

Reduce, Recycle, Reuse

You might be able to reuse a random choice multiple times. In the example of a web page displaying an advertisement described at the start of this chapter, the same random ad may be shown to all visitors for five minutes, then a new random ad is chosen for the next time period.

The following Python Flask app uses a function decorator @lru_cache that makes a function cache its result. The next time the function is called, it skips the code in that function, and instead just returns the cached advertisement.

Random/soln/rand-cached.py
```python
import mysql.connector
from flask import Flask, Response, jsonify, request
from functools import lru_cache

app = Flask(__name__)

@app.route('/advert')
def advert():
    if request.args.get("reset"):
        get_random_advert.cache_clear()
    return jsonify(get_random_advert())

@lru_cache(maxsize=1)
def get_random_advert():
    cnx = mysql.connector.connect(user='scott', database='test')
    cursor = cnx.cursor()
    cursor.execute("SELECT * FROM Adverts ORDER BY RAND() LIMIT 1")
    columns = [col[0] for col in cursor.description]
```

```
    advert = dict(zip(columns, cursor.fetchone()))
    cnx.commit()
    return advert
if __name__ == '__main__':
    app.run()
```

This web page checks if an optional request parameter "reset" is present. If so, the cache is emptied, and then the function runs the SQL query to choose a new random advertisement. The web page owner runs a script to reset the cache every five minutes. Then only that script will experience a slower page load.

> Some queries cannot be optimized; take a different approach.

Mini-Antipattern: Query for Multiple Random Rows

The solutions in this chapter focus on returning a single random row from a table, but some applications may need a set of multiple rows selected randomly. The solutions for this can be more difficult to optimize.

The naive solution is to fall back to the expensive query at the start of this chapter, but increase the LIMIT:

```
SELECT * FROM Bugs ORDER BY RAND() LIMIT 5;
```

That's a simple and straightforward query, but it's still too costly if the table has many rows. An alternative is to use any of the solutions shown previously, which each choose a single random row, then simply run that query repeatedly, until you have the number of rows you need. Running a well-optimized query five times might still be superior to running the poorly optimized query once.

There are caveats to this practice.

Selecting a single random row repeatedly might choose a given row more than once. If you need a specific number of rows chosen randomly but with no duplicates, you would need code to check the result and continue to repeat the query until you get enough distinct results.

If the table is too small, re-trying could cause an infinite loop. You'll be waiting a long time before you get five distinct rows from a table that has only four rows. You would need to include logic to check for such a case.

This is solved clearly in the naive solution using ORDER BY RAND() LIMIT 5. It's up to you to choose between the solution that runs with better performance vs. the solution that requires you to write less code.

Some people, when confronted with a problem, think "I know, I'll use regular expressions." Now they have two problems.

     Jamie Zawinski

## CHAPTER 17

Poor Man's Search Engine

I was working in a technical support job in 1995, at a time when companies were just starting to adopt the web as a way to provide information to their customers. I had a collection of short documents describing solutions to common support questions, and I wanted to put them on the web in a knowledge base application.

As the collection grew, it needed to be searchable, because customers didn't want to browse through hundreds of articles to find their answers. One strategy would be to organize the articles in categories, but even these groups were too large, and many articles belonged in multiple groups.

The most flexible and straightforward interface was to allow the customer to enter any set of words and show them the articles in which those words appear. An article was weighted higher if it matched the search terms more fully. Also, the search solution should allow matching word forms. For example, a search for the word *crash* should also match *crashed*, *crashes*, and *crashing*. Of course, the search had to work in a growing collection of documents quickly enough to be useful in a web application.

If that careful description sounds superfluous to you, that shouldn't be surprising. Searching through text online has become so common that it's hard to recall the time before it was available. Unfortunately, using SQL to search by keywords, while also making the solution both fast and accurate, is deceptively difficult.

Objective: Full-Text Search

Any application that stores text needs to search for words or phrases within that text. Databases store more textual data than ever, and at the same time users demand to be able to search for matching text at greater speeds. Web applications especially need high-performance and scalable database techniques for searching text.

One fundamental principle of SQL (and relational theory from which SQL is derived) is that a value in a column is *atomic*. That is, you can compare a value to another value, but you always compare the *whole* value when you do that. Comparing substrings is bound to be inefficient or inaccurate in SQL.

Antipattern: Pattern Matching Predicates

SQL provides pattern-matching predicates for comparing strings, and this is the first solution most programmers use when searching for keywords. The most widely supported of these is the LIKE predicate.

The LIKE predicate supports a wildcard (%) that matches zero or more characters. Using this wildcard before and after a keyword matches any string that contains that word. The first wildcard matches any text preceding the word, and the second wildcard matches any text following the word.

Search/anti/like.sql
```
SELECT * FROM Bugs WHERE description LIKE '%crash%';
```

Regular expressions are also supported by many database brands. You don't need wildcards, because conventionally, regular expressions match the pattern against any substring anyway. Although SQL-99 defines the predicate SIMILAR TO for matching regular expressions, most brands of SQL database still use nonstandard syntax. Here's an example using MySQL's regular expression predicate:

Search/anti/regexp.sql
```
SELECT * FROM Bugs WHERE description REGEXP 'crash';
```

The most important disadvantage of pattern-matching operators is that they have poor performance. They can't benefit from a conventional index, so they must scan every row in a table. Since matching a pattern against a string column is an expensive operation (relative to, for instance, comparing two integers for equality), the total cost of a table scan for this search is very high.

A second problem of simple pattern matching using LIKE or regular expressions is that it can find unintended matches.

Search/anti/like-false-match.sql
```
SELECT * FROM Bugs WHERE description LIKE '%one%';
```

The previous example matches text that contains the words *one*, but it also matches strings *money*, *prone*, *lonely*, and so on. Searching for a pattern with the keyword delimited by spaces doesn't match occurrences of the word with punctuation or occurrences of the word at the start or end of the text. The regular expressions supported by your database might support a special pattern for a *word boundary* to solve this issue in MySQL 8.0:

```
Search/anti/regexp-word.sql
SELECT * FROM Bugs WHERE description REGEXP '\\bone\\b';
```

Given the problems of performance and scalability and the gymnastics you have to do to prevent irrelevant matches, simple pattern matching is a poor technique for searching for keywords.

How to Recognize the Antipattern

Some questions like the following commonly indicate that the Poor Man's Search Engine antipattern is being employed:

- "How do I insert a variable in between two wildcards in a LIKE expression?"

  The question usually comes up when the programmer wants to do a pattern-matching search using input from a user.

- "How can I write a regular expression to check that a string contains multiple words, that the string *doesn't* contain a certain word, or that the string contains any form of a given word?"

  If a complex problem seems too hard to solve with a regular expression, it probably is.

- "The search feature of our website has become unusably slow as we've added more documents to the database. What's wrong?"

  As the volume of data goes up, the antipattern solution shows poor scalability.

Legitimate Uses of the Antipattern

The expressions shown in the antipattern section are legal SQL queries, and they have a straightforward and simple usage. That counts for a lot.

Performance is often important, but some queries are run so infrequently that it doesn't make sense to invest a lot of resources to optimize them. Maintaining indexes to benefit a rarely used query could be just as costly as running that query in an inefficient manner. If the nature of the query is ad hoc, there's no guarantee that the index you defined would benefit that given query anyway.

It's hard to use pattern-matching operators for complex queries, but if you design the patterns for simple cases, they can help you get the right results with a minimum of fuss.

Solution: Use the Right Tool for the Job

It's best to use a specialized search engine technology instead of plain SQL pattern-matching conditions.

The following sections describe some of the technologies offered as built-in extensions by different database brands and technologies offered by independent projects. Also, you'll see a solution that uses standard SQL but is more efficient on average than substring matching.

Vendor Extensions

Every major brand of database has invented their own answer to the common requirement of full-text search. If you use a single brand (or are willing to use vendor-dependent features), these features are the best way to get high-performance text search, with the greatest integration with SQL queries.

The following are brief descriptions of full-text search features in several brands of SQL database. You should note from these examples that the solution provided by each brand uses different syntax and has different features from the solutions of other brands. Learning one doesn't help much to know the others. In addition, the examples shown here are minimal. Each brand's full-text search solution has many options, so you should read the current documentation for the brand of database you use.

Full-Text Index in MySQL

MySQL provides a simple full-text index type. You can define a full-text index over columns of type CHAR, VARCHAR, or TEXT. Here's an example that defines a full-text index that includes content from the bug summary and description columns:

Search/soln/mysql/alter-table.sql
```
ALTER TABLE Bugs ADD FULLTEXT INDEX bugfts (summary, description);
```

Use the MATCH() function to search for a keyword among the indexed text. The columns you name as arguments to the MATCH() function must be the same columns, in the same order that you used when creating the index.

Search/soln/mysql/match.sql
```
SELECT * FROM Bugs WHERE MATCH(summary, description) AGAINST ('crash');
```

You can also use a simple boolean expression notation in the pattern. This example demonstrates how to search for rows that contain the word "crash" but do not contain the word "save":

Search/soln/mysql/match-boolean.sql
```
SELECT * FROM Bugs WHERE MATCH(summary, description)
  AGAINST ('+crash -save' IN BOOLEAN MODE);
```

Text Indexing in Oracle

Oracle has supported text-indexing features since Oracle 8 in 1997, when it was part of a data cartridge called ConText. The technology has been updated several times, and the feature is now integrated into the database software.

The text indexing in Oracle is complex and rich, so here is a greatly simplified summary:

- CONTEXT

  Create an index of this type for a single text column. Use the CONTAINS() operator to search using this index. The index doesn't stay consistent with changes to data unless you define the index with PARAMETERS ('SYNC (ON COMMIT)').

  Search/soln/oracle/create-index.sql
  ```
  CREATE INDEX BugsText ON Bugs(summary) INDEXTYPE IS CTXSYS.CONTEXT;

  SELECT * FROM Bugs WHERE CONTAINS(summary, 'crash') > 0;
  ```

- CTXCAT

  This index type is specialized for short text samples such as those used in online catalogs, along with other structured columns from the same table. The index stays consistent as transactions update the indexed data.

  Search/soln/oracle/ctxcat-create.sql
  ```
  CTX_DDL.CREATE_INDEX_SET('BugsCatalogSet');
  CTX_DDL.ADD_INDEX('BugsCatalogSet', 'status');
  CTX_DDL.ADD_INDEX('BugsCatalogSet', 'priority');

  CREATE INDEX BugsCatalog ON Bugs(summary) INDEXTYPE IS CTXSYS.CTXCAT
    PARAMETERS('BugsCatalogSet');
  ```

  The CATSEARCH() operator takes two arguments for searching the text column and the structured column set, respectively.

  Search/soln/oracle/ctxcat-search.sql
  ```
  SELECT * FROM Bugs
  WHERE CATSEARCH(summary, '(crash save)', 'status = "NEW"') > 0;
  ```

- CTXXPATH

  This index type is specialized for searching an XML document with the existsNode() operator.

  Search/soln/oracle/ctxxpath.sql
  ```
  CREATE INDEX BugTestXml ON Bugs(testoutput) INDEXTYPE IS CTXSYS.CTXXPATH;

  SELECT * FROM Bugs
  WHERE testoutput.existsNode('/testsuite/test[@status="fail"]') > 0;
  ```

- CTXRULE

  Suppose you have a large collection of documents in your database and you need to classify them based on their content.

  With the CTXRULE index, you can design rules to analyze documents and report their classification. Alternatively, you can provide a sample set of documents with your idea of their classifications and have Oracle design the rules to apply to the rest of the document collection. You can even fully automate the process, letting Oracle analyze your document collection and come up with a set of rules and classifications for identifying them.

  Examples using CTXRULE indexes are beyond the scope of this book.

- Oracle 12 introduced syntax to create a kind of text index for JSON data. Suppose your table has a JSON column called properties to store dynamic attributes.

  Search/soln/oracle/create-index-json.sql
  ```
  CREATE SEARCH INDEX BugsJson ON Bugs(properties) FOR JSON;

  SELECT * FROM Bugs
  WHERE json_textcontains(properties, '$.summary', 'crash');
  ```

Full-Text Search in Microsoft SQL Server

SQL Server 2000 and later support full-text searching, with complex configuration options for languages, a thesaurus, and automatic synchronization with data changes. SQL Server provides a series of stored procedures for creating full-text indexes, and you can use the CONTAINS() operator in queries to employ the full-text index.

To perform the familiar example of searching for bugs that include the word *crash*, first enable the full-text feature, and define a catalog in your database:

Search/soln/microsoft/catalog.sql
```
CREATE FULLTEXT CATALOG BugsCatalog;
```

Next, define a full-text index on the Bugs table, add columns to the index, and activate the index:

Search/soln/microsoft/create-index.sql

```
CREATE FULLTEXT INDEX ON Bugs(summary, description)
  KEY INDEX bug_id ON BugsCatalog
  WITH CHANGE_TRACKING AUTO;
```

Finally, run a query using the CONTAINS() operator or FREETEXT() operator:

Search/soln/microsoft/search.sql

```
SELECT * FROM Bugs WHERE CONTAINS(summary, 'crash');

SELECT * FROM Bugs WHERE FREETEXT(summary, 'crash bug error');
```

Text Search in PostgreSQL

PostgreSQL provides a sophisticated and highly configurable way of converting text into a searchable collections of lexical elements and matching these documents against patterns. Keeping text indexes in sync became easier in PostgreSQL 12, by using generated columns.

Search/soln/postgresql/create-table.sql

```
CREATE TABLE Bugs (
  bug_id SERIAL PRIMARY KEY,
  summary      VARCHAR(80),
  description  TEXT,
  ts_bug_text  TSVECTOR GENERATED ALWAYS AS (to_tsvector('english',
      COALESCE(summary, '') || COALESCE(description, ''))) STORED
  -- other columns
);
```

You should also create a *generalized inverted index* (GIN) index on the TSVECTOR column:

Search/soln/postgresql/create-index.sql

```
CREATE INDEX bugs_ts ON Bugs USING GIN(ts_bug_text);
```

After this, you can use the PostgreSQL text search operator @@ to search efficiently, aided by the full-text index:

Search/soln/postgresql/search.sql

```
SELECT * FROM Bugs WHERE ts_bug_text @@ to_tsquery('crash');
```

There are many other options for customizing searchable content, search queries, and search results.

Full-Text Search (FTS) in SQLite

Standard tables in SQLite don't support efficient full-text searches, but you can use an optional extension for SQLite to store searchable text in a *virtual table* specialized for searching text. The implementation of this extension has changed several times. FTS1 and FTS2 are obsolete. You can use FTS3 in SQLite 3.5.0 and later, or FTS4 in SQLite 3.7.4 and later.

FTS extensions are not typically enabled in a default build of SQLite, so you need to build it from source with the FTS extensions enabled. Enabling FTS3 implicitly enables FTS4. Add the following options when you run configure.

Search/soln/sqlite/configure
```
CPPFLAGS="-DSQLITE_ENABLE_FTS3 -DSQLITE_ENABLE_FTS3_PARENTHESIS" ./configure
```

Once you have a version of SQLite with FTS enabled, you can create a virtual table for the searchable text. Any data type, constraints, or other column options are ignored.

Search/soln/sqlite/create-table.sql
```
CREATE VIRTUAL TABLE BugsText USING fts4(summary, description);
```

If you are indexing text from another table (as in this example using the Bugs table), you must copy the data into the virtual table. The FTS virtual table always contains a primary key column called docid, so you can correlate rows to those in a source table.

Search/soln/sqlite/insert.sql
```
INSERT INTO BugsText (docid, summary, description)
  SELECT bug_id, summary, description FROM Bugs;
```

Now you can query the FTS virtual table BugsText using the efficient full-text search predicate MATCH, and you can join matching rows to the source table Bugs. Using the name of the FTS table as a pseudocolumn matches the pattern against any column.

Search/soln/sqlite/search.sql
```
SELECT b.* FROM BugsText t JOIN Bugs b ON (t.docid = b.bug_id)
WHERE BugsText MATCH 'crash';
```

The matching pattern also supports limited boolean expressions.

Search/soln/sqlite/search-boolean.sql
```
SELECT * FROM BugsText WHERE BugsText MATCH 'crash -save';
```

Third-Party Search Engines

If you need to search text in a way that works the same regardless of which database brand you use, you need a search engine that runs independently from the SQL database. This section briefly describes two such products, Sphinx Search and Apache Lucene.

Sphinx Search

Sphinx Search[1] is an open source search engine technology that integrates well with MySQL and PostgreSQL.

Indexing and searching is fast in Sphinx Search, and it supports distributed queries as well. It's a good choice for high-scale searching applications that have data that updates infrequently.

You can use Sphinx Search to declare a search index with multiple fields using a configuration file sphinx.conf. The index has fields which are searchable, and optionally other attribute fields.

```
Search/soln/sphinx/sphinx.conf
searchd
{
    log = ./data/searchd.log
    pid_file = ./data/searchd.pid
}

index bugs
{
    type = rt
    path = ./data/bugs
    rt_field = summary
    rt_field = description
    stored_fields = summary, description
}
```

Once you declare this configuration in sphinx.conf, any client that can connect to a MySQL instance can connect to Sphinx Search, because Sphinx Search implements a service that mimics the MySQL client/server protocol.

```
Search/soln/sphinx/mysql-client.sh
mysql -h 127.0.0.1 -P 9306
```

You can insert data into the index as if it's an SQL table:

```
Search/soln/sphinx/insert.sql
INSERT INTO Bugs (id, summary, description)
  VALUES (1234, 'crash when I save', '...');
```

Then you can search the index using a limited SQL language:

```
Search/soln/sphinx/search.sql
SELECT * FROM Bugs WHERE MATCH('crash');
```

Sphinx Search also has a daemon process and an API with which to invoke searches from any programming language that has client interface for MySQL.

---

1. https://sphinxsearch.com/

Apache Lucene

Lucene[2] is a mature search engine for Java applications.

Lucene builds an index in its proprietary format for a collection of text *documents*. The Lucene index doesn't stay in sync with the source data it indexes. If you insert, delete, or update rows in the database, you must apply matching changes to a Lucene index.

Using the Lucene search engine is a bit like using a car engine; you need quite a bit of supporting technology around it to make it useful. Lucene doesn't read data collections from an SQL database directly; you have to write documents in the Lucene index. For example, you could run an SQL query and, for each row of the result, create one Lucene document and save it to the Lucene index. You can use Lucene through its Java API.

Fortunately, Apache also offers a complementary project called Solr.[3] Solr is a server that provides a gateway to a Lucene index. You can add documents to Solr and submit search queries using a REST-like interface so you can use it from any programming language.

Solr has tools for importing data in XML or CSV format, or for indexing document formats such as Microsoft Word, PDF, or other proprietary formats. You can also direct Solr to connect to an SQL database, run a query, and index the query results using Solr's DataImportHandler tool.

Elasticsearch and OpenSearch

Like Apache Solr, both Elasticsearch[4] and OpenSearch[5] utilize the Apache Lucene engine.

Elasticsearch has many additional features for analytics and visualization. It is combined with Logstash, a tool for importing a stream of data to the search engine, and Kibana, a graphical user interface for searching data stored in Elasticsearch. These products were developed by the company Elastic, Inc., and called the *ELK stack*. Originally developed as open source software, in 2021 Elastic changed the license for future versions of the ELK stack products, to encourage users to use only Elastic's own managed service.

In response, Amazon forked the technology of Elasticsearch 7.10.2 and Kibana 7.10.2, the last versions available under the open source Apache License.

---

2.   https://lucene.apache.org/
3.   https://lucene.apache.org/solr/
4.   https://www.elastic.co/elasticsearch/
5.   https://aws.amazon.com/elasticsearch-service/the-elk-stack/what-is-opensearch/

Amazon's product is called OpenSearch. You can use either Logstash or other Amazon data-streaming services to import data into an OpenSearch index.

Undoubtedly, both Elastic and Amazon will continue to develop their respective products. Expect future versions to diverge with new features, and eventually become incompatible. This is a natural outcome when a technology is forked. If you need to choose one of these products, then you should try both, evaluate which one has the features most useful to your needs, and decide which vendor you want to do business with.

Roll Your Own

Suppose you don't want to use proprietary search features, nor do you want to install an independent search engine product. You need an efficient, database-independent solution to make text searchable. This section shows a design called an *inverted index*. Basically, an inverted index is a list of all words one might search for. In a many-to-many relationship, the index associates these words with the text entries that contain the respective word. That is, a word like *crash* can appear in many bugs, and each bug may match many other keywords. This section shows how to design an inverted index.

First, define a table Keywords to list the keywords for which users will search, and define an intersection table BugsKeywords to establish a many-to-many relationship:

Search/soln/inverted-index/create-table.sql
```
CREATE TABLE Keywords (
  keyword_id   SERIAL PRIMARY KEY,
  keyword      VARCHAR(40) NOT NULL,
  UNIQUE KEY (keyword)
);

CREATE TABLE BugsKeywords (
  keyword_id   BIGINT UNSIGNED NOT NULL,
  bug_id       BIGINT UNSIGNED NOT NULL,
  PRIMARY KEY (keyword_id, bug_id),
  FOREIGN KEY (keyword_id) REFERENCES Keywords(keyword_id),
  FOREIGN KEY (bug_id) REFERENCES Bugs(bug_id)
);
```

Next, add a row to BugsKeywords for every keyword that matches the description text for a given bug. A substring-match query determines these matches using LIKE or regular expressions. This is just as costly as the naive searching method described in the "Antipattern" section, but you only need to perform the search once. If the result is saved in the intersection table, all subsequent searches for the same keyword are much faster.

Next, write a MySQL stored procedure to make it easier to search for a given keyword. If the word has already been searched, the query is faster because the rows in BugsKeywords are a list of the documents that contain the keyword. If no one has searched for the given keyword before, you need to search the collection of text entries the hard way.

Search/soln/inverted-index/search-proc.sql

```sql
CREATE PROCEDURE BugsSearch(IN p_keyword VARCHAR(40))
BEGIN
  DECLARE v_keyword_id BIGINT UNSIGNED;

  SELECT MAX(keyword_id) INTO v_keyword_id FROM Keywords
  WHERE keyword = p_keyword;

  IF (v_keyword_id IS NULL) THEN
    INSERT INTO Keywords (keyword) VALUES (p_keyword);

    SELECT LAST_INSERT_ID() INTO v_keyword_id;

    INSERT INTO BugsKeywords (bug_id, keyword_id)
      SELECT bug_id, v_keyword_id FROM Bugs
      WHERE summary REGEXP CONCAT('\\b', p_keyword, '\\b')
        OR description REGEXP CONCAT('\\b', p_keyword, '\\b');
  END IF;

  SELECT b.* FROM Bugs b
  JOIN BugsKeywords k USING (bug_id)
  WHERE k.keyword_id = v_keyword_id;
END
```

❶ Search for the user-specified keyword. Return either the integer primary key from Keywords.keyword_id or null if the word has not been seen previously.

❷ If the word was not found, insert it as a new word.

❸ Query for the primary key value generated in Keywords.

❹ Populate the intersection table by searching Bugs for rows containing the new keyword.

❺ Finally, query the full rows from Bugs that match the keyword_id, whether the keyword was found or had to be inserted as a new entry.

Now you can call this stored procedure and pass the desired keyword. The procedure returns the set of matching bugs, whether it has to calculate the matching bugs and populate the intersection table for a new keyword or whether it simply benefits from the result of an earlier search.

Search/soln/inverted-index/search-proc.sql

```sql
CALL BugsSearch('crash');
```

There's another piece to this solution: you need a trigger to populate the intersection table as each new bug is inserted. If you need to support edits to bug descriptions, you may also have to write a trigger to reanalyze text and add or delete rows in the BugsKeywords table.

Search/soln/inverted-index/trigger.sql
```
CREATE TRIGGER Bugs_Insert AFTER INSERT ON Bugs
FOR EACH ROW
BEGIN
  INSERT INTO BugsKeywords (bug_id, keyword_id)
    SELECT NEW.bug_id, k.keyword_id FROM Keywords k
    WHERE NEW.description REGEXP CONCAT('\\b', k.keyword, '\\b')
      OR NEW.summary REGEXP CONCAT('\\b', k.keyword, '\\b');
END
```

The keyword list is populated naturally as users perform searches, so you don't need to fill the keyword list with every word found in the knowledge base articles. On the other hand, if you anticipate words that users are likely to search for, you can run a search for them, thus bearing the initial cost of being the first to search for each keyword so that doesn't fall on your users.

I used an inverted index for my knowledge base application that I described at the start of this chapter. I also enhanced the Keywords table with an additional column num_searches. I incremented this column each time a user searched for a given keyword so I could track which searches were most in demand.

Today, you can use a variety of text-indexing tools, either indexing features built into the SQL database you use, or one of the complementary software products that specialize in text search. There isn't any solution that is clearly best for all projects, so you need to try several and evaluate their strengths and limits against the needs of your project before choosing one.

> SQL treats a column as an atomic value. If you need to optimize searching for a substring, then you need to use an extension to SQL or a complementary technology.

Entia non sunt multiplicanda praeter necessitatem (Latin, "entities must not be multiplied beyond necessity").

> *Irish Franciscan philosopher John Punch, 1639*

## CHAPTER 18

Spaghetti Query

Your boss is on the phone with his boss, and he waves to you to come over. He covers his phone receiver with his hand and whispers to you, "The executives are in a budget meeting, and we're going to have our staff cut unless we can feed my VP some statistics to prove that our department keeps a lot of people busy. I need to know how many products we work on, how many developers fixed bugs, the average bugs fixed per developer, and how many of our fixed bugs were reported by customers. Right now!"

You leap to your SQL tool and start writing. You want all the answers at once, so you make one complex query, hoping to do the least amount of duplicate work and so produce the results faster.

Spaghetti-Query/anti/complex-report.sql
```sql
SELECT COUNT(bp.product_id) AS how_many_products,
  COUNT(dev.account_id) AS how_many_developers,
  COUNT(b.bug_id)/COUNT(dev.account_id) AS avg_bugs_per_developer,
  COUNT(cust.account_id) AS how_many_customers
FROM Bugs b JOIN BugsProducts bp ON (b.bug_id = bp.bug_id)
JOIN Accounts dev ON (b.assigned_to = dev.account_id)
JOIN Accounts cust ON (b.reported_by = cust.account_id)
WHERE cust.email NOT LIKE '%@example.com'
GROUP BY bp.product_id;
```

The numbers come back, but they seem wrong. How did we get dozens of products? How can the average bugs fixed be exactly 1.0? And it wasn't the number of customers; it was the number of bugs reported by customers that your boss needs. How can all the numbers be so far off? This query will be a lot more complex than you thought.

Your boss hangs up the phone. "Never mind," he sighs. "It's too late. Let's clean out our desks."

Objective: Decrease SQL Queries

One of the most common places where SQL programmers get stuck is when they ask, "How can I do this with a single query?" This question is asked for virtually any task. Programmers have been trained that one SQL query is difficult, complex, and expensive, so they reason that two SQL queries must be twice as bad. More than two SQL queries to solve a problem is generally out of the question.

Programmers can't reduce the complexity of their tasks, but they want to simplify the solution. They use terms like "elegant" or "efficient," and they think they've achieved those qualities by solving the task with a single query.

Antipattern: Solve a Complex Problem in One Step

SQL is a very expressive language—you can accomplish a lot in a single query or statement. That doesn't mean it's mandatory or even a good idea to aim to solve every problem in one line of code. Do you have this habit with any other programming language you use? Probably not.

Unintended Products

One common consequence of producing all your results in one query is a *Cartesian product*. This happens when two of the tables in the query have no condition restricting their relationship. Without such a restriction, the join of two tables pairs each row in the first table to *every* row in the other table. Each such pairing becomes a row of the result set, and you end up with many more rows than you expect. For example, suppose you want to query the bugs database to count the tags used to label a given bug, and also count the products the bug affects. Some programmers would try to use a query like the following:

Spaghetti-Query/anti/cartesian.sql
```
SELECT b.bug_id,
  COUNT(t.tag) AS count_tags,
  COUNT(bp.product_id) AS count_products
FROM Bugs b
LEFT OUTER JOIN Tags t ON (t.bug_id = b.bug_id)
LEFT OUTER JOIN BugsProducts bp ON (bp.bug_id = b.bug_id)
WHERE b.bug_id = 1234
GROUP BY b.bug_id;
```

The result immediately looks wrong, given what you know about your database.

bug_id	count_tags	count_products
1234	8	8

How can the count of products be 8, when you know there are only 3 different products currently in the database? It seems unusual that a bug would be given 8 tags. Isn't it an odd concidence that this bug has a count of 8 for both products and tags?

A coworker suggests to filter the results to the distinct values before counting them. Then the results appear more like what you expect.

Spaghetti-Query/anti/cartesian-distinct.sql

```
SELECT b.bug_id,
  COUNT(DISTINCT t.tag) AS count_tags,
  COUNT(DISTINCT bp.product_id) AS count_products
FROM Bugs b
LEFT OUTER JOIN Tags t ON (t.bug_id = b.bug_id)
LEFT OUTER JOIN BugsProducts bp ON (bp.bug_id = b.bug_id)
WHERE b.bug_id = 1234
GROUP BY b.bug_id;
```

bug_id	count_tags	count_products
1234	4	2

Counting only distinct values won't work for other queries, if it's expected that the data have multiple matches with the same value. It would be better to understand what caused the counts to be multiplied, so you can avoid it. You can try to query without the GROUP BY to see what the result set would have looked like without using aggregation.

Spaghetti-Query/anti/cartesian-no-group.sql

```
SELECT b.bug_id, t.tag, bp.product_id
FROM Bugs b
LEFT OUTER JOIN Tags t ON (t.bug_id = b.bug_id)
LEFT OUTER JOIN BugsProducts bp ON (bp.bug_id = b.bug_id)
WHERE b.bug_id = 1234;
```

bug_id	tag	product_id
1234	crash	1
1234	crash	3
1234	save	1
1234	save	3
1234	v3.0	1
1234	v3.0	3
1234	windows	1
1234	windows	3

Even though the query looked like it correctly joins Bugs and Tags, and correctly joins Bugs and BugsProducts, there's a Cartesian product "hiding" in the query, because no join condition applies between the Tags and BugsProducts. In other words, the results are multiplied because each row in Tags matches *every* row in BugsProducts.

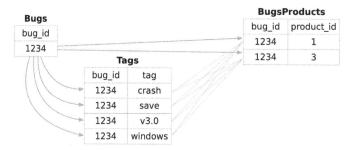

It's all too easy to produce a Cartesian product unintentionally when you try to make a query do double-duty like this. If you try to do another unrelated join in the same query without a condition restricting the results, the total could be multiplied yet again, producing another Cartesian product.

As Though That Weren't Enough...

Besides the fact that you can get the wrong results, it's important to consider that these queries are simply hard to write, hard to modify, and hard to debug. You should expect to get regular requests for incremental enhancements to your database applications. Managers want more complex reports and more fields in a user interface. If you design intricate, monolithic SQL queries, it's more costly and time consuming to make enhancements to them. Your time is worth something, both to you and to your project.

There are runtime costs, too. An elaborate SQL query that has to use many joins, correlated subqueries, and other operations will be harder for the SQL engine to optimize and execute quickly than a more straightforward query would have been. Programmers have an instinct that the fewer SQL queries, the better the performance. This may be true, but only if the SQL queries in question are of equal complexity. The cost of a single monster query can increase exponentially, until it's more economical to use several simpler queries.

How to Recognize the Antipattern

If you hear the following statements from members of your project, it could indicate a case of the Spaghetti Query antipattern:

- "Why are my sums and counts impossibly large?"

  An unintended Cartesian product has multiplied two joined data sets.

- "I've been working on this monster SQL query all day!"

  SQL isn't this difficult—really. If you've been struggling with a single query for too long, you should reconsider your approach. This advice applies to any other programming language, too. If a tasks seems too difficult, then break it into smaller tasks. Take a step back and question the assumptions in your application design. Could a different algorithm or a different data model make the task easier?

- "We can't add anything to our database report, because it will take too long to figure out how to recode the SQL query."

  The person who coded the query will be responsible for maintaining it forever, even if they have moved on to other projects. That person could be you, so don't write overly complex SQL that no one else can maintain!

- "Try putting another DISTINCT into the query."

  Compensating for the explosion of rows in a Cartesian product, programmers reduce duplicates using the DISTINCT keyword as a query modifier or an aggregate function modifier. This hides the evidence of the malformed query but causes extra work for the RDBMS to generate the interim result set only to sort it and discard duplicates.

Another clue that a query might be a Spaghetti Query is simply that it has an excessively long execution time. Poor performance could be symptomatic of other causes, but as you investigate such a query, you should consider that you may be trying to do too much in a single SQL statement.

Legitimate Uses of the Antipattern

The most common reason that you might need to run a complex task with a single query is that you are using a programming framework or a visual component library that connects to a data source and presents data in an application. Simple business intelligence and reporting tools also fall into this category, although more sophisticated BI software can merge results from multiple data sources.

A component or reporting tool that assumes its data source is a single SQL query may have a simpler usage, but it encourages you to design monolithic queries to synthesize all the data for your report. If you use one of these reporting applications, you may be forced to write a more complex SQL query than if you had the opportunity to write code to process the result set.

If the reporting requirements are too complex to be satisfied by a single SQL query, it might be better to produce multiple reports. If your boss doesn't like this, remind him or her of the relationship between the report's complexity and the hours it takes to produce it.

Sometimes, you may want to produce a complex result in one query because you need all the results combined in sorted order. It's easy to specify a sort order in an SQL query. It's usually more efficient for the database to do it, and less work for you than writing custom code in your application to sort the results of several queries.

Is there a legitimate use for a Cartesian product?

You might wonder why SQL allows joins without conditions. Surely it would be better to prevent Cartesian products if they cause so much trouble.

SQL supports Cartesian products with CROSS JOIN syntax. You might run this type of join deliberately to generate every possible combination between two sets of rows.

For example, suppose you want a quick way to generate a set of integers from 0 to 99 using SQL. You can do this by creating a small table with ten rows, integers from 0 to 9. Then generate a Cartesian product query by joining the table to itself twice. Each number in that table is joined to all ten numbers, giving the result set 10 * 10 rows. Use an expression that adds the number from the first table to the number from the second table, times ten. The result is 100 rows, with numbers from 0 to 90+9, or 99.

Spaghetti-Query/soln/cartesian-good.sql
```
CREATE TABLE integers (
  num INT PRIMARY KEY
);

INSERT INTO integers (num) VALUES (0), (1), (2), (3), (4), (5), (6), (7), (8), (9);

SELECT 10*digit10.num + digit1.num AS num
FROM integers AS digit1
CROSS JOIN integers AS digit10;
```

If you need numbers from 0 to 999, then make another cross join to the same table. Use its numbers as the hundreds place in the values returned by the expression.

Spaghetti-Query/soln/cartesian-good.sql
```
SELECT 100*digit100.num + 10*digit10.num + digit1.num AS num
FROM integers AS digit1
CROSS JOIN integers AS digit10
CROSS JOIN integers AS digit100;
```

This is just one example. There are other good uses for CROSS JOIN. They're uncommon, but when you need one, it's handy that SQL supports syntax for it.

Solution: Divide and Conquer

The quote at the beginning of this chapter is similar to the *law of parsimony*:

The Law of Parsimony
When you have two competing theories that make exactly the same predictions, the simpler one is the better.

What this means to SQL is that when you have a choice between two queries that produce the same result set, choose the simpler one. We should keep this in mind when straightening out instances of this antipattern.

One Step at a Time

If you can't see a logical join condition between the tables involved in an unintended Cartesian product, that could be because there simply is no such condition. To avoid the Cartesian product, you have to split up a Spaghetti Query into several simpler queries.

In the simple example shown earlier, you need only two queries:

Spaghetti-Query/soln/split-query.sql
```
SELECT b.bug_id, COUNT(t.tag) AS count_tags
FROM Bugs b
LEFT OUTER JOIN Tags t ON (b.bug_id = t.bug_id)
WHERE b.bug_id = 1234
GROUP BY b.bug_id;

SELECT b.bug_id, COUNT(bp.product_id) AS count_products
FROM Bugs b
LEFT OUTER JOIN BugsProducts bp ON (b.bug_id = bp.bug_id)
WHERE b.bug_id = 1234
GROUP BY b.bug_id;
```

The counts reported by these two queries are 4 and 2, as expected.

bug_id	count_tags
1234	4

bug_id	count_products
1234	2

You may feel slight regret at resorting to an "inelegant" solution by splitting this into multiple queries, but this should be replaced by relief as you realize this has advantages for development, maintenance, and performance:

- The query doesn't produce an unwanted Cartesian product, as shown in the earlier examples, so it's easier to be sure the query is giving you accurate results.

- When new requirements are added to the report, it's easier to add another simple query than to integrate more calculations into an already-complicated query.

- The SQL engine can usually optimize and execute a simple query more easily and reliably than a complex query. Even if it seems like the work is duplicated by splitting the query, it may nevertheless be a net win.

- In a code review or a teammate training session, it's easier to explain how several straightforward queries work than to explain one intricate query.

Solving Your Boss's Problem

How could you have solved the urgent request for statistics about your project? Your boss said, "I need to know how many products we work on, how many developers fixed bugs, the average bugs fixed per developer, and how many of our fixed bugs were reported by customers."

The best solution is to split up the work:

- How many products:

Spaghetti-Query/soln/count-products.sql
```
SELECT COUNT(*) AS how_many_products
FROM Products;
```

- How many developers fixed bugs:

Spaghetti-Query/soln/count-developers.sql
```
SELECT COUNT(DISTINCT assigned_to) AS how_many_developers
FROM Bugs
WHERE status = 'FIXED';
```

- Average number of bugs fixed per developer:

Spaghetti-Query/soln/bugs-per-developer.sql
```
SELECT AVG(bugs_per_developer) AS average_bugs_per_developer
FROM (SELECT dev.account_id, COUNT(*) AS bugs_per_developer
      FROM Bugs b JOIN Accounts dev
        ON (b.assigned_to = dev.account_id)
      WHERE b.status = 'FIXED'
      GROUP BY dev.account_id) t;
```

- How many of our fixed bugs were reported by customers:

```
Spaghetti-Query/soln/bugs-by-customers.sql
SELECT COUNT(*) AS how_many_customer_bugs
FROM Bugs b JOIN Accounts cust ON (b.reported_by = cust.account_id)
WHERE b.status = 'FIXED' AND cust.email NOT LIKE '%@example.com';
```

Some of these queries are tricky enough by themselves. Trying to combine them all into a single pass would be a nightmare.

Writing SQL Automatically—with SQL

When you split up a complex SQL query, the result may be many similar queries, perhaps varying slightly depending on data values. Writing these queries is a chore, so it would be a good place to use code generation.

Code generation is the technique of writing code whose output is new code you can compile or run. This can be worthwhile if the new code is laborious to write by hand. A code generator can eliminate repetitive work for you.

Multitable Updates

During a consulting job, I was called to solve an urgent SQL problem for a manager.

I went to the manager's office and found a harried-looking fellow who was clearly at the end of his rope. We had barely exchanged greetings when he began sharing with me his woes. "I sure hope you can solve this problem quickly; our inventory system has been offline *all day*." He was no amateur with SQL, but he told me he had been working for hours on a statement that could update a large set of rows.

His problem was that he couldn't use a consistent SQL expression in his UPDATE statement for all values of rows. In fact, the change he needed to apply was different on each row. His database tracked inventory for a computer lab and the usage of each computer. He wanted to set a column called last_used to the most recent date each computer had been used.

He was too focused on solving this complex task in a single SQL statement, another example of the Spaghetti Query antipattern. In the hours he had been struggling to write the perfect UPDATE, he could have made the changes manually.

Instead of writing one SQL statement to solve his complex update, I wrote a script to generate a set of simpler SQL statements that had the desired effect:

```
Spaghetti-Query/soln/generate-update.sql
SELECT CONCAT('UPDATE Inventory '
  ' SET last_used = ''', MAX(u.usage_date), '''',
  ' WHERE inventory_id = ', u.inventory_id, ';') AS update_statement
FROM ComputerUsage u
GROUP BY u.inventory_id;
```

The output of this query is a series of UPDATE statements, complete with semicolons, ready to run as an SQL script:

---
update_statement

UPDATE Inventory SET last_used = '2002-04-19' WHERE inventory_id = 1234;

UPDATE Inventory SET last_used = '2002-03-12' WHERE inventory_id = 2345;

UPDATE Inventory SET last_used = '2002-04-30' WHERE inventory_id = 3456;

UPDATE Inventory SET last_used = '2002-04-04' WHERE inventory_id = 4567;

...

With this technique, I solved in minutes what that manager had been struggling with for hours.

Executing so many SQL queries or statements may not be the most efficient way to accomplish a task. You should balance the goal of efficiency against the goal of getting the task done.

> Although SQL seems powerful enough to solve a complex problem in a single query, don't be tempted to build a house of cards.

CHAPTER 19

Implicit Columns

A PHP programmer asked for help troubleshooting the confusing result of a seemingly straightforward SQL query against his library database:

Implicit-Columns/intro/join-wildcard.sql
```
SELECT * FROM Books b JOIN Authors a ON (b.author_id = a.author_id);
```

This query returned all book titles as null. Even stranger, when he ran a different query without joining to the Authors, the result included the real book titles as expected.

The cause of his trouble was that the PHP database extension he was using returned each row resulting from the SQL query as an associative array. For example, he could access the Books.isbn column as $row["isbn"]. In his tables, both Books and Authors had a column called title (the latter was for titles like *Dr.* or *Rev.*). A single-result array element $row["title"] can store only one value; in this case, Authors.title occupied that array element. Most authors in the database had no title, so the result was that $row["title"] appeared to be null. When the query skipped the join to Authors, no conflict existed between column names, and the book title occupied the array element as expected.

The solution was to declare a column alias to give one or the other title column a different name so that each would have a separate entry in the array.

Implicit-Columns/intro/join-alias.sql
```
SELECT b.title, a.title AS salutation
FROM Books b JOIN Authors a ON (b.author_id = a.author_id);
```

His second question was, "How do I give one column an alias but also request other columns?" He wanted to continue using the wildcard (SELECT *) but apply an alias to one column covered by the wildcard.

Objective: Reduce Typing

Software developers don't like to type, which in a way makes their choice of career ironic, like the twist ending in an O. Henry story.

One example that programmers cite as requiring too much typing is when writing all the columns used in an SQL query:

Implicit-Columns/obj/select-explicit.sql
```
SELECT bug_id, date_reported, summary, description, resolution,
  reported_by, assigned_to, verified_by, status, priority, hours
FROM Bugs;
```

It's no surprise that software developers gratefully use the SQL *wildcard* feature. The * symbol means *every column*, so the list of columns is implicit rather than explicit. This helps make queries more concise.

Implicit-Columns/obj/select-implicit.sql
```
SELECT * FROM Bugs;
```

Likewise, when using INSERT, it seems smart to take advantage of the default: the values apply to all the columns in the order they're defined in the table.

Implicit-Columns/obj/insert-explicit.sql
```
INSERT INTO Accounts (account_name, first_name, last_name, email,
  password, portrait_image, hourly_rate)
VALUES ('bkarwin', 'Bill', 'Karwin', 'bill@example.com',
  SHA2('xyzzy', 256), NULL, 49.95);
```

It's shorter to write the statement without listing the columns.

Implicit-Columns/obj/insert-implicit.sql
```
INSERT INTO Accounts
VALUES (DEFAULT, 'bkarwin', 'Bill', 'Karwin', 'bill@example.com',
  SHA2('xyzzy', 256), NULL, 49.95);
```

If you use INSERT statement with implicit columns, the VALUES() clause must include the same number of values as the number of columns in the table. You can use the DEFAULT keyword in the VALUES() clause to set a column to its default value in the new row.

Antipattern: A Shortcut That Gets You Lost

Although using wildcards and unnamed columns satisfies the goal of less typing, this habit creates several hazards.

Breaking Refactoring

Suppose you need to add a column to the Bugs table, such as date_due for scheduling purposes.

Implicit-Columns/anti/add-column.sql
```
ALTER TABLE Bugs ADD COLUMN date_due DATE;
```

Your INSERT statement now results in an error, because you listed eleven values instead of the twelve the table now expects.

Implicit-Columns/anti/insert-mismatched.sql
```
INSERT INTO Bugs
VALUES (DEFAULT, CURDATE(), 'New bug', 'Test T987 fails...',
    NULL, 123, NULL, NULL, DEFAULT, 'Medium', NULL);

-- SQLSTATE 21S01: Column count doesn't match value count at row 1
```

In an INSERT statement that uses implicit columns, you must give values for all columns in the same order that columns are defined in the table. If the columns change, the statement produces an error—or even assigns values to the wrong columns.

Suppose you run a SELECT * query, and since you don't know the column names, you reference columns based on their ordinal position:

Implicit-Columns/anti/ordinal.py
```
import mysql.connector

cnx = mysql.connector.connect(user='scott', database='test')
cursor = cnx.cursor()

query = "SELECT * FROM Bugs WHERE bug_id = %s"
cursor.execute(query, (1234,))
for (row) in cursor:
    print(row[10])
```

Unknown to you, another person on the team dropped a column:

Implicit-Columns/anti/drop-column.sql
```
ALTER TABLE Bugs DROP COLUMN verified_by;
```

The hours column is no longer at position 10. Your application is using the value in another column by mistake. As columns are renamed, added, or dropped, your query result could change in ways your code doesn't support. You can't predict how many columns your query returns if you use a wildcard.

These errors can propagate through your code, and by the time you notice the problem in the output of the application, it's hard to trace back to the line where the mistake occurred.

Hidden Costs

The convenience of using wildcards in queries can harm performance and scalability. The more columns your query fetches, the more data must travel over the network between your application and the database server.

You probably have many queries running concurrently in your production application environment. They compete for access to the same network bandwidth. Even a very high-bandwidth network can be saturated by a hundred application clients querying for thousands of rows at a time.

Object-relational mapping (ORM) techniques such as Active Record often use SELECT * by default to populate the fields of an object representing a row in a database. Even if the ORM offers the means to override this behavior, most programmers don't bother.

You Asked for It, You Got It

"Is there a shortcut to request all columns, except a few that I don't want?" This is a common questions from programmers using the SQL wildcard. Perhaps these programmers are trying to avoid the resource cost of fetching bulky TEXT columns that they don't need, but they do want the convenience of using a wildcard. Or else they have so many columns in a given table that they think it would be easier to specify the columns to exclude.

The answer is no, SQL does not support any syntax, which means, "all the columns I want but none that I don't want." Either you use the wildcard to request all columns from a table, or else you have to list the columns you want explicitly.

Imagine what it would look like, if there were SQL query syntax to request all columns with the * wildcard, except specific columns to exclude. This syntax doesn't exist in SQL, but hypothetically, it might look like the following:

Implicit-Columns/anti/wildcard-except-fake.sql
```
SELECT * EXCEPT reported_by, assigned_to, verified_by, priority, hours
FROM Bugs;
```

SQL can't guess which columns you don't want. You would have to name them explicitly. So it wouldn't save you much typing after all. In fact, it could require *more* typing, if your typical query needs fewer than half the columns.

Any other developer who reads your code would naturally have the question, "if those columns are excluded, what columns are returned by this query?" Or they might overlook the EXCEPT keyword, and mistakenly think the columns named are to be included, instead of excluded.

How to Recognize the Antipattern

The following scenarios may indicate that your project is using implicit columns inappropriately, and it's causing trouble:

- "The application broke because it's still referencing columns in the database result set by the old column names. We tried to update all the code, but I guess we missed some."

  You've changed a table in the database—adding, deleting, renaming, or changing the order of columns—but you failed to change your application code that references the table. It's laborious to track down all these references.

- "It took us days to track down our network bottleneck, and we finally narrowed it down to excessive traffic to the database server. According to our statistics, the average query fetches more than 2MB of data but displays less than a tenth of that."

  You're fetching a lot of data you don't need.

Legitimate Uses of the Antipattern

A well-justified use of wildcards is in ad hoc SQL when you're writing quick queries to test a solution or as a diagnostic check of current data. A single-use query benefits less from maintainability.

The examples in this book use wildcards to save space and to avoid distracting from the more interesting parts of the example queries. In production application code, you should avoid using SQL wildcards.

If your application needs to run a query that adapts when columns are added, dropped, renamed, or repositioned, you may find it best to use wildcards. Be sure to plan for the extra work it takes to troubleshoot the pitfalls.

You can use wildcards for each table individually in a join query. Prefix the wildcard with the table name or alias. This allows you to specify a short list of specific columns you need from one table, while using the wildcard to fetch all columns from the other table. For example:

Implicit-Columns/legit/wildcard-one-table.sql
```
SELECT b.*, a.first_name, a.email
FROM Bugs b JOIN Accounts a
  ON (b.reported_by = a.account_id);
```

Keying in a long list of column names can be time-consuming. For some people, development efficiency is more important than runtime efficiency.

Likewise, you might place a priority on writing queries that are shorter and more readable. Using wildcards does reduce keystrokes and result in a shorter query, so if this is your priority, then use wildcards.

Some developers assume that a long SQL query passing from the application to the database server causes too much network overhead. In theory, query length could make a difference in some cases. It's more common that the rows of data that your query returns use much more network bandwidth than your SQL query string. Use your judgment about exception cases, but don't sweat the small stuff.

Solution: Name Columns Explicitly

Always spell out all the columns you need, instead of relying on wildcards or implicit column lists.

Implicit-Columns/soln/select-explicit.sql
```sql
SELECT bug_id, date_reported, summary, description, resolution,
  reported_by, assigned_to, verified_by, status, priority, hours
FROM Bugs;
```

Implicit-Columns/soln/insert-explicit.sql
```sql
INSERT INTO Accounts (account_name, first_name, last_name, email,
  password_hash, portrait_image, hourly_rate)
VALUES ('bkarwin', 'Bill', 'Karwin', 'bill@example.com',
  SHA2('xyzzy'), NULL, 49.95);
```

All this typing seems burdensome, but it's worth it in several ways.

Mistake Proofing

Remember poka-yoke, the practice from the Japanese manufacturing industry of designing mistake-proof systems (Chapter 5, Keyless Entry, on page 53)? You make your SQL queries more resistant to the errors and confusion described earlier when you specify the columns in the select-list of the query.

- If a column has been repositioned in the table, it doesn't change position in a query result.

- If a column has been added in the table, it doesn't appear in the query result.

- If a column has been dropped from the table, your query raises an error —but it's a good error, because you're led directly to the code that you need to fix, instead of left to hunt for the root cause.

You get similar benefits when you specify columns in INSERT statements. The order of columns you specify overrides the order in the table definition, and values are assigned to the columns you intend. Newly added columns you haven't named in your statement are given default values or null. If you reference a column that has been deleted, you get an error, but troubleshooting is easier.

This is an example of the *fail early* principle.

You Ain't Gonna Need It

If you're concerned about the scalability and throughput of your software, you should look for possible wasteful use of network bandwidth. The bandwidth of an SQL query can seem harmless during software development and testing, but it bites you when your production environment is running thousands of SQL queries per second.

Once you abandon the SQL wildcard, you're naturally motivated to think about which columns you really need in a given query, and leave out the columns you don't need. This helps you to type less, and promotes more efficient use of bandwidth too.

Implicit-Columns/soln/yagni.sql
```
SELECT date_reported, summary, description, resolution, status, priority
FROM Bugs;
```

You Need to Give Up Wildcards Anyway

When you buy a bag of candies from the vending machine, the wrapper is a convenience, making it easy to carry the package of candies back to your desk. Once you open the bag, however, you need to treat the candies as individuals. They roll, slide, and bounce all over the place. If you're not careful, some may fall under your desk and attract bugs. But there's no way to eat one until you tear open the bag.

In an SQL query, if you need to use a function or expression in the select-list, or use a column alias, or exclude columns, you need to break open the "container" provided by the wildcard. You lose the convenience of treating the collection of columns as a single package, but you gain access to all of its contents.

Implicit-Columns/soln/select-expr.sql
```
SELECT bug_id, SUBSTRING(summary FROM 1 FOR 16) AS summary_shortened, ...
FROM Bugs;
```

You inevitably need to treat columns individually. If you avoid using wildcards from the beginning, it'll be easier to change your query later.

> Take all you want, but eat all you take.

Part IV

Application Development Antipatterns

SQL is supposed to be used in the context of applications written in another language, such as Python, Java, C, C++, C#, JavaScript, Elixir, and so on. There are right ways and wrong ways to employ SQL in an application, and this part of the book describes some common blunders.

The enemy knows the system.
    ▷ *Shannon's maxim*

## CHAPTER 20

Readable Passwords

Suppose you receive a phone call from a man using one of the applications you support. The caller is having trouble logging in.

"This is Pat Johnson in Sales. I must have forgotten my password. Can you just look it up and tell me what it is?" Pat sounds a bit sheepish but also strangely in a hurry.

"I'm sorry, I'm not supposed to do that," you answer. "I can reset your account, and that'll send an email to the address you registered for your account. You can use the instructions in that email to set a new password."

The man becomes more impatient and assertive. "That's ridiculous," he says. "At my last company the support staff could look up my password. Are you unable to do your job? Do you want me to call your manager?"

Naturally, you want to preserve a smooth relationship with your users, so you run an SQL query to look up the plain-text password for Pat Johnson's account and read it to him over the phone.

The man hangs up. You comment to your co-worker, "That was a close call. I almost had an escalation from Pat Johnson. I hope he doesn't complain."

Your co-worker looks puzzled. "*He?* Pat Johnson in Sales is a woman. I think you just gave her password to a con artist."

Objective: Recover or Reset Passwords

It's a sure bet that in any application that has passwords, a user will forget their password. Most modern applications handle this by giving the user a chance to recover or reset their password through email or SMS. This requires the user to have access to the email or mobile device associated with the user profile in the application.

Antipattern: Store Password in Plain Text

The frequent mistake in these kinds of password-recovery solutions is that the application allows the user to request an email containing their password in clear text. This is a dire security flaw related to the database design, and it leads to several security risks that could allow unauthorized people to gain privileged access to the application.

Let's explore these risks in the following sections, assuming our example bug-tracking database has a table Accounts, where each user's account is stored as a row in this table.

Storing Passwords

A password is typically stored in the Accounts table as a string attribute column:

Passwords/anti/create-table.sql
```sql
CREATE TABLE Accounts (
  account_id    SERIAL PRIMARY KEY,
  account_name  VARCHAR(20) NOT NULL,
  email         VARCHAR(100) NOT NULL,
  password      VARCHAR(30) NOT NULL
);
```

You can create an account simply by inserting one row and specifying the password as a string literal:

Passwords/anti/insert-plaintext.sql
```sql
INSERT INTO Accounts (account_id, account_name, email, password)
  VALUES (123, 'billkarwin', 'bill@example.com', 'xyzzy');
```

It's not secure to store a password in clear text or even to pass it over the network in the clear. If an attacker can read the SQL statement you use to insert a password, they can see the password plainly. This is also true for SQL statements to change a password or verify that user input matches a stored password. Hackers have several opportunities to steal a password, including the following:

- Intercepting network packets as the SQL statement is sent from the application client to the database server when not encrypting communications with TLS. This is easier than it sounds; free software tools such as Wireshark[1] or tcpdump[2] allow a third party to "wiretap" TCP/IP, and read packets between your client and the server.

---

1. https://www.wireshark.org/
2. https://www.tcpdump.org/

- Searching SQL query logs on the database server. The attacker may need access to the database server host, but assuming they have that, they can access log files that include a record of SQL statements executed by that database server.

- Reading data from database backup files on the server or on backup media. Backup media is sometimes even easier to hack than the database itself, because owners don't enforce secure access to the backups as strictly as they do for the database.

Hackers use techniques like these to acquire information about your password system, so you must take care to block not only their access to your database, but also to your network, logs, and backups.

Authenticating Passwords

Later, when the user tries to log in, your application compares the user's input to the password string stored in the database. This comparison is done as plain text, since the password itself is stored in plain text. For example, you can use a query like the following to return a 0 (false) or 1 (true), indicating whether the user's input matches the password in the database:

```
Passwords/anti/auth-plaintext.sql
SELECT CASE WHEN password = 'opensesame' THEN 1 ELSE 0 END
  AS password_matches
FROM Accounts
WHERE account_id = 123;
```

In this example, the password the user entered, *opensesame*, is incorrect, and the query returns a zero value.

Like in the previous section on storing passwords, interpolating the user's input string into the SQL query in plain text exposes it to discovery by an attacker.

Many programmers design an authentication query with conditions for both the account_id and password columns in the WHERE clause:

```
Passwords/anti/auth-lumping.sql
SELECT * FROM Accounts
WHERE account_name = 'bill' AND password = 'opensesame';
```

This query lumps two different cases together: it returns an empty result set if the account doesn't exist or if the user tried to log in with the wrong password. You might want to treat these two reasons for failed authentication differently.

For example, you may want to lock an account temporarily if you detect many failed password guesses in a row, because this might indicate an attempted intrusion. However, you can't detect this pattern if you can't tell the difference between a wrong account name and a wrong password.

Sending Passwords in Email

Since the password is stored in plain text in the database, retrieving the password in your application is simple:

Passwords/anti/select-plaintext.sql
```sql
SELECT account_name, email, password
FROM Accounts
WHERE account_id = 123;
```

Your application can then send to a user's email address on request. You've probably seen one of these emails as part of the password reminder feature of any number of websites you use. An example of this kind of email is shown here:

Example of Password Recovery Email:
```
From: daemon
To: bill@example.com
Subject: password request

You requested a reminder of the password for your account "bill".
Your password is "xyzzy".

Click the link below to log in to your account:

https://www.example.com/login
```

Sending an email with the password in plain text is a serious security risk. Email can be intercepted, logged, and stored in multiple ways by hackers. It's not good enough that you use a secure protocol to view mail or that the sending and receiving mail servers are managed by responsible system administrators. Since email is routed across the Internet, it can be intercepted at other sites. Secure protocols for email aren't necessarily widespread or under your control.

How to Recognize the Antipattern

Any application that can recover your password and send it to you must be storing it in plain text or at least with some reversible encoding. This is the antipattern.

It's not just about sending passwords in email. Any form of password recovery reveals that the password is stored in an inappropriate way. If your application can read a password for a legitimate purpose, then it's possible that a hacker can read the password illicitly.

Legitimate Uses of the Antipattern

Your application may need to use a password to access another third-party service—that is, your application can be a client. In this case, you must store that password in a readable format. Preferably, you use some encoding that your application can reverse, instead of using plain text in the database.

You can make a distinction between *identification* and *authentication*. A user can identify themself as anyone they want, but authentication is proving they are who they say they are. Passwords are the most common way of doing this.

If you can't enforce security strong enough to defeat skilled and determined attackers, then you effectively have an identification mechanism but not a reliable authentication mechanism. This isn't necessarily a deal-breaker.

Not every software application is at risk for attack, and not every application contains sensitive information that must be protected. For example, an intranet application may be accessed by only a few people who are known to be honest and cooperative. In this case, an identification mechanism may be enough for the application to work, and in those informal environments, a simpler login design may be adequate. The additional work necessary to create a strong authentication system may not be justified.

Be careful, though—applications have a tendency to evolve beyond their original environment or role. Before you make your quaint little intranet application available outside your company firewall, you should get a qualified security expert to evaluate it.

Ethics of Software Development

If you're developing an application that supports passwords and you're asked to design a feature to recover users' passwords, you should push back respectfully, warn the project decision makers about the risks, and offer an alternative solution that provides similar value: password reset, instead of password recovery.

Just as an electrician should recognize and correct a wiring design that poses an unsafe fire risk, it's your responsibility as a software engineer to be aware of safety issues and to promote safer software.

A good book you should read is *24 Deadly Sins of Software Security [HLV09]*. Another good resource is the Open Web Application Security Project.[a]

---

a.   https://owasp.org/

Solution: Store a Salted Hash of the Password

The chief problem in this antipattern is that the original form of the password is readable. Instead, you should authenticate the user's input against a password without reading it. This section describes how to implement this kind of secure password storage in an SQL database.

Understanding Hash Functions

Encode the password using a one-way *cryptographic hash function*. This transforms its input string into a new string, called the *hash*, that is unrecognizable. Even the length of the original string is obscured, because the hash returned by a hash function is a fixed-length string. For example, the SHA-256 algorithm converts our example password, *xyzzy*, to a 256-bit string of bits, usually represented as a 64-character string of hexadecimal digits:

Passwords/soln/sha256.py
```
import hashlib

m = hashlib.sha256()
m.update(b'xyzzy')
print(m.hexdigest())

# Output:
# 184858a00fd7971f810848266ebcecee5e8b69972c5ffaed622f5ee078671aed
```

Another characteristic of a cryptographic hash is that it's not reversible. You can't recover the input string from its hash because the hashing algorithm is designed to "lose" some information about the input. A good hashing algorithm should take as much work to crack as it would to simply guess the input through trial and error.

A popular algorithm in the past has been SHA-1, but researchers have proved this 160-bit hashing algorithm has insufficient cryptographic strength; bad guys can infer the input from a hash string. This technique is very time-consuming but nevertheless takes less time than it would take to guess the password by trial and error.

The National Institute of Standards and Technology (NIST) phased out SHA-1 as an approved secure hashing algorithm after 2010 in favor of these stronger variants: SHA-224, SHA-256, SHA-384, and SHA-512.[3] Then, in 2015, NIST approved the SHA3 family of hash algorithms. Whether you need to comply with NIST standards or not, it's a good idea to use at least SHA-256 for passwords.

---

3. https://csrc.nist.gov/projects/hash-functions

MD5() is another popular hash function, producing hash strings of 128 bits. MD5() has also been shown to be cryptographically weak, so you shouldn't use it for encoding passwords. Weaker algorithms still have uses, but not for sensitive information like passwords.

Using a Hash in SQL

The following is a redefinition of the Accounts table. The SHA-256 password hash is always 64 characters long, so define the column as a fixed-length CHAR column of that length.

Passwords/soln/create-table.sql
```
CREATE TABLE Accounts (
  account_id      SERIAL PRIMARY KEY,
  account_name    VARCHAR(20),
  email           VARCHAR(100) NOT NULL,
  password_hash   CHAR(64) NOT NULL
);
```

Hashing functions aren't part of the standard SQL language, so you may need to rely on your database brand to support hashing as an extension. For example, MySQL 5.5 with SSL support includes a function SHA2().

Passwords/soln/insert-hash.sql
```
INSERT INTO Accounts (account_id, account_name, email, password_hash)
  VALUES (123, 'billkarwin', 'bill@example.com', SHA2('xyzzy', 256));
```

You can validate a user's input by applying the same hash function to it and comparing the result to the value stored in the database.

Passwords/soln/auth-hash.sql
```
SELECT CASE WHEN password_hash = SHA2('xyzzy', 256) THEN 1 ELSE 0 END
  AS password_matches
FROM Accounts
WHERE account_id = 123;
```

Suppose a user's account needs to be disabled, if they must be locked out of the system. Ideally, the authentication system should use a separate attribute to mark an account as disabled. If this feature is not supported, you can disable an account by changing its password. There is a chance that the user could guess the new password, but if you change the string stored as the password hash to a string that the hash function could never produce, then no password input could be validated against it. For example, the string *noaccess* contains letters that aren't hexadecimal digits.

Adding Salt to Your Hash

If you store hashes instead of passwords and the attacker gains access to your database (by searching your trash for backup storage media, for example), they can still attempt to guess passwords by trial and error. Guessing each password may take a long time, but they can prepare their own database of hashes of likely passwords against which to compare the hash strings they find in your database. If only one user chose a password that is a word in the dictionary, it's easy for an attacker to find it by searching your password database for hashes that match his prepared table of hashes. They can even do this with SQL:

Passwords/soln/dictionary-attack.sql

```sql
CREATE TABLE DictionaryHashes (
  password         VARCHAR(100),
  password_hash  CHAR(64)
);

SELECT a.account_name, h.password
FROM Accounts AS a JOIN DictionaryHashes AS h
  ON a.password_hash = h.password_hash;
```

One way to defeat this kind of "dictionary attack" is by including a *salt* in your password-encoding expression. A salt is a string of meaningless bytes you concatenate with the user's password, before passing the resulting string to the hash function. Even if the user chose a word in the dictionary as their password, the hash produced from a salted password won't match the hash in the attacker's hash database. For example, if the password is *"xyzzy"*, you can see that the hash of this word is different from a hash of the word with a few random bytes appended:

Passwords/soln/sha256-salt.py

```python
import hashlib

m = hashlib.sha256()
m.update(b'xyzzy')
print(m.hexdigest())

# Output:
# 184858a00fd7971f810848266ebcecee5e8b69972c5ffaed622f5ee078671aed

# append the salt to the previous password content, so the hex digest
# is the hash of both strings concatentated.
m.update(b'-0xT!sp9')
print(m.hexdigest())

# Output:
# 741b8aabe2e615e1c12876e66075199d602116ffb40b822dd5596baa7dafd40e
```

Each password should use a different salt value to make an attacker have to generate a new dictionary table of hashes for each password. Then they're back to square one, because cracking passwords in your database takes as much time as guessing them with trial and error. The following code is an example of storing a salt value and combining it with the password before hashing, then validating a password input by combining it with the same salt.

```
Passwords/soln/salt.sql
CREATE TABLE Accounts (
  account_id      SERIAL PRIMARY KEY,
  account_name    VARCHAR(20),
  email           VARCHAR(100) NOT NULL,
  password_hash   CHAR(64) NOT NULL,
  salt            BINARY(8) NOT NULL
);

INSERT INTO Accounts (account_id, account_name, email,
    password_hash, salt)
  VALUES (123, 'billkarwin', 'bill@example.com',
    SHA2(CONCAT('xyzzy', '-0xT!sp9'), 256), '-0xT!sp9');

SELECT (password_hash = SHA2(CONCAT('xyzzy', salt), 256))
  AS password_matches
FROM Accounts
WHERE account_id = 123;
```

A good salt is at least 8 bytes long, generated randomly for each password. The previous examples show a salt string containing printable characters, but you can (and should) make a salt using printable and unprintable bytes.

A related, and more sophisticated, technique to recover passwords from their hashes is called a *rainbow table*. Employing a salt defends against this technique too.

Hiding the Password from SQL

Now that you're using a strong hashing function to encode the password before you store it and you use a salt to thwart dictionary attacks, you would think this is enough to ensure security. Unfortunately, the password still appears in plain text in the SQL expression, which means that it's readable if an attacker can intercept network packets or if SQL queries are logged and the log files fall into the wrong hands.

You can protect against this kind of exposure if you don't put the plain-text password into the SQL query. Instead, compute the hash in your application code, and use only the hash in the SQL query. It does an attacker little good to intercept the hash, because they can't reverse it to get the password.

You do need the salt before you can compute the hash.

The following Python example gets a salt, computes a hash, and runs a query to validate the password against the salted hash stored in the database:

Passwords/soln/auth-salt.py

```python
import mysql.connector
import hashlib

cnx = mysql.connector.connect(user='scott', database='test')
cursor = cnx.cursor()

# For the sake of simplicity in this code example, the name and password
# are fixed values. In a real application, they would be inputs.
name = 'bill'
password = 'xyzzy';

query = "SELECT password_hash, salt FROM Accounts WHERE account_name = %s"
cursor.execute(query, (name,))
for (row) in cursor:
    stored_hash = row[0]
    # salt is stored as binary bytes, so it must be decoded to a string.
    salt = row[1].decode()

# Concatenate the input password with the stored salt, and produce a hash.
m = hashlib.sha256()
m.update(f"{password}{salt}".encode('utf-8'))
input_hash = m.hexdigest()

# Compare the hash of the input against the hash stored in the database.
if input_hash == stored_hash:
    print("match successful!")
```

In web applications, attackers can also intercept data on the network, between the user's browser and the web server. When the user submits a login form, the browser sends his password in plain text to the server. It's a good defense against network interceptors if you use a secure HTTP connection whenever sending a password from the browser to the application. Some developers also hash the password using browser-side code before sending the HTTP request, as a defense-in-depth technique.

Resetting the Password Instead of Recovering the Password

Now that the password is stored in a more secure way, you still need to solve the original objective: help users who have forgotten their password. You can't recover their password, because now your database stores a hash instead of the password. Even though you cannot reverse the hash any more easily than an attacker could, you can allow a user access in other ways. Two sample implementations are described here.

The first alternative is that when a user who has forgotten their password requests help, instead of emailing their password, your application can send an email with a temporary password generated by the application. The password reset code in your application knows the plaintext password, so it can send it in an email. Only the hashed version of that password is stored in the database.

For additional security, the application may expire the temporary password after a short time, so if the email is intercepted, it's more likely that it will not allow unauthorized access.

Example of Email with a System-Generated Temporary Password
```
From: daemon
To: bill@example.com
Subject: password reset

You requested to reset your password for your account.

Your temporary password is "p0trz3b1e".
This password will cease to allow access after one hour.

Click the link below to log in to your account and
set your new password:

https://www.example.com/login
```

In a second alternative, instead of including a new temporary password in an email, the user's reset request is logged in a database table and assigned a unique token as an identifier:

Passwords/soln/reset-request.sql
```
CREATE TABLE PasswordResetRequest (
  account_id  BIGINT UNSIGNED PRIMARY KEY,
  token       CHAR(32) NOT NULL,
  expiration  TIMESTAMP NOT NULL,
  FOREIGN KEY (account_id) REFERENCES Accounts(account_id)
);

SET @token = MD5('billkarwin' || CURRENT_TIMESTAMP || RAND());

# Use REPLACE instead of INSERT in MySQL, so the statement overwrites
# any existing row for the given account_id.
REPLACE INTO PasswordResetRequest (account_id, token, account_id, expiration)
  VALUES (123, @token, CURRENT_TIMESTAMP + INTERVAL 1 HOUR);
```

Then you include the token in an email. You could also send the token in some other message, such as SMS, as long as it's sent to an address that's already associated with the account requesting a password reset. That way, if a stranger requests a password reset illicitly, it sends a spurious email only to the actual owner of the account.

Example of Email with a Temporary Link to a Password Reset Page

```
From: daemon
To: bill@example.com
Subject: password reset

You requested to reset your password for your account.

Click the link below within one hour to change your password.
After one hour, the link below will no longer work and your
password will remain unchanged.

https://www.example.com/reset_password?token=f5cabff22532bd0025118905bdea50da
```

When the application receives a request for the special reset_password screen, the value in the token parameter must match a row in the PasswordResetRequest table, and the expiration timestamp on this row must still be upcoming, not past. The account_id on this row references the Accounts table, so the token is restricted to enable a password reset of only one specific account.

With either of the two previous methods, the user must be forced to change their password before they are allowed to do any other action on the website. Once they have changed their password, then only they know it, because only the hash is stored in the database, not the plaintext password.

The state of cryptography is constantly advancing, trying to stay ahead of attack technology. The techniques in this chapter are still relevant regardless of the type of cryptographic hash algorithm you use, but you should use current recommended algorithms such as the following:

- Argon2[4] is a password hashing algorithm that won the Password Hashing Competition (PHC) in 2015.

- PBKDF2[5] is a widely used *key strengthening* standard.

- Bcrypt[6] implements an *adaptive hashing* function.

This list will eventually become outdated too. If you're responsible for implementing an authentication system, then you should keep yourself up to date on the latest NIST standards for recommended algorithms.

> If you can read passwords, so can a hacker.

---

4. https://www.argon2.com/
5. https://tools.ietf.org/html/rfc2898
6. https://en.wikipedia.org/wiki/Bcrypt

Mini-Antipattern: Storing Hash Strings in VARCHAR

"What data type should I use to store a hash?"

The result of a hash is commonly stored as a string of hexadecimal digits, and most developers default to using VARCHAR to store any string. If they don't know how much space the string requires, they choose VARCHAR(255) because that is greatest length supported by the most implementations of SQL.

Each hash algorithm is different, but they have the property that no matter what the length of the input, all inputs return the same length result for a given hash algorithm. This determines the length of storage you need to store the hash. You don't need to use a VARCHAR, since the length is fixed. Instead, use a fixed-length CHAR column.

A string of hexadecimal digits can be stored as binary bytes in half the space. For example, the hexadecimal value FF uses two characters when stored as a string, but the same value occupies one binary byte. So, each fixed-length hash string can be stored either in a CHAR column, or a BINARY column of half the length. Every programming language should have a built-in function for converting between a string of hexadecimal digits and the binary form.

Another choice is to encode the same bytes in base64 format. Whereas hexadecimal encodes three bytes of binary data using six characters, base64 encodes the same three bytes using four characters. This means base64 is 50% more compact than hexadecimal. Base64 is more friendly to human readers than binary, because base64 uses only printable characters.

Using binary or base64 reduces storage space used both by data storage and any index on that data.

Algorithm	Bits	Type for Hex Digits	Type for Base64	Type for Bytes
MD5	128	CHAR(32)	CHAR(22)	BINARY(16)
SHA-1	160	CHAR(40)	CHAR(27)	BINARY(20)
SHA-256	256	CHAR(64)	CHAR(43)	BINARY(32)
SHA-512	512	CHAR(128)	CHAR(86)	BINARY(64)

Password-hashing functions like Argon2, PBKDF2, or Bcrypt have options that result in minor differences in output format. The format encodes the options you choose, and also the salt used. Here is an example of using the Argon2 command-line tool. It returns a string of 84 characters, so given these options, use a CHAR(84) to store this string.

```
echo "mypassword" | argon2 "salt1234" -e
$argon2i$v=19$m=4096,t=3,p=1$c2FsdDEyMzQ$61QNJTDZzd7eL6u5HDE0jCyhoLrGmH...
```

The result follows the PHC format, with five fields separated by $ characters: the algorithm, version, options, the base-64 encoded salt, and the base-64 encoding of the 256-bit hash result. Normally you don't need to inspect this string; you would just validate a new input password by hashing it, and comparing the result to the stored result.

Quote me as saying I was misquoted.

    > *Groucho Marx*

## CHAPTER 21

SQL Injection

In March 2010, a serial computer hacker was convicted and sentenced to 20 years in US federal prison for his role in the largest identity theft in history.[1] He acquired an estimated 130 million credit and debit card numbers by hacking into ATM machines and payment systems, using a technique called *SQL injection.*

SQL injection vulnerabilities are reported in popular software products and websites regularly, and any one report may refer to a breach of millions of records of personal information. For example, the WordPress blogging platform or one of its plugins has an urgent SQL security patch several times per year.[2] Every operating system, database brand, and programming language has been the subject of SQL injection vulnerabilties.

SQL injection was first publicly identified in 1998, so why does this flaw still affect so many software products and websites today? The answer is that it's not really a bug in vendor software—it's a programming mistake, committed every day by many of the estimated 24.3 million software developers worldwide (as of 2021).[3]

Computer science education seldom trains developers in secure coding practices (except in classes specifically about code security). This is a skill they are expected to learn on the job. Robert C. Martin, author of *Clean Code [Mar08]*, claims the population of programmers doubles about every five years, which means at any given time, at least half of working software developers

---

1.   https://www.justice.gov/opa/pr/leader-hacking-ring-sentenced-massive-identity-thefts-payment-processor-and-us-retail

2.   https://www.bleepingcomputer.com/news/security/wordpress-related-vulnerabilities-saw-a-30-percent-uptick-in-2018/

3.   https://www.developernation.net/developer-reports/de20

have less than five years of experience.[4] If many software development shops employ mostly junior programmers, then those programmers may get no mentoring for good security habits. Employers are more concerned with releasing software as quickly as possible, not time-consuming code reviews or "nice to have" security testing. Both businesses and programmers often prioritize repairing vulnerabilities only after getting hacked.

SQL injection attacks remain an easy target for hackers, because enough software developers don't understand the nature of the vulnerability and they keep creating the vulnerability in new code.

Objective: Write Dynamic SQL Queries

SQL is intended to be integrated with application code. When you build SQL queries as strings and combine application variables into the string, this is commonly called *dynamic SQL*. In the following example, a variable is interpolated into a Python f-string. By the time the database receives the query, the value of bugid is part of the query.

SQL-Injection/obj/dynamic-sql.py
```
bugid = 1234
query = f"SELECT * FROM Bugs WHERE bug_id = {bugid}";
cursor.execute(query)
```

Dynamic SQL queries are a natural way to get the most out of a database. When you use application data to specify how you want to query a database, you're using SQL as a two-way language. Your application is having a kind of dialogue with the database.

It's not too hard to make your software do tasks that you want it to do—the harder challenge is making your software prevent actions that you don't want it to do. SQL injection flaws are examples of the latter.

Antipattern: Execute Unverified Input As Code

SQL injection happens when you interpolate some content into an SQL query string and the content modifies the syntax of your query in ways you didn't intend. In the classic example of SQL injection, the value you interpolate into your string finishes the SQL statement and executes a second complete statement. For instance, if the value of bugid is *1234; DELETE FROM Bugs*, the resulting SQL shown earlier would look like this:

SQL-Injection/anti/delete.sql
```
SELECT * FROM Bugs WHERE bug_id = 1234; DELETE FROM Bugs
```

---

4. https://www.youtube.com/watch?v=BHnMItX2hEQ

This type of SQL injection can be spectacular (cartoon by Randall Munroe,[5] used with permission).

Usually these flaws are more subtle, but still dangerous.

Accidents May Happen

Suppose you are writing a web interface to view the bugs database and one page allows you to view a project based on its name. The following example shows this implemented with Python and Flask.

SQL-Injection/anti/ohare.py
```
import mysql.connector
import json
from flask import Flask, Response, request

app = Flask(__name__)

cnx = mysql.connector.connect(user='scott', database='test')
cursor = cnx.cursor()

@app.route('/products', methods = ['GET'])
def get_products():
    product_name = request.args.get("name")

    # UNSAFE!
    sql = f"SELECT * FROM Products WHERE product_name = '{product_name}'"

    cursor.execute(sql)
    return json.dumps(cursor.fetchall())

if __name__ == '__main__':
    app.run()
```

❶ Create an instance of a Flask web application.

❷ Open a connection to the MySQL database on the local host.

❸ Define a route so http GET requests to the web application at the named path are handled by the function that follows.

---

5. https://xkcd.com/327/

❹ Define a request handler function.

❺ Assign the value of the GET request parameter *name* to a variable.

❻ Format a string containing an SQL query, using a Python f-string to interpolate the variable.

❼ Execute the string as an SQL query.

❽ Start the Flask web application when the Python script is invoked.

The trouble begins when your team is hired to develop software for O'Hare International Airport in Chicago. You naturally give the project a name like "O'Hare." You might use a request like the following to view the project in your web application:

http://bugs.example.com/project/view?name=O'Hare

Your code interpolates the value of that request parameter into the SQL query, but it produces an invalid query:

SQL-Injection/anti/ohare.sql
```
SELECT * FROM Products WHERE product_name = 'O'Hare'
```

Because a string is terminated by the first quote character it finds, the resulting expression contains a short string, *'O'*, followed by some extra characters, *Hare'*, which cause the database to return a syntax error. This is an honest accident. The risk of anything bad happening is low, because a statement with a syntax error can't execute. The greater risk is that the statement executes without error but does something you didn't intend.

One of the Top Web Security Threats

SQL injection becomes a greater threat when an attacker can use this to manipulate your SQL statements. For example, your application may allow a user to change their password:

SQL-Injection/anti/set-password.py
```
def set_password():
    userid = request.form["userid"]
    password = request.form["password"]

    # UNSAFE!
    query = f"""UPDATE Accounts
        SET password_hash = SHA2('{password}', 256)
        WHERE account_id = {userid}"""

    cursor.execute(query)
    cnx.commit()
    return "OK"
```

A clever attacker who can guess how the request parameters are used in your SQL statement can post a carefully chosen string to exploit it:

password=xyzzy&userid=123 OR TRUE

After interpolating the string from the userid parameter into your SQL expression, the string has changed the syntax of the statement. Now it changes the password for *every* account in the database, not for one specific account:

SQL-Injection/anti/set-password.sql
```
UPDATE Accounts SET password_hash = SHA2('xyzzy', 256)
WHERE account_id = 123 OR TRUE;
```

SQL injection works by changing the syntax of the SQL statement before the statement is parsed. As long as you insert dynamic portions to the statement before it's parsed, you have a risk of SQL injection.

There are countless ways a maliciously chosen string can alter the behavior of your SQL statements. It's limited only by the imagination of the attacker and your ability to protect your SQL statements.

The Quest for a Cure

Now that you know the threat of SQL injection, the next natural question is, what do you need to do to protect code from being exploited? You may have read a blog or an article that described some single technique and claimed it's the universal remedy against SQL injection. In reality, none of these techniques is proof against all forms of SQL injection, so you need to use all of them in different cases.

Escaping Values

The oldest way to protect SQL queries from accidental unmatched quote characters is to *escape* any quote characters to prevent them from becoming the end of the quoted string. In standard SQL, you can use two quote characters to make one literal quote character:

SQL-Injection/anti/ohare-escape.sql
```
SELECT * FROM Products WHERE product_name = 'O''Hare'
```

Most brands of database also support the backslash to escape the following quote character, just like most other programming languages do:

SQL-Injection/anti/ohare-escape.sql
```
SELECT * FROM Products WHERE product_name = 'O\'Hare'
```

The idea is that you transform application data before you interpolate it into SQL strings. Most SQL programming interfaces provide a convenience function.

The Python connector for MySQL provides a function called escape() for this purpose. The following example shows how this function is used:

SQL-Injection/anti/ohare-escape.py

```python
def get_products():
    product_name = cnx.converter.escape(request.args.get("name"))

    # SAFE!
    sql = f"SELECT * FROM Products WHERE product_name = '{product_name}'"

    cursor.execute(sql)
    return json.dumps(cursor.fetchall())
```

This technique reduces the risk of SQL injection resulting from unmatched quote characters within the dynamic content. However, it's an extra step to remember to escape the input every time you need to interpolate a variable into an SQL query, and it's an easy step to forget.

It's also useful only for values in quoted string literals in SQL. The following example shows using the escape function to protect the string input, but escaping special characters doesn't work for a variable that is used as a numeric literal.

SQL-Injection/anti/set-password-escape.py

```python
def set_password():
    userid = request.form["userid"]
    password = cnx.converter.escape(request.form["password"])

    # STILL UNSAFE!
    query = f"""UPDATE Accounts
        SET password_hash = SHA2('{password}', 256)
        WHERE account_id = {userid}"""

    cursor.execute(query)
    cnx.commit()
    return "OK"
```

If the userid input has malicious content, the query could still run as if it had been written like the following:

SQL-Injection/anti/set-password-escape.sql

```sql
UPDATE Accounts SET password_hash = SHA2('xyzzy', 256)
WHERE account_id = 123 OR TRUE
```

You can't compare a numeric column directly to a string containing digits in all brands of database. Some databases may implicitly cast the string to a sensible numeric equivalent, but in standard SQL you have to use the CAST() function deliberately to convert a string to a numeric data type.

There are also obscure corner cases where strings in non-ASCII character sets can pass through a function intended to escape the quote characters but leave unescaped quote characters intact.[6,7]

Query Parameters

The solution most frequently cited as a panacea to SQL injection is to use *query parameters*. Instead of interpolating dynamic values into your SQL string, leave *parameter placeholders* in the string as you prepare the query. Then provide a parameter value as you execute the prepared query.

The MySQL Connector for Python uses *%s* as placeholders in the following example. That connector also supports the *%(name)s* placeholder format if the parameter values are provided in a Python *dict* (a dict in Python is a set of key/value pairs, similar to a Hash in Ruby or Perl, or a HashMap in Java).

```
SQL-Injection/anti/parameter.py
name = request.args.get("name")
cnx.execute("SELECT * FROM Products WHERE product_name = %s", [name])
```

Many programmers recommend this solution because you don't have to escape dynamic content or worry about flawed escaping functions. In fact, query parameters are a very strong defense against SQL injection. Unfortunately, parameters aren't a universal solution because the value of a query parameter is always interpreted as a single literal value. The following list describes cases where dynamic SQL cannot use a parameter.

A list of values cannot be a single parameter:

```
SQL-Injection/anti/parameter.py
bugid_list = "1234,3456,5678"
cnx.execute("SELECT * FROM Bugs WHERE bug_id IN ( %s )", [bugid_list])
```

This works as though you provided a single string value composed of digits and commas, which doesn't work the same as a series of integers:

```
SQL-Injection/anti/parameter.sql
SELECT * FROM Bugs WHERE bug_id IN ( '1234,3456,5678' )
```

A table identifier cannot be a parameter:

```
SQL-Injection/anti/parameter.py
table = "Bugs"
cnx.execute("SELECT * FROM %s WHERE bug_id = 1234", [table])
```

This works as though you had entered a string literal in place of the table name, which is simply a syntax error:

---

6.   https://bugs.mysql.com/bug.php?id=8378
7.   https://shiflett.org/blog/2006/addslashes-versus-mysql-real-escape-string

```
SQL-Injection/anti/parameter.sql
SELECT * FROM 'Bugs' WHERE bug_id = 1234
```

A column identifier cannot be a parameter:

```
SQL-Injection/anti/parameter.py
column = "date_reported"
cnx.execute("SELECT * FROM Bugs ORDER BY %s", [column]);
```

In this example, the sort is a no-op, because the expression is a constant string, the same on every row:

```
SQL-Injection/anti/parameter.sql
SELECT * FROM Bugs ORDER BY 'date_reported';
```

An SQL keyword cannot be a parameter:

```
SQL-Injection/anti/parameter.py
keyword = "DESC"
cnx.execute("SELECT * FROM Bugs ORDER BY date_reported %s", [keyword]);
```

The parameter is interpreted as a literal string, not an SQL keyword. In this example, the result is a syntax error.

```
SQL-Injection/anti/parameter.sql
SELECT * FROM Bugs ORDER BY date_reported 'DESC'
```

What Was My Complete Query?

Many people think that using SQL query parameters is a way to quote values into an SQL statement automatically. This isn't accurate, and thinking about query parameters this way leads to misunderstanding about how they work.

The RDBMS server parses your SQL as you *prepare* the query. After this, nothing can change the syntax of that SQL query.

You provide values as you *execute* a prepared query. Each value you provide is used for each placeholder, one for one.

You can execute a prepared query again, substituting new parameter values for the old values. So, the RDBMS must keep track of the query and the parameter values separately. This is good for security.

This means that if you retrieve the prepared SQL query string, it doesn't contain any parameter values. It would be handy to see the SQL statement including parameter values if you're debugging or logging queries, but these values are never combined with the query in its human-readable SQL form.

Debug your dynamic SQL by logging both the query with parameter placeholders and the parameter values separately.

Stored Procedures

Use of stored procedures is another method that many software developers claim is proof against SQL injection vulnerabilities. Typically, stored procedures contain fixed SQL statements, parsed when you define the procedure.

However, it's possible to use dynamic SQL unsafely in stored procedures. In the following example, the input_userid argument is interpolated into the SQL query verbatim, which is unsafe.

```
SQL-Injection/anti/procedure.sql
CREATE PROCEDURE UpdatePassword(
  IN input_password VARCHAR(20),
  IN input_userid VARCHAR(20))
BEGIN
  SET @sql = CONCAT('UPDATE Accounts
    SET password_hash = SHA2(', QUOTE(input_password), ', 256)
    WHERE account_id = ', input_userid);
  PREPARE stmt FROM @sql;
  EXECUTE stmt;
END
```

Using dynamic SQL in a stored procedure is no more and no less safe than using dynamic SQL in application code. The input_userid argument can contain harmful content and produce an unsafe SQL statement:

```
SQL-Injection/anti/set-password.sql
UPDATE Accounts SET password_hash = SHA2('xyzzy', 256)
WHERE account_id = 123 OR TRUE;
```

Data Access Frameworks

You might see advocates of data access frameworks claim that their library protects your code from SQL injection risks. This is a false claim for any framework that allows you to write SQL statements as strings. This gives the wrong idea that merely using the framework means that unsafe coding habits magically become safe.

No framework can force you to write safe SQL code. A framework typically provides convenience functions to help you, but it's up to you to use them. It's easy to bypass these functions and use common string interpolation to build an SQL statement unsafely.

How to Recognize the Antipattern

Practically every database application builds SQL statements dynamically. If you build any portion of an SQL statement by concatenating strings together or interpolating variables into strings, then the statement potentially exposes your application to SQL injection attacks. SQL injection vulnerabilities are so common that you should assume that you have some in any application that uses SQL, unless you've just completed a code review specifically to find and correct these issues.

Legitimate Uses of the Antipattern

This antipattern is different from most of the others in this book, in that there aren't any legitimate reasons for allowing your application to have a security vulnerability because of SQL injection. It's your responsibility as a software developer to write code defensively and to help your peers to do so as well. Software is only as secure as its weakest link—make sure you're not responsible for that weakest link!

Solution: Trust No One

There is no single technique for securing your SQL code. You should learn all of the following techniques and use them in appropriate cases.

Filter Input

Instead of wondering whether some input contains harmful content, you should strip away any characters that aren't valid for that input.

For example, if you need an integer, use a function like int()() for simple cases like numbers:

SQL-Injection/soln/casting.py
```python
def get_products():
    bugid = int(request.args.get("bugid"))

    # SAFE!
    sql = f"SELECT * FROM Bugs WHERE bug_id = {bugid}"

    cursor.execute(sql)
    return json.dumps(cursor.fetchall())
```

Another type of filtering is to use regular expressions to match safe substrings. If the input doesn't match the regular expression, then don't use that input. Either transform the input, use a default value in place of the input, or else return an error.

SQL-Injection/soln/regexp.py
```python
def get_bugs():
    o = request.args.get("order")

    if re.search('^\w+$', o):
        sortorder = o
```

```
   else:
       sortorder = "date_reported"
   # SAFE!
   sql = f"SELECT * FROM Bugs ORDER BY {sortorder}"

   cursor.execute(sql)
   return json.dumps(cursor.fetchall())
```

❶ Assign the value of the GET request parameter *order* to a variable.

❷ Use a regular expression to check that the value is a string of one or more characters that are alphanumeric or _. If it does match that pattern, assign it to the sortorder variable.

❸ If the value does not match the regular expression pattern, assign a default value to sortorder.

❹ Format a string containing an SQL query, using a Python f-string to interpolate the variable. By this time, you know that the string is safe to use as a column name, because it's either the default value, or else at least it contains no quotes or other special characters.

Rule #31: Check the Back Seat

If you like to watch monster movies, you know that creatures like to hide behind the driver seat of your car and grab you after you get in. The lesson is that you shouldn't assume there's no danger inside a familiar space like your car.

SQL injection can take indirect forms. Any string could contain special characters, and thus be unsafe to use as-is in an SQL query. In the following example, a name is queried from the Accounts table, then interpolated into a fulltext search function.

SQL-Injection/anti/second-order.py
```
sql1 = "SELECT last_name FROM Accounts WHERE account_id = 123"
cursor.execute(sql1)

for row in cursor:
    # UNSAFE!
    sql2 = f"SELECT * FROM Bugs WHERE MATCH(description) AGAINST ('{row["last_name"]}')"
    cursor.execute(sql2)
    print(cursor.fetchall())
```

This could cause a problem in the previous query if the user had spelled their name as *O'Hara*. Just because the string was stored in your database doesn't "bless" it—the string could cause an error if you use it as part of a subsequent SQL query.

This type of SQL injection flaw is called *second-order SQL injection*. It usually only results in errors, but it has been used by malicious attackers too.

Parameterize Dynamic Values

When the dynamic parts of your query are simple values, you should use query parameters, as mentioned on page 245.

SQL-Injection/soln/parameter.py
```python
def set_password():
    userid = request.form["userid"]
    password = request.form["password"]

    # SAFE!
    sql = """UPDATE Accounts
        SET password_hash = SHA2(%s, 256)
        WHERE account_id = %s"""

    cursor.execute(sql, [password, userid])
    cnx.commit()
    return "OK"
```

The examples in the "Antipattern" section showed a parameter can substitute only for a single value, after the RDBMS has parsed the SQL statement. So, no attempted SQL injection attack can change the syntax in a parameterized query. Even if an attacker tries to use a malicious parameter value such as *123 OR TRUE*, the RDBMS interprets the parameter as a single string value. At worst, the query fails to apply to any rows; it's not likely to apply to the wrong rows.

The malicious value would result in a relatively safe SQL statement equivalent to the following:

SQL-Injection/soln/parameter.sql
```sql
UPDATE Accounts SET password_hash = SHA2('xyzzy', 256)
WHERE account_id = '123 OR TRUE'
```

It looks strange to compare the account_id to a string, but it does no harm. Because account_id is a numeric column, the string is cast to its numeric value, based on the leading digits *123*. The remaining characters are ignored.

You should use query parameters when you need to combine application variables as literal values in SQL expressions.

Quoting Dynamic Values

Query parameters are usually the best solution, but in rare cases a query with parameter placeholders causes the query optimizer to make odd decisions about which indexes to use.

For example, suppose you have a column in the Accounts table called is_active. This column stores a true value for 99 percent of the rows, giving it an uneven distribution of values. A query that searches for is_active = false would benefit from an index, but it would be a waste to read the index for a query searching for is_active = true. However, if you used a parameter in the expression is_active = %s, the optimizer can't know which value you will supply when you execute the prepared query, so it's liable to choose the wrong optimization plan.

It can be tricky to know when this optimizer variation happens. If you suspect the query is too slow (that is, you observed unsatisfactory performance in your application), then test the query execution plan with EXPLAIN (see Explain, on page 148), with both common and uncommon values, and see if the plan is different.

In exotic cases like this, it could be better to interpolate values directly into the SQL statement, in spite of the general recommendation to use query parameters. If you do this, you should quote the strings carefully.

SQL-Injection/soln/interpolate.py
```python
def get_account():
    account_name_escaped = cnx.converter.escape(request.args.get("name"))

    # SAFE!
    sql = f"""SELECT * FROM Accounts
        WHERE account_name = '{account_name_escaped}'"""

    cursor.execute(sql)
    return json.dumps(cursor.fetchall())
```

Make sure you use a function that is mature and well tested against obscure SQL security issues. Most data access libraries include such a string-quoting function. Don't try to implement your own quoting function unless you have studied the security risks thoroughly. Don't use functions that are irrelevant to SQL, for example, HTML entity encoding.

Isolate User Input from Code

Query parameters and escaping techniques help you combine literal values into SQL expressions, but they don't help with other parts of a statement, such as table or column identifiers or SQL keywords. You need another solution to make these parts of a query dynamic.

Suppose your users want to choose how to sort lists of bugs, for instance by status or by date created. They also want to choose the direction of sorting.

SQL-Injection/soln/orderby.sql
```sql
SELECT * FROM Bugs ORDER BY status ASC;

SELECT * FROM Bugs ORDER BY date_reported DESC;
```

> ## Parameterizing an IN() Predicate
>
> We've seen that you can't pass a comma-separated string in a single parameter. You need as many parameters as the number of items in your list.
>
> For example, say you need to query six bugs by their primary keys:
>
> SQL-Injection/soln/in-predicate.py
> ```python
> bug_list = [123, 234, 345, 456, 567, 678]
> sql = "SELECT * FROM Bugs WHERE bug_id IN (%s, %s, %s, %s, %s, %s)"
> cursor.execute(sql, bug_list)
> ```
>
> This works only if you have exactly six items in bug_list, matching the number of parameter placeholders. You should build the SQL IN predicate dynamically, using a number of placeholders equal to the number of items in bug_list.
>
> The following example produces an array of placeholders the same length as bug_list and then joins that array with commas before using it in the SQL expression.
>
> SQL-Injection/soln/in-predicate.py
> ```python
> bug_list = [123, 234, 345, 456, 567, 678]
> placeholders = ",".join(["%s"] * len(bug_list))
> sql = f"SELECT * FROM Bugs WHERE bug_id IN ({placeholders})"
> cursor.execute(sql, bug_list)
> ```

In the following example, a Python script accepts request parameters order and dir, and the code naively uses interpolation to use these inputs in the SQL query as a column name and a keyword.

SQL-Injection/soln/mapping.py
```python
def get_bugs_unsafe():
    sortorder = request.args.get("order")
    direction = request.args.get("dir")

    # UNSAFE!
    sql = f"SELECT * FROM Bugs ORDER BY {sortorder} {direction}"

    cursor.execute(sql)
    return json.dumps(cursor.fetchall())
```

The script assumes that the request input order contains the name of a column and that dir contains either ASC or DESC. This is not a safe assumption, because a user can send any parameter values in a web request.

Instead, you should look up the values of the inputs in a map, and then use the respective mapped values in your SQL query. The following code shows an example of this.

SQL-Injection/soln/mapping.py
```python
def get_bugs_safe():
```
❶   `sortorders = {"status": "status", "date": "date_reported"}`
❷   `directions = {"up": "ASC", "down": "DESC"}`

```
s = request.args.get("order")
if s in sortorders:
    sortorder = sortorders[s]
else:
    sortorder = "bug_id"

d = request.args.get("dir")
if d in directions:
    direction = directions[d]
else:
    direction = "ASC"

# SAFE!
sql = f"SELECT * FROM Bugs ORDER BY {sortorder} {direction}"

cursor.execute(sql)
return json.dumps(cursor.fetchall())
```

❶ Declare a Python dict sortorders, to map valid user choices as keys and SQL column names as values.

❷ Declare a Python dict directions, to map valid user choices as keys and SQL keywords ASC and DESC as values.

❸ If the user's choices match array keys in sortorders, then use the corresponding values. Otherwise use a default value.

❹ Likewise, if the user's choices match array keys in directions, then use the corresponding values. Otherwise use a default value.

❺ Now the sortorder and direction variables are safe to use in your SQL query, because they can contain only values you declared explicitly in your code.

This technique has several advantages:

• You never combine user input with your SQL query, so you reduce the risk of SQL injection.

• You can make any part of an SQL statement dynamic, including identifiers, SQL keywords, and even entire expressions.

• You have an easy and efficient way to validate user choices.

• You decouple the internal details of your queries from the user interface.

The choices are hard-coded in your application, but this is appropriate for table names, column names, and SQL keywords. Allowing arbitrary input is typical for data values, but not for identifiers or keywords.

Isn't It Harder to Use Query Parameters?

You've probably seen many code examples and tutorials that use string concatenation or variable interpolation for SQL queries. A score of programming books and blogs can't be wrong, right? Old habits die hard.

Using SQL query parameters is usually easier than the traditional code. The following old-school PHP example shows how an escaping function can be more trouble than it's worth, and how query parameters can improve it.

```
SQL-Injection/soln/concat.php
$sql = "INSERT INTO Accounts (account_id, account_name, email, password)
  VALUES (".intval($account_id)."."
  .mysqli_real_escape_string($conn, $account_name)."', '"
  .mysqli_real_escape_string($conn, $email)."' SHA256('"
  .mysqli_real_escape_string($conn, $password).", 256)";
mysqli_query($sql);
```

There are two missing quotes, a missing comma, and a missing parenthesis in the preceding example. How long does it take you find them? They're hard to spot because the SQL syntax is laced with PHP expressions. The double quotes open and close a PHP string repeatedly, and within the string, single quotes open and close SQL string literal syntax repeatedly. You might spend hours debugging code like this example. Compare with the following equivalent PHP code using query parameters.

```
SQL-Injection/soln/parameter-mysqli.php
$sql = "INSERT INTO Accounts (account_id, account_name, email, password)
  VALUES (?, ?, ?, SHA256(?, 256))";
$stmt = mysqli_prepare($conn, $sql);
mysqli_stmt_bind_param($stmt, "isss", $account_id, $account_name, $email, $password);
mysqli_stmt_execute($stmt);
```

This is much easier to write, easier to read, and easier to debug. You don't need quotes around the parameter placeholders, so you can't miss one. You can see mistyped commas and parentheses quickly. Another programmer who reads your code can understand the logic of the query more easily, too.

PHP's PDO extension makes using query parameters even more streamlined.

```
SQL-Injection/soln/parameter-pdo.php
$sql = "INSERT INTO Accounts (account_id, account_name, email, password)
  VALUES (?, ?, ?, SHA256(?, 256))";
$stmt = $pdo->prepare($sql);
$stmt->execute([$account_id, $account_name, $email, $password]);
```

Learning to use query parameters takes only a little effort, and once you do, it will make you more productive many times over. The reliable protection from SQL injection is only one of the benefits.

Get a Buddy to Review Your Code

The best way to catch flaws is to get another pair of eyes to look at it. Ask a teammate who is familiar with SQL injection risks to help you inspect your code. Don't let pride or ego keep you from doing the right thing—you may be embarrassed now over missing a coding mistake, but would you rather have to admit responsibility later for a security flaw that allowed hackers to exploit your website?

In an inspection for SQL injection, use the following guidelines:

1. Find SQL statements that are formed using application variables, string concatenation, or replacement.

2. Trace the origin of all dynamic content used in your SQL statements. Find any data that comes from an external source, such as user input, files, environment, web services, third-party code, or even a string fetched from the database.

3. Assume any external content is potentially hazardous. Use filters, validators, and mapping arrays to transform untrusted content.

4. Combine external data into your SQL statements using query parameters or robust escaping functions.

5. Don't forget to inspect your stored procedures and other places where you may find dynamic SQL statements.

Code inspection is the most accurate and economical way to find SQL Injection flaws. You should budget your time for this and treat it as a mandatory activity. You can also return the favor by inspecting your teammates' code.

You may also use an SQL query log or an application performance monitoring (APM) technology to watch for unexpected SQL queries, which could be the result of SQL injection attacks.

> Let users input values, but never let users input code.

Mini-Antipattern: Query Parameters inside Quotes

"Why does my query fail to find any data when I use a parameterized query? When I interpolate a variable into the SQL string, it works."

A common mistake is to put the query parameter placeholder inside quotes (the following example uses ? as the placeholder, the default for MySQL):

```
SELECT * FROM Bugs WHERE bug_id = '?'
```

This treats the question mark symbol as a string literal, not a parameter placeholder. The bug_id, being an integer, is compared to the numeric value of the string literal, which is zero. In this table, the bug_id values start at 1, so a value of zero will not match any row.

If you think about it, it must do this, because otherwise there would be no way to use a plain question mark character in a string.

```
SELECT * FROM Bugs WHERE summary = 'Is this a bug?'
```

This also comes up when programmers want to combine a query parameter with some literal text. The following example shows a case where the intent is to add the % wildcards before and after the query parameter placeholder, for a pattern-matching expression with LIKE:

```
SELECT * FROM Bugs WHERE summary LIKE '%?%'
```

You must treat the parameter placeholder as its own token in the query syntax. It behaves as if it were a string literal. You can use it in an expression, such as string concatenation:

```
SELECT * FROM Bugs WHERE summary LIKE CONCAT('%', ?, '%')
```

Alternatively, you could use a placeholder alone in the query, and pass a parameter value that is the result of a string formatting expression in your client application code. The following Python example uses an f-string to sandwich a variable with % wildcards before and after, then passes the resulting string as the query parameter.

```
query = "SELECT * FROM Bugs WHERE summary LIKE %s"
pattern = f"%{word}%"
cursor.execute(query, [pattern])
```

Notice the placeholder in the query is not inside single quotes.

Those who matter don't mind, and those who mind don't matter.

> *Bernard Baruch (on seating arrangements for his dinner party guests)*

## CHAPTER 22

Pseudokey Neat-Freak

Your manager approaches you, holding two report printouts. "The bean counters are saying we have discrepancies between this quarter's report and last quarter's. I'm looking at them, and they're absolutely right. Most of the later assets have disappeared. What happened?"

You look at the reports, and the pattern of discrepancies rings a bell. "No, everything is still there. You asked me to clean up the rows in the database so there are no missing rows. You said the accountants kept asking you questions about missing assets, because of gaps in the numbering.

"So, I renumbered some of the rows to make them all fit into the places where there were missing rows before. There aren't any missing rows now—every number between 1 and about 12,340 is used. They're all still there, but some have just changed number and moved up. You told me to do this."

Your manager shakes his head. "But that's not what I want. The accountants have to track depreciation by the asset numbers. The number for each piece of equipment has to stay the same in each quarterly report. Besides, all the asset ID numbers are printed on labels on each piece. It'd take weeks to relabel everything in the company. Can you please change all the ID numbers back to their original values?"

You want to be cooperative, so you turn back to your keyboard to start working, but suddenly you think of a new problem. "What about new assets we bought this month, after I consolidated the asset IDs? The new assets have been assigned ID values that were in use before I did the renumbering. If I change the asset IDs back to their old values, what should I do about the duplicates?"

Objective: Tidy Up the Data

There's a certain type of person who is unnerved by a gap in a series.

bug_id	status	product_name
1	OPEN	Open RoundFile
2	FIXED	ReConsider
4	OPEN	ReConsider

On one hand, it's understandable to be concerned, because it's unclear what happened to the row with bug_id 3. Why didn't the query return that bug? Did the database lose it? What was in that bug? Was the bug reported by one of our important customers? Am I going to be held responsible for the lost data?

The objective of one who practices the *Pseudokey Neat-Freak* antipattern is to resolve these troubling questions. This person is accountable for data integrity issues, but typically they don't have enough understanding of, or confidence in, the database technology to feel confident of the report results.

Antipattern: Filling in the Corners

There are two ways you might fill the perceived gap.

Assigning Numbers Out of Sequence

Instead of allocating a new primary key value using the automatic pseudokey mechanism, you might want to make any new row use the first unused primary key value. This way, as you insert data, you naturally make gaps fill in.

bug_id	status	product_name
1	OPEN	Open RoundFile
2	FIXED	ReConsider
4	OPEN	ReConsider
3	NEW	Visual TurboBuilder

However, you have to run an unnecessary self-join query to find the lowest unused value:

```
Neat-Freak/anti/lowest-value.sql
SELECT b1.bug_id + 1
FROM Bugs b1
LEFT OUTER JOIN Bugs AS b2 ON (b1.bug_id + 1 = b2.bug_id)
WHERE b2.bug_id IS NULL
ORDER BY b1.bug_id LIMIT 1;
```

Earlier in the book, we looked at a concurrency issue when you try to allocate a unique primary key value by running a query such as SELECT MAX(bug_id)+1 FROM Bugs (see Special Scope for Sequences, on page 46). This has the same flaw when two applications may try to find the lowest unused value at the same time. As both try to use the same value as a primary key value, one succeeds, and the other gets an error. This method is both inefficient and prone to errors.

Renumbering Existing Rows

You might find it's more urgent to make the primary key values be contiguous, and waiting for new rows to fill in the gaps won't fix the issue quickly enough. You might think to use a strategy of updating the key values of existing rows to eliminate gaps and make all the values contiguous. This usually means you find the row with the highest primary key value and update it with the lowest unused value. For example, you could update the value 4 to 3:

Neat-Freak/anti/renumber.sql
```
UPDATE Bugs SET bug_id = 3 WHERE bug_id = 4;
```

bug_id	status	product_name
1	NEW	Open RoundFile
2	FIXED	ReConsider
3	DUPLICATE	ReConsider

To accomplish this, you need to find an unused key value using a method similar to the previous one for inserting new rows. You also need to run the UPDATE statement to reassign the primary key value. Either one of these steps is susceptible to concurrency issues. You need to repeat the steps many times to fill a wide gap in the numbers.

You must also propagate the changed value to all child records that reference the rows you renumber. This is easiest if you declared foreign keys with the ON UPDATE CASCADE option, but if you didn't, you would have to disable constraints, update all child records manually, and restore the constraints. This is a laborious, error-prone process that can interrupt service in your database, so if you feel you want to avoid it, you're right.

Even if you do accomplish this cleanup, it's short lived. When a pseudokey generates a new value, the value is greater than the last value it generated (even if the row with that value has since been deleted or changed), *not* the highest value currently in the table, as some database programmers assume. Suppose you update the row with the greatest bug_id value 4 to the lower unused value to fill a gap. The next row you insert using the default pseudokey generator will allocate 5, leaving a new gap at 4.

Manufacturing Data Discrepancies

The story at the beginning of this chapter describes some hazards of renumbering primary key values. If another system external to your database depends on identifying rows by their primary keys, then your updates invalidate the data references in that system.

It's not a good idea to reuse the row's primary key value, because a gap could be the result of deleting or rolling back a row for a good reason. For example, suppose a user with account_id 789 is barred from your system for sending offensive emails. Your policies require you to delete the offender's account, but if you recycle primary keys, you would subsequently assign 789 to another user. Since some offensive emails are still waiting to be read by some recipients, you could get further complaints about *account 789*. Through no fault of his own, the poor user who now has that number catches the blame.

Don't reallocate pseudokey values just because they seem to be unused.

How to Recognize the Antipattern

The following quotes can be hints that someone in your organization is about to use the Pseudokey Neat-Freak antipattern.

- "How can I reuse an autogenerated identity value after I roll back an insert?"

  Pseudokey allocation doesn't roll back; if it did, the RDBMS would have to allocate pseudokey values within the scope of a transaction. This would cause either race conditions or blocking when multiple clients are inserting data concurrently.

- "What happened to bug_id 4?"

  This is an expression of misplaced anxiety over unused numbers in the sequence of primary keys.

- "How can I query for the first unused ID?"

  The reason to do this search is almost certainly to reassign the ID.

- "What if I run out of numbers?"

  This is used as a justification for reallocating unused ID values. See Mini-Antipattern: Is a BIGINT Big Enough?, on page 51.

Legitimate Uses of the Antipattern

There's no reason to change the value of a pseudokey, since the value should have no significance anyway. If the values in the primary key column carry some meaning, then this column is a *natural key*, not a pseudokey. It's not unusual to change values in a natural key.

Solution: Get Over It

The values in any primary key must be unique and non-null so you can use them to reference individual rows, but that's the only rule—they don't have to be consecutive numbers to identify rows.

Numbering Rows

Pseudokey generators return numbers that look almost like row numbers, because they're *monotonically increasing* (each successive value is one greater than the preceding value), but this is only a coincidence of their implementation. Generating values in this way is a convenient way to ensure uniqueness.

Don't confuse row numbers with primary keys. A primary key identifies one row in one table, whereas row numbers identify rows in a result set. Row numbers in a query result set don't correspond to primary key values in the table, especially when you use query operations like JOIN, GROUP BY, or ORDER BY.

There are good reasons to use row numbers, for example, to return a subset of rows from a query result. This is often called *pagination*, like a page of an Internet search. To select a subset in this way, use true row numbers that are increasing and consecutive, regardless of the form of the query.

SQL:2003 specifies *window functions* including ROW_NUMBER(), which returns consecutive numbers specific to a query result set. A common use of row numbering is to limit the query result to a range of rows:

```
Neat-Freak/soln/row_number.sql
SELECT t1.* FROM
  (SELECT a.account_name, b.bug_id, b.summary,
    ROW_NUMBER() OVER (ORDER BY a.account_name, b.date_reported) AS rn
   FROM Accounts a JOIN Bugs b ON (a.account_id = b.reported_by)) AS t1
WHERE t1.rn BETWEEN 51 AND 100;
```

These functions are now supported by nearly every popular brand of SQL database.

Using GUIDs

You could also generate random pseudokey values, as long as you don't use any number more than once. Some databases support a *globally unique identifier* (GUID) for this purpose.

A GUID is a pseudorandom number of 128 bits (usually represented by at least 32 hexadecimal digits). For practical purposes, a GUID is unique, so you can use it to generate a pseudokey.

The following example uses Microsoft SQL Server 2005 syntax:

```
Neat-Freak/soln/uniqueidentifier-sql2005.sql
CREATE TABLE Bugs (
  bug_id UNIQUEIDENTIFIER DEFAULT NEWID(),
  -- . . .
);

INSERT INTO Bugs (bug_id, summary)
VALUES (DEFAULT, 'crashes when I save');
```

This creates a row like the following:

bug_id	summary
0xff19966f868b11d0b42d00c04fc964ff	Crashes when I save

Using GUIDs has at least two advantages over pseudokey generators:

- You can generate pseudokeys on multiple database servers concurrently without using the same values.

- No one will complain about gaps—they'll be too busy complaining about typing thirty-two hex digits for primary key values.

The latter point leads to some of the disadvantages:

- The values are long and hard to type.

- The values are random, so you can't infer any pattern or rely on a greater value indicating a more recent row.

- Storing a GUID requires at least 16 binary bytes. This takes more space and runs more slowly than using a typical 4-byte integer pseudokey.

The Most Important Problem

Now that you know the problems caused by renumbering pseudokeys and some alternative solutions for related goals, you still have one big problem to solve: how do you fend off an order from a boss who wants you to tidy up the database by closing the gaps in a pseudokey? This is a problem of communication, not technology. Nevertheless, you might need to *manage your manager* to defend the data integrity of your database.

- *Explain the technology.* Honesty is usually the best policy. Be respectful and acknowledge the request. For example, tell your manager this:

  "The gaps do look strange, but they're harmless. It's normal for rows to be skipped, rolled back, or deleted from time to time. We allocate a new number for each new row in the database, instead of writing code to figure out which old numbers we can reuse safely. This makes our code cheap to develop, makes it faster to run, and reduces errors."

- *Be clear about the costs.* Changing the primary key values seems like a trivial task, but you should give realistic estimates for the work to calculate new values, write and test code to handle duplicate values, cascade changes throughout the database, investigate the impact to other systems, and train users and administrators to manage the new procedures.

  Most managers prioritize based on cost of a task, and they should back down from requesting frivolous, micro-optimizing work when they're confronted with the real cost.

  If the manager still wants you to do this, then ask them if this should delay your other assignments. Remind them of the other tasks you would need to postpone, and ask if your manager still thinks renumbering pseudokeys rises to the top of that list.

- *Use natural keys.* If your manager or other users of the database insist on interpreting meaning in the primary key values, then let there be meaning. Don't use pseudokeys—use a string or a number that encodes some identifying meaning. Then it's easier to explain any gaps within the context of the meaning of these natural keys.

  You can also use both a pseudokey and another attribute column you use as a natural identifier. Hide the pseudokey from reports if gaps in the numeric sequence make readers anxious.

> Use pseudokeys as unique row identifiers; they're not row numbers.

Mini-Antipattern: Auto-Increment per Group

"I need an auto-increment column, but it must start over at 1 for each subgroup of rows."

This request takes many forms. Rankings of sports players per team, or per year. Invoices per customer. Regardless of the reason for it, there are a few problems with this requirement.

First, allocating new incremental values becomes more complex. Inserting a row needs to check the most recent value generated for the same subgroup, which means blocking concurrent inserts while it examines the current set of rows. This can result in a bottleneck and hinder fast inserts.

An alternative is that inserts must create new sequence generators on the fly, for each new subgroup. This might lead to an explosion in the number of sequence generators. If the subgroups each have just one row, then there will be as many sequence generators as rows in the table itself.

Second, numbering rows per subgroup sounds like it will serve as an ordinal ranking. Remember that pseudokeys are intended to be unique, but it's more difficult to ensure they use consecutive values. If rows are deleted, or transactions rolled back, the consecutive values must be reassigned, possibly for many rows.

A better solution is to number rows when you query them, which is easy to do with the ROW_NUMBER() window function. This ensures that you get a sequence of ordinal integers with no gaps, restarting for each subgroup defined by the PARTITION BY option.

```
SELECT bug_id, author, comment,
  ROW_NUMBER() OVER (PARTITION BY bug_id
    ORDER BY comment_date) AS comment_number
FROM Comments;
```

It is a capital mistake to theorize before you have all the evidence.

> Sherlock Holmes

## CHAPTER 23

See No Evil

"I found *another* bug in your product," the voice on the phone said.

I got this call while working as a technical support engineer for an SQL RDBMS product. We had one customer who was well known for making spurious reports against our database. Nearly all of his reports turned out to be simple mistakes on his part, not bugs.

"Good morning, Mr. Davis. Of course, we'd like to fix any problem you find," I answered. "Can you tell me what happened?"

"I ran a query against your database, and nothing came back." Mr. Davis said sharply. "But I know the data is in the database—I can verify it in a test script."

"Was there any problem with your query?" I asked. "Did the API return any error or warning?"

Davis replied, "Why would I look at the return value of an API function? The function should just run my SQL query. If it returns an error, that indicates your product has a bug in it. If your product didn't have bugs, there would be no errors. I shouldn't have to work around your bugs."

I was stunned, but I had to let the facts speak for themselves. "OK, let's try a test. Copy and paste the *exact* SQL query from your code into the query tool, and run it. What does it say?" I waited for him.

"Syntax error at SELCET." After a pause, he said, "You can close this issue," and he hung up abruptly.

Mr. Davis was the sole developer for an air traffic control company, writing software that logged data about international airplane flights. We heard from him every week.

Objective: Write Less Code

Everyone wants to write *elegant code*. That is, we want to do cool work with less code. The cooler the work is and the less code it takes us, the greater the ratio of elegance. If we can't make our work cooler, it stands to reason that at least we can improve the elegance ratio (the ratio of coolness to code volume) by doing the same work in fewer lines of code.

That's a superficial reason, but there are better reasons to write concise code:

- We'll finish coding a working application more quickly.
- We'll have less code to test, to document, or to have peer reviewed.
- We'll have fewer bugs if we have fewer lines of code.

It's therefore an instinctive priority for programmers to eliminate any code they can, especially if that code fails to increase coolness.

Antipattern: Making Bricks Without Straw

Developers commonly practice the See No Evil antipattern in two forms: first, ignoring the return values of a database API, and second, reading fragments of SQL code interspersed with application code. In both cases, developers fail to use information that is easily available to them.

Diagnoses Without Diagnostics

The following code example contains errors, but no error checking.

```
See-No-Evil/anti/no-check.py
import mysql.connector
```
❶
```
cnx = mysql.connector.connect(user='scottt', database='test')

cursor = cnx.cursor()

query = '''SELCET bug_id, summary, date_reported FROM Bugs
    WHERE assigned_to = %s AND status = %s'''

parameters = (1, 'NEW')
```
❷
```
cursor.execute(query, parameters)

for row in cursor:
    print(row)
```

This code is concise, but there are several places in this code where status values returned from functions could indicate a problem. You'll never know about it if you ignore the return values.

Probably the most common error from a database API occurs when you try to create a database connection, for example at ❶. You could accidentally mistype the database name or server hostname or you could use the wrong user or password, or the database server could be down or unreachable. Depending on the language and database connector, such an accident may throw an exception, which would terminate the example script. In other languages, exceptions are not thrown, but the result of the connection is an invalid object.

The mistake in the username used in the previous Python example results in an error like the following:

```
mysql.connector.errors.ProgrammingError: 1045 (28000):
Access denied for user 'scottt'@'localhost'
```

If you fix the misspelled username, then the call to execute() at ❷ could throw an exception if you have a simple syntax error caused by a typo, an imbalanced parenthesis, or a misspelled column name.

```
mysql.connector.errors.ProgrammingError: 1064 (42000):
You have an error in your SQL syntax;
check the manual that corresponds to your MySQL server version
for the right syntax to use near 'SELCET bug_id, ...
```

Programmers with attitudes like Mr. Davis aren't uncommon. They may feel that checking return values and exceptions adds nothing to their code, because those cases aren't supposed to happen anyway. Also, the extra code is repetitive and makes an application ugly and hard to read. Checking errors definitely adds no coolness, but it does add lines of code, so unfortunately it reduces the ratio of coolness to lines of code.

Users don't see the code; they only see the output. When a fatal error goes unhandled, the user may see an incomprehensible exception message, or a blank white screen:

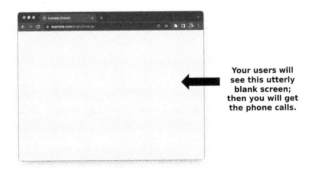

Your users will see this utterly blank screen; then you will get the phone calls.

When this happens, it's no consolation that the code is tidy and concise.

Lines Between the Reading

Another common bad habit that fits the See No Evil antipattern is to debug by staring at application code that builds an SQL query as a string. This is difficult because it's hard to visualize the resulting SQL string after you build it with application logic, string concatenation, and extra content from application variables.

Trying to debug in this way is like trying to solve a jigsaw puzzle without looking at the photo on the box.

For a simple example, let's look at a type of question I see frequently from developers. The following code builds a query conditionally by concatenating a WHERE clause if the script needs to search for a specific bug instead of a collection of bugs.

See-No-Evil/anti/white-space.py
```python
import mysql.connector

bug_id = int(input() or '0')

cnx = mysql.connector.connect(user='scott', database='test')

cursor = cnx.cursor()

query = '''SELECT * FROM Bugs'''

parameters = tuple()

if bug_id > 0:
    query = query + '''WHERE bug_id = %s'''
    parameters = parameters + (bug_id,)

cursor.execute(query, parameters)

for row in cursor:
    print(row)
```

Why would the query in this example give an error? The answer is clearer if you look at the full query string resulting from the concatenation:

See-No-Evil/anti/white-space.sql
```sql
SELECT * FROM BugsWHERE bug_id = 1234
```

There's no whitespace between Bugs and WHERE, which gives the query invalid syntax, as though it were reading a table called BugsWHERE, followed by an SQL expression in an invalid context. The code has concatenated the strings with no space between them.

Developers waste an unbelievable amount of time and energy trying to debug problems like this by looking at the code that builds the SQL, instead of looking at the SQL itself.

How to Recognize the Antipattern

Though you might think that it's difficult to spot code when it is missing, modern IDE products highlight code when it ignores a function's return value, or neglects to handle a checked exception. You might also recognize the See No Evil antipattern from the following phrases:

- "My program crashes after I query the database."

  Often the crash happens because your query failed, and you tried to use the result in an illegal manner, such as calling a method on a nonobject or dereferencing a null pointer.

- "Can you help me find my SQL error? Here's my code..."

  First, start by looking at the SQL, not the code that builds it.

- "I don't bother cluttering up my code with error handling."

  Some computer scientists have estimated that up to 50 percent of the lines of code in a robust application are devoted to handling error cases. This may seem like a lot, unless you think of all the steps that you could include under error handling: detecting, classifying, reporting, and compensating. You can also get a feel for the variety of errors by examining your automated tests, and counting how many unit test cases are required to validate handling of all the potential error cases. It's important for any software to be able to do all that.

Legitimate Uses of the Antipattern

You can omit error checking when there's really nothing for you to do in response to the error. For example, the close() function for a database connection returns a status, but if your application is about to finish and exit anyway, it's likely that the resources for that connection will be cleaned up regardless.

Exceptions in object-oriented languages allow you to trigger an exception without being responsible for handling it. Your code trusts that whatever code called yours is the code that's responsible for handling the exception. Your code can then allow the exception to pass back up the calling stack.

Solution: Recover from Errors Gracefully

Anyone who enjoys dancing knows that missteps are inevitable. The secret to remaining graceful is to know how to recover. Give yourself a chance to notice the cause of the mistake. Then you can react quickly and seamlessly, getting back into rhythm before anyone has noticed your gaffe.

Maintain the Rhythm

Checking return status and exceptions from database API calls is the best way to ensure that you haven't missed a step. The following example shows code that checks the status after each call that could cause an error:

See-No-Evil/soln/check.py

```python
import mysql.connector
from mysql.connector import errorcode

try:
    cnx = mysql.connector.connect(user='scott', database='test')
❶ except mysql.connector.Error as err: # check for errors
    if err.errno == errorcode.ER_ACCESS_DENIED_ERROR:
        print("Something is wrong with your user name or password")
    elif err.errno == errorcode.ER_BAD_DB_ERROR:
        print("Database does not exist")
    else:
        print(err)

cursor = cnx.cursor()

try:
    query = '''SELECT bug_id, summary, date_reported FROM Bugs
        WHERE assigned_to = %s AND status = %s'''
    parameters = (1, 'NEW')
    cursor.execute(query, parameters)
❷ except mysql.connector.Error as err:
    print(err)
```

The code at ❶ catches the exception that is thrown if a database connection fails, and outputs the exception message. It's even better to log the SQL exception for the developer to inspect, and show a more friendly message to the user instead. Likewise, you should handle exceptions for the query execution, as shown at ❷.

Retrace Your Steps

It's also important to use the actual SQL query to debug a problem, instead of the code that produces an SQL query. Many simple mistakes, such as misspellings or imbalanced quotes or parentheses, are apparent instantly, even though they're obscure and puzzling otherwise.

- Build your SQL query in a variable, instead of building it ad hoc in the arguments of the API method to prepare the query. This will give you the opportunity to examine the variable before you use it.

- Choose a place to output SQL that is not part of your application output, such as a log file, an IDE debugger console, or a browser extension to show diagnostic output.

- Do not print the SQL query within HTML comments of a web application's output. Any user can view your page source. Reading the SQL query gives hackers a lot of knowledge about your database structure.

Using an object-relational mapping (ORM) framework that builds and executes SQL queries transparently can make debugging harder, because the SQL query is generated on the fly by the ORM code. Some ORM frameworks solve this by sending generated SQL to a log. A common example for most web application languages is that the code errors are output to the http server error log. You should learn which log is used by your language in your code environment, and watch the log while you are debugging.

Finally, most database brands provide their own logging mechanism on the database servers instead of in application client code. If you can't enable SQL logging in the application, you can still monitor queries as the database server executes them.

> Assume any line of code will fail, instead of assuming it will work. You need to collect information about the nature and cause of the failure before you can troubleshoot it.

Mini-Antipattern: Reading Syntax Error Messages

In the case of SQL syntax errors, MySQL provides useful information: exactly what part of the SQL query followed the part where the syntax parser got confused or was expecting something different.

In Mini-Antipattern: Reserved Words, on page 128, you saw how a query that uses a reserved keyword in an unexpected position can result in a syntax error. Other types of syntax errors can be caused by missing keywords, extra keywords, or mistakes using punctuation.

The following should use the ORDER BY syntax, but the keyword BY is missing.

```
SELECT * FROM Bugs ORDER date_reported;
                          ^ error starts here
```

> ERROR 1064 (42000): You have an error in your SQL syntax; check the manual that corresponds to your MySQL server version for the right syntax to use near 'date_reported' at line 1

The following shows a misunderstanding about how to write an expression in a WHERE clause; the WHERE keyword should appear only once, followed by a boolean expression.

```
SELECT * FROM Bugs WHERE status = 'NEW' AND WHERE assigned_to = 123;
                                            ^ error starts here
```

> ERROR 1064 (42000): You have an error in your SQL syntax; check the manual that corresponds to your MySQL server version for the right syntax to use near 'WHERE assigned_to = 1' at line 1

The next example shows the syntax parser got confused at the very end of the query, because it ended without closing the parentheses. Since the error occurs at the end of the query, what follows is an empty string. You saw in the previous example that the excerpt following the mistake is shown between single quotes. Since the excerpt after the end of a query is an empty string, the following error message shows two single quotes with nothing inside.

```
SELECT * FROM Bugs WHERE (status = 'NEW';
                                        ^ error starts here
```

> ERROR 1064 (42000): You have an error in your SQL syntax; check the manual that corresponds to your MySQL server version for the right syntax to use near '' at line 1

In each case, you should inspect the query carefully at the point where the error message indicates, and you'll have a lead on what part you need to fix.

Error messages are often hard to understand. Some are worse than others (for example, Oracle's error messages are famously bad), but you should try to learn what you can from them.

If it's not written down, it didn't happen.

> common aphorism

## CHAPTER 24

Diplomatic Immunity

One of my earliest jobs gave me a lesson in the importance of using software engineering best practices, after a tragic accident left me responsible for an important database application.

I interviewed for a contract job at Hewlett-Packard to develop and maintain an application on UNIX, written in C with HP ALLBASE/SQL. The manager and staff interviewing me told me sadly that their programmer who had worked on that application was killed in a traffic accident. No one else in their department knew how to use UNIX or anything about the application.

After I started the job, I found that the developer had never written documentation or tests for this application, and he never used a version control system for his code, or even code comments. All his code resided in a single directory, including code that was part of the live system, code that was under development, and code that was no longer used.

This project had high *technical debt*—a consequence of using shortcuts instead of best practices. Technical debt causes risk and extra work in a project until you pay it off by refactoring, testing, and documenting.

I worked for six months to organize and document the code for what was really a fairly modest application, because I had to spend a lot of my time supporting its users and continuing development.

There was obviously no way that I could ask my predecessor to help me come up to speed on the project. The experience really demonstrated the impact of letting technical debt get out of control.

Objective: Employ Best Practices

Professional programmers strive to use good software engineering habits in their projects, such as the following:

- Keeping application code under version control using tools such as Git or Subversion.

- Developing and running automated unit tests or functional tests for applications.

- Writing code with documentation, specifications, comments, and consistent code style to support the requirements, implementation strategies, operation, and maintenance of an application.

The time you take to develop software using best practices is a net win, because it reduces a lot of needless or repetitive work. Most experienced developers know that sacrificing these practices for the sake of expediency is a recipe for failure.

Antipattern: Make SQL a Second-Class Citizen

Even among developers who accept best practices when developing application code, there's a tendency to think of database code as exempt from these practices. This antipattern is called *Diplomatic Immunity* because it assumes that the rules of application development don't apply to database development.

Developers make this assumption for a variety of reasons:

- The role of software engineer and database administrator are separate in some companies. The DBA typically works with several teams of programmers, so there's a perception that they're not a full-time member of any one of these teams. They're treated like a visitor, and they're not subject to the same responsibilities as the software engineers.

- The SQL language used for relational databases differs from conventional programming. Even the way you invoke SQL statements as a specialized language within application code suggests a kind of guest-like status.

- Advanced IDE tools are popular for application code languages, making editing, testing, and version control quick and painless. But tools for database development are not as advanced, or at least not as widely used. Developers can code applications with best practices easily, but applying these practices to SQL feels clumsy by comparison. Developers tend to find other things to do.

- In IT, it's ordinary for knowledge and operation of the database to be focused on one person—the DBA. Because the DBA is the only one who has access to the database server, they serve as a living knowledge base and version control system.

The database is the foundation of an application, and quality matters. You know how to develop application code with high quality, but you may be building your application on top of a database that has failed to solve the needs of the project or that no one understands. The risk is that you're developing an application only to find that you have to scrap it.

How to Recognize the Antipattern

You might think it's hard to show evidence of not doing something, but that isn't always true. The following are some telltale signs of cutting corners:

- "We are adopting the new engineering process—that is, a lightweight version of it."

  Lightweight in this context means that the team intends to skip some tasks that the engineering process calls for. Some of these may be legitimate to skip, but it could also be a euphemism for not following important best practices.

- "We don't need the DBA staff to attend training for our new version control system, since they don't use it anyway."

  Excluding some technical team members from training (and probably access) *ensures* that they won't use those tools.

- "How can we track which tables and columns contain *personally identifiable information* (PII) or *sensitive personal information* (SPI)? We have to prove that we are handling sensitive data correctly, to comply with audits and privacy laws."

  Data privacy is now a very important topic even for small businesses. If you don't keep accurate and current documentation for your database schema, you have to resort to treating all the data as sensitive. This makes your project more costly, because it adds continual work and expense for ensuring compliance and paying for storage to retain data.

- "Is there a tool to compare two database schemas, report the differences, and create a script to alter one to reconcile with the other?"

  If you don't follow a process of deploying changes to database schema, they can get out of sync, and then it's a complicated task to bring them back into order.

- "My code is self-documenting."

  This is often given as an excuse for absent documentation or code comments. This has become a cliché, but it's hardly ever true.

Legitimate Uses of the Antipattern

While documentation, tests, and version control are good habits for any code you want to use more than once, you may also write code that is truly ad hoc, such as a one-time test of an API function, or code you write as a proof of concept or to teach a colleague some technique.

A quick test for whether code is really temporary is to delete it immediately after you've used it. If you can't bring yourself to do that, then it's probably worth keeping. If it's worth keeping, then you should commit it in a version control repository and write at least some brief notes about what the code is for and how to use it.

As a compromise, some developers have the habit of storing ad hoc code in a "gist," or a special repository for code or notes for which they haven't found a more official home.

Solution: Establish a Big-Tent Culture of Quality

Quality is simply testing to most software developers, but that's only *quality control*—just a part of the story. The full life cycle of software engineering involves *quality assurance*, which includes three parts:

1. Specify project requirements and deliverables clearly and in writing.
2. Design and develop a solution for your requirements.
3. Validate and test that your solution matches the requirements.

You need to do all three of these to perform QA correctly, although in some software methodologies, you don't necessarily have to do them in that order.

You can achieve quality assurance in database development by following best practices in *documentation*, *source code version control*, and *testing*.

Exhibit A: Documentation

There's no such thing as self-documenting code. Although it's true that a skilled programmer can decipher most code through a combination of careful analysis and experimentation, this is laborious (if code were readable, one wouldn't call it *code*). Also, code can't tell you about missing features or unsolved problems.

You should document the requirements and implementation of a database just as you do application code. Whether you're the original designer of the database or you're inheriting a database designed by someone else, use the following checklist to document a database:

Entity-relationship diagram: The single most important piece of documentation for a database is an ER diagram showing the tables and their relationships. Several chapters in this book use a simple form of ER diagrams. More complex ER diagrams have notation for columns, keys, indexes, and other database objects.

Some diagramming software packages include elements for ER diagram notation. Some tools can even reverse-engineer an SQL script or a live database and produce an ER diagram.

One caveat is that databases can be complex and have so many tables that it's impractical to use a single diagram. In this case, you should decompose it into several diagrams. Usually you can choose natural sub-groups of tables so each diagram is readable enough to be useful and not overwhelming to the reader.

Tables, columns, and views: You also need written documentation for your database, because an ER diagram isn't the right format to describe the purpose and usage of each table, column, and other object.

Tables need a description of what type of entity the table models. For example, Bugs, Products, and Accounts are pretty clear, but what about a lookup table like BugStatus or an intersection table like BugsProducts or a dependent table like Comments? Also, how many rows do you anticipate each table to have? What queries against this table do you expect?

Columns each have a name and a data type, but that doesn't tell the reader what the column's values mean, or what values make sense in that column (it's probably not every value allowed for the data type). For columns storing a quantitative value, the unit of measurement should be clear. Does the column allow nulls or not, and why?

Views store frequently used queries against one or more tables. What made it worthwhile to create a given view? What application or user is expected to use the view? Was the view intended to abstract a complex relationship of tables? Was it intended to allow unprivileged users to run prescribed queries? Is the view updatable?

Relationships: Referential integrity constraints implement dependencies between tables, but this might not tell everything that you intend the constraints to model. For example, Bugs.reported_by is not nullable, but Bugs.assigned_to is nullable. Does that mean a bug can be fixed before it's assigned? If not, when must the bug be assigned?

In some cases, you may have implicit relationships but no constraints for them. Without documentation, it's hard to know where these relationships exist.

Triggers: Data validation, data transformation, and logging database changes are examples of tasks for a trigger. What business rules are you implementing in triggers?

Stored procedures: Document your stored procedures like an API. What problem is the procedure solving? Does a procedure perform any changes to data? What are the data types and meanings of the input and output parameters? Do you intend the procedure to replace a certain type of query to eliminate a performance bottleneck? Do you use the procedure to grant unprivileged users access to privileged tables?

SQL Security: What database users do you define for applications to use? What access privileges do each of these users have? What SQL roles do you provide, and which users can use them? Are any users designated for specific tasks, such as backups or reports? What system-level security provisions do you use, such as if the client must reach the RDBMS server via SSL? What measures do you take to detect and block attempts at illicit authentication, like brute-force password guessing? Have you done a thorough code review for SQL Injection vulnerabilities?

Database infrastructure: This information is chiefly used by IT staff and DBAs, but developers need to know some of it too. What RDBMS brand and version do you operate? What is your database server hostname? Do you use multiple database servers, replication, clusters, proxies, and so on? What is your network organization and the port number used by the database server? What connection options do client applications need to use? What are the database user passwords? What are your database backup policies?

Object-relational mapping: Your project may implement some database-handling logic in application code, as part of a layer of ORM-based code classes. What business rules are implemented in this way? Data validation, data transformation, logging, caching, or profiling?

Developers don't like to maintain engineering documentation. It's hard to write, it's hard to keep up-to-date, and it's dispiriting when few people read what you do write. But even battle-hardened, extreme programmers know that they need to document the database, even if they document no other part of their software.

No Code Documentation, Except for the Database

Joel Spolsky is a co-founder of the popular programmer help site Stack Overflow. In the Stack Overflow podcast #80,[a] he said he saw little value in documenting code.

> *Joel:* There is definitely a feeling among programmers that there's never enough documentation of the code they've been told to go work on, ever. And there's also a pretty clear reluctance to ever write any documentation, because documentation in and of itself almost never gets written.

He feels documentation that is not updated to match code changes fails to be helpful, and if documentation is not helpful, then other developers usually don't bother to read it, and so there's no purpose to writing it at all. A moment later in the same podcast, Spolsky makes an exception. He says that documenting at least the *database* is important.

> *Joel:* I found that if you have a database, and you don't carefully document every column, that after a year or two you start to have a really, really brittle world.

---

a. https://stackoverflow.blog/2010/01/21/podcast-80/

Trail of Evidence: Source Code Control

If your database server failed completely, how would you recreate a database? What's the best way to track a complex upgrade to your database design? How would you back out a change?

You are accustomed to using a version control system to manage application code, solving similar problems of software development. A project under version control should include *everything* you need to rebuild and redeploy the project. Source control also serves as a history of changes and an incremental backup so you can reverse any of these changes.

You should also use version control with your database code and get similar benefits for development. Check into the repository the files related to your database development, including the following:

Data definition scripts: All brands of database provide ways to execute *SQL scripts* containing CREATE TABLE and other statements that define the database objects.

Triggers and procedures: Many projects supplement application code with routines stored in the database. Your application probably won't work without these routines, so they count as part of your project's code.

Bootstrap data: Lookup tables may contain some set of data that represents an initial state of your database, before any users enter new data. You should keep bootstrap data to help if you need to recreate a database from your project source. Also called *seed data*.

ER diagrams and documentation: These files aren't code, but they're closely tied to the code, describing database requirements, implementation, and integration with the application. As the project evolution results in changes to both the database and the application, you should keep these files up-to-date. Make sure the documents describe the current designs.

DBA scripts: Most projects have a collection of data-handling jobs that run outside the application. These include tasks for import/export, synchronization, reporting, backups, validation, testing, and so on.

Make sure your database code files are associated with the application code that uses that database. Part of the benefit of using version control is that if you check out your project from the repository given a certain revision number, date, or milestone, the files should work together. Use the same repository for both application code and database code.

Schema Evolution Tools

Your code is under version control, but your database isn't. Ruby on Rails popularized a technique called *migrations* to manage upgrades to a database instance under version control. Migrations automate most of the work of synchronizing a database instance with the structure expected in a given revision of your code under version control.

To develop a migration for a database schema change, you write a script with code to upgrade a database by one step, based on Rails' abstract class for making database changes. Also write a downgrade function that reverses the changes from those in the upgrade function.

```
class AddHoursToBugs < ActiveRecord::Migration
  def self.up
    add_column :bugs, :hours, :decimal
  end

  def self.down
    remove_column :bugs, :hours
  end
end
```

The Rails tool that runs migrations automatically creates a table to record the revision or revisions that apply to your current database instance. For example, if you need to change your database to version 5, then you would specify that as an argument to the migration tool.

```
$ rake db:migrate VERSION=5
```

You accumulate a set of these migration scripts; each one can upgrade or downgrade the database schema one step.

There's a lot more to learn about Rails migrations in *Agile Web Development with Rails 7 [Rub22]* or Alembic migrations in *Essential SQLAlchemy [MC15]*.

Other development frameworks, such as Liquibase or Flyway for Java, Doctrine for PHP, SqlAlchemy for Python, or Microsoft ASP.NET, support features similar to Rails' migrations.

Burden of Proof: Testing

The final part of quality assurance is quality control—validating that your application does what it set out to do. Most professional developers are familiar with techniques to write automated tests to validate application code behavior. One important principle of testing is *isolation*, testing only one part of the system at a time so that if a defect exists, you can narrow down where it exists as precisely as possible.

You can extend the practice of isolation testing to the database by validating the database structure and behavior independently from your code. The following example shows a unit test script in Python:

Diplomatic_immunity/DatabaseTest.py
```python
import unittest
import mysql.connector

class TestDatabase(unittest.TestCase):

    def setUp(self):
        self.cnx = mysql.connector.connect(user='scott', database='test')
        self.cursor = self.cnx.cursor()

    def test_table_bugs_exists(self):
        query = '''SELECT true FROM Bugs LIMIT 1'''
        self.cursor.execute(query)

    def test_table_bugs_column_bugid_exists(self):
        query = '''SELECT bug_id FROM Bugs LIMIT 1'''
        self.cursor.execute(query)

    # the issue_id column was removed, so this should fail
    def test_table_bugs_column_issueid_not_exists(self):
        with self.assertRaises(mysql.connector.errors.ProgrammingError) as e:
            query = '''SELECT issue_id FROM Bugs LIMIT 1'''
            self.cursor.execute(query)

if __name__ == '__main__':
    unittest.main()
```

You can use the following checklist for tests that validate your database:

Tables, columns, views: You should test that tables and views you expect to exist in the database do exist. Each time you enhance the database with a new table, view, or column, add a new test that confirms that the object is present. You can also use *negative tests* to confirm that a table or column you removed in the current revision of your project is in fact no longer present.

Constraints: This is another use of negative testing. Try to execute INSERT, UPDATE, or DELETE statements that should result in an error because of a constraint. For example, try to violate not-null, unique constraints, or foreign keys. If the statement doesn't return an error, then your constraint isn't working. You can catch many bugs early by identifying these failures.

Triggers: Triggers can enforce constraints too. Triggers can perform cascading effects, transform values, log changes, and so on. You should test these scenarios by executing a statement that spawns the trigger and then querying to confirm that the trigger performed the action you intended.

Stored procedures: Testing procedures in the database is closest to conventional unit testing of application code. A stored procedure has input parameters, which could throw errors if you try to pass values outside the range of valid input. Logic within the body of the procedure could allow multiple execution paths. The procedure could return a single value or a query result set, depending on the inputs and the state of data in the database. Also, the procedure could have *side effects* in the form of updating the database. You can test all of these features of procedures.

Bootstrap data: Even a supposedly empty database typically needs some initial data, such as in lookup tables. You can run queries to validate that the initial data is present.

Queries: Application code is laced with SQL queries. You can execute queries in a test environment to validate syntax and results. Confirm that the result set includes the column names and data types you expect, just like testing tables and views.

ORM classes: Like triggers, ORM classes contain logic, including validation, transformation, or monitoring. You should test your ORM-based database abstraction code as you would any other application code. Confirm that these classes do the expected actions with input and also that they reject invalid input.

If any of your tests fail, your application could be using the wrong database instance. For example, you may have intended to connect to a staging database, but you accidentally have the tests configured to connect to the production database, or a replica database instance, or a test database where the schema changes have not been fully executed yet. Double-check your configuration, correct it if needed, and try again. If you're sure you're connection is proper but you need to alter the database, then you can run a *migration script* (see Schema Evolution Tools, on page 280) to synchronize this database instance to match what your application expects.

Case Load: Working in Multiple Branches

While you develop your application, you could work on multiple revisions of the code. You might even work on different revisions in the same day. For example, you could fix an urgent bug in the branch of the application currently deployed and then moments later resume working on long-term development in the main branch.

The database your application uses isn't under revision control. It's not practical to set up and tear down a database on a moment's notice, even if the database brand you use is relatively agile and easy to use.

Ideally, create a separate instance of your database for each revision of the application you need to develop, test, stage, or deploy. Also, each developer in your project team needs a separate database instance so they can work without interfering with the rest of the team.

Make your application support a configurable means to specify database connection parameters so that whichever application revision you work on, you can specify which database to use without overwriting code.

Today every RDBMS brand, both commercial and open source, offers a free solution for development and testing. Cloud services or containerization technology such as Docker allow every developer to launch a virtual server at very low cost, and use it for testing. There is no reason that software developers can't develop and test in a fully functional environment that matches the production environment.

> Use software development best practices, including documentation, testing, and version control, for your database as you do for your application code.

Mini-Antipattern: Renaming Things

If you want to rename a table that is already in use, then you have a chicken-and-egg problem.

If you change a table name in the database first, the application will get an error, because it's still querying by the old table name. You realize you need to update the code to use the new name, and then redeploy the application —but you can't do this with split-second timing. Deployment usually takes a few minutes, during which time the application continues to generate errors. Conversely, if you update and deploy the code first, then you must change the table name in the database, also with sensitive timing.

If your application is deployed to multiple servers, code updates will deploy on each server independently, so multiple versions of your application can be active on different servers.

If you have the freedom to interrupt service for your application until both the table rename and the code change can be done in tandem, then you have no problem. However, modern businesses expect applications to run without downtime as much as possible.

When confronted with this level of complexity, many developers realize that changing the names of tables or columns is even harder than adding tables or adding columns or indexes to a table in use. They might even decide that changing names is not worth the work and the risk of downtime.

Sometimes there's a legitimate and important reason to change names. It's not just personal preference or style.

- The old table name is offensive, and continuing to use sensitive words creates a legal liability for the business.

- The old table name refers to a name for a technology, a partner company, or a corporate brand that is no longer used. After a corporate acquisition, there might be a need to change references to the old name.

- The old table name conflicts with a trademarked name, and the owners of that trademark require their name stop being used in an unauthorized way.

- The old name is too close to a different word used within the project or company. For example, an application named "Raffle" had to be renamed, because a different application named "Rattle" existed in the same company, and using both names is confusing.

Changing column names has similar considerations. There are potential solutions to change a table name or a column name while minimizing downtime for the application. Each of the solutions has to be done with careful planning and testing.

The first solution is to rename the table or column in a new table, then gradually transition the application code to use it. This allows code deployments to happen independently, without downtime.

1. Create a table with the changed table name or column name.

2. Change the code to apply every write to both the old and the new table, but query only the old table, which is the only one with completely up-to-date data. Deploy this code.

3. Gradually copy all old data from the old table to the new table.

4. Change the code to read from the new table, while still applying writes to both tables. Deploy this code.

5. Change the code to stop writes to the old table. Deploy this code.

6. Drop the old table.

A second alternative is to use a *view*. Rename the table to the new name you want, then nearly simultaneously, create a view using the old name, that serves as a kind of "alias" for the new table name. Your application should be able to use the view for most types of queries, even INSERT or UPDATE. You need to test carefully to make sure your queries work against the view as well as they did against the base table. After the name switch is successful, you may change the application code at your convenience to use the table by its new name.

CHAPTER 25

Standard Operating Procedures

I visited a startup company as an SQL performance consultant. They were telling me about the software developer team and application design. They had made an effort to hire the best PHP developers in their city. Their architecture used a dozen load-balanced PHP application servers, and another server dedicated to hosting a MySQL database.

The performance problem they asked me to solve was that their database server was overloaded, while the servers running their PHP code were practically idle. Their application was often waiting for the database. The business owners wanted me to improve the performance of the database server.

The first thing I did was examine the database query log to identify the queries that were running most frequently, so we could optimize them. What I saw in the query log was that most queries in the log were executing stored procedures with statements like CALL ListCustomersProc(); These calls were taking too long. The application needed them to take no more than 50 milliseconds, but they were taking 20 times that long, often well over a full second.

I asked if I could examine the code for the stored procedures. "Sure," the manager said, "I'll ask the lead developer to explain the code for one of our stored procedures, because he's the only one who understands it. We've struggled with developing and optimizing stored procedure code in MySQL."

The stored procedures they had developed used a lot of complex and inefficient code, building queries from fragments, and executing them as dynamic SQL.

"The code you've written in your procedures is the cause of the performance problems," I explained. "You should do more of the logic to build queries in PHP. This would spread the workload out over your multiple application servers instead of forcing it all to run on the database server in these stored procedures, and since your team is more expert with PHP than with the

MySQL stored procedure language, they'll probably write the code more quickly, write unit tests more easily, and also develop efficiencies like helper functions to generate similar queries."

"But we decided at the start of the project that all the SQL code should be implemented in stored procedures," the developer said.

"Why?" I asked. "Your team is full of expert PHP developers, and your PHP application layer has many servers that can scale out. Why would you make them write code in an unfamiliar language, and run it on only a single server?"

"We were told that's the way to develop database applications," the developer replied. "The company founder said he did that on other projects using Oracle PL/SQL or Microsoft SQL Server T-SQL."

Objective: Use Stored Procedures

Stored procedures are a feature of SQL that developers can use to put custom code into the database itself, and call those procedures from their client application.

The following example shows a MySQL stored procedure that closes any outstanding bugs for a specified product. This is implemented in a procedure so that we can run this as an update, but in a prescribed way: only bugs that currently have a status of *NEW* or *OPEN* are closed by this action. If the application had direct access to update the bugs table, they might change the status of the wrong bugs.

Procedures/anti/close-bugs.sql
```sql
CREATE PROCEDURE CloseUnresolvedBugsForProduct(
  IN given_product_id BIGINT UNSIGNED)
BEGIN
  START TRANSACTION;
  UPDATE Bugs JOIN BugsProducts USING (bug_id)
  SET status = 'WONTFIX'
  WHERE product_id = given_product_id
  AND status IN ('NEW', 'OPEN');
  COMMIT;
END
```

The developer of a client application only needs to call the procedure, and pass one product id as an argument. They don't need to know how to write the SQL to update the bugs in the proper way.

Procedures/anti/close-bugs.sql
```sql
CALL CloseUnresolvedBugsForProduct(1234);
```

In the early days of SQL databases, software engineering was done differently than it is today. Because of the languages and programming paradigms used then, it was desirable to consolidate database-related business logic into a single callable interface, to avoid code duplication. It made sense to store the routines implementing this business logic in the database, to be invoked by any client application. This way there was some assurance against each client implementing the logic differently.

Besides this, the database administrator may have been the only member of the team who was expert in writing efficient SQL queries, and they were given the work of implementing the queries in the stored procedures. Then all clients would call those procedures with the right arguments, and trust that the database-related work was done efficiently and consistently.

The SQL procedure language used by database administrators at that time became known as PL/SQL. It resembled legacy procedural languages like Algol or Pascal, more than the object-oriented, functional, or scripting languages that are more popular today.

This isn't necessarily a good software development model for modern projects. Projects probably don't have a database administrator specialist who has more experience at writing efficient SQL queries than the other software developers. Code duplication is less of a risk factor, because it's common to use object-oriented frameworks or functional programmer frameworks to implement a *data access layer* (DAL).

Using stored procedures isn't an objective or a goal; it's an implementation choice. Yet some software development teams still make the assumption that one must use stored procedures because "we've always done it this way."

Antipattern: Follow the Leader

The real antipattern in this chapter is not the use of stored procedures. The antipattern is to use any technology feature—stored procedures is just a good example—because it was done before you. Just because stored procedures were right in some prior project doesn't necessarily make it a good choice for your current project.

Stored procedures (or more broadly, *stored routines*, which also includes functions, triggers, and packages) are a traditional part of application development if you use one of the major commercial SQL database platforms such as Oracle, Microsoft SQL Server, IBM DB2, Informix, or Sybase. However, there are several hidden costs to using stored procedures.

Procedure Language

Despite the fact that ANSI/ISO SQL defines a standard stored procedure language, each brand of SQL database implements the syntax differently, making procedures not portable. For example, if you develop a procedure for Microsoft SQL Server, and then your project switches to MySQL (or vice versa), you will need to rewrite each procedure. Developers need to know the specific syntax supported by both brands of database, as well as built-in functions and other procedure code idioms. They need to painstakingly analyze the intended logic of each procedure, and think of how best to implement equivalent logic in the procedure language of the other brand.

Many SQL brands implement extensions to the standard stored procedure language to give it support for object-oriented features, packages, libraries of built-in functions, or data types for arrays or collections. Unfortunately, they implement these features in non-standard ways, so each implementation is different.

Development and Deployment

Today, developers enjoy many sophisticated code editors and IDE products. Some are open source, such as IntelliJ Community Edition, Eclipse, NetBeans, or Microsoft Visual Studio. Some are commercial developer tools, such as Apple's Xcode, or the various JetBrains products.

Developers who use a debugger for client languages like Java or Python are used to being able to set breakpoints and inspect the content of variables dynamically. Few of the most popular IDE's for application programming support SQL stored procedures. To develop and debug stored procedures, you need to use a more specialized code tool, such as Oracle SQL Developer, Microsoft SQL Server Management Studio, or Toad by Quest Software.

Deploying stored procedures is different from deploying applications. Deploying a procedure looks about the same as creating a procedure using CREATE PROCEDURE. To deploy a code change later, different brands use different statements: Oracle, IBM DB2, Informix, or PostgreSQL use CREATE OR REPLACE PROCEDURE; Microsoft SQL Server uses CREATE OR ALTER PROCEDURE.

Deploying a project that has a strict requirement for high availability has special challenges. You can deploy client applications with no downtime, because applications are provisioned on multiple application servers. As you deploy them, you can restart one instance of the application at a time, while allowing the other instances to continue serving requests. For a single database implementation, there are no redundant instances. Using CREATE OR

REPLACE PROCEDURE to modify the code of a procedure on a busy database server must wait for any clients currently executing the procedure to finish, and meanwhile it blocks any further calls to the procedure. If the procedure execution takes long enough, it can make clients wait, and it seems like the whole database has locked up.

As described in Schema Evolution Tools, on page 280, some applications organize their database changes using migration tools. The application framework typically supports a special configuration format or API for defining tables, columns, and indexes, to help developers create database objects without making syntax mistakes. Unfortunately, most migration tools don't support stored procedure syntax in this way. At best, they delegate stored procedures to a general feature for executing an SQL script, and the developer must code the CREATE PROCEDURE statements in the SQL script. Likewise, migration tools provide a path to reverse or "downgrade" changes to tables, columns, or indexes, but not for stored procedures.

Performance and Scalability

Running code uses resources on the server where it runs. The database server must parse and execute SQL queries, and that requires resources too. Stored procedures also run in the database server, and the more complex the code, the more CPU resources it demands on that server. If you implement a lot of complex code in stored procedures, and clients run procedures frequently, then the CPU on the database server could become overloaded, and cause all the concurrent procedure calls and queries to execute more slowly.

Meanwhile, the clients who called those procedures are idle, waiting for the procedures to finish and return their results. While the clients are waiting, the CPU resources on the application servers are underutilized. Those servers have ample computing power that could be used, but instead they're just waiting. The illustration on page 292 depicts several application servers with low activity (indicated by the gauge leaning to the left), connected to a single database server that is overloaded. With such high load, the database server is now a bottleneck for the whole system, because it can't take on any further increase in load.

An exception in the case of Oracle is that PL/SQL routines may run on an application server, as part of Oracle Forms. Otherwise, PL/SQL routines are executed in the database server.

Some SQL implementations provide a compiler for stored procedures, so they execute more efficiently. The procedure may be called many times by different

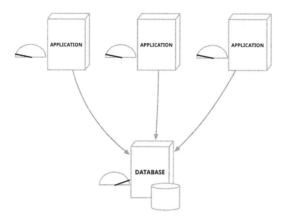

clients before the next time you change it. You need to recompile the procedure after changing its code (in this way, it's similar to any other compiled language such as Java or C++). If indexes or data change in a way that could affect the query optimizer, then the procedure may need to be recompiled. It can be confusing to know when to recompile a procedure, and if it is not done properly, it can lead to poorly optimized queries.

Depending on the brand of SQL database product, syntax errors in procedure code may be reported immediately when you try to define the procedure. Other brands don't check syntax until the first time you execute the procedure. This difference can be confusing. If you don't remember to test procedures, you won't know about the error until later, perhaps after you deploy the procedure to production. You must learn habits for developing and testing stored procedures in the database brand you use.

Scalability is a concern too. A database may grow large enough that it needs to be split, so shards of the data are distributed over multiple servers. But a stored procedure executes within a single database server, so it can only access data on the same server. PostgreSQL, Oracle, and Microsoft SQL Server support features called *foreign data wrapper*, *Database Link*, or *Linked Server*, so a procedure or query running in one server can access data that resides on a remote server. However this takes configuration to link servers, there are some limitations for SQL queries and transactions, and there's an increased risk of connectivity problems between the servers.

How to Recognize the Antipattern

The following are examples of things you might hear others saying during a database development project, or you might even say them yourself.

- "Why do I get a syntax error in DECLARE when I am creating my stored procedure?"

  Differences in syntax and usage of stored procedure statements between brands can be confusing. For example, developers who use MySQL after having learned on other brands often get confused because DECLARE can be used only at the top of the procedure's main BEGIN...END block, and local variables declared in this way do not use the @ symbol. You need to study the documentation of both brands carefully to understand how to translate procedure code between brands.

- "What tool can I use to migrate 500 or more stored procedures from T-SQL to MySQL?"

  The developer incorrectly assumes that such a tool exists that can rewrite any arbitrary T-SQL procedure as a MySQL procedure (the same is true of any other pair of SQL database brands).

- "We always use procedures because they give better performance."

  It's not a good idea to make such unequivocal policies, because few features provide better performance in all cases. To truly optimize, developers need to evaluate the architecture on a case by case basis, instead of following arbitrary rules.

Legitimate Uses of the Antipattern

As mentioned earlier, stored procedures per se are not an antipattern. This is true especially in SQL database brands whose implementation is more mature, featureful, and high performance than that of MySQL.

Edge cases occur where you can use a stored procedure as the best solution for a given task. For example, if you have a slow network between the client application and the database server, and your task involves several individual steps of running SQL queries to get interim results, implementing code in a stored procedure eliminates at least the latency caused by the network round-trips.

Tasks which are run infrequently, or run with no client application, are another good candidate for a stored procedure. Procedures are sometimes used for database administration tasks like auditing privileges, emptying caches or logs, measuring performance or resource usage, or running scheduled tasks.

Encapsulating SQL queries that require elevated privileges is another good use of stored procedures. The database administrator can grant privileges to the procedure itself, and then grant users the privilege to run the procedure. That allows users to be more self service, by running a procedure that performs a sensitive operation in a prescribed way. Working with sensitive data (PII or SPI) in a stored procedure avoids any risk of attackers intercepting network traffic.

Solution: Adopt Modern Application Architecture

Client programming languages have come a long way since SQL introduced stored procedures. Preferring a language such as Java, Python, or Go to run queries resolves the disadvantages mentioned earlier. Developers are undoubtedly more familiar and productive with their favorite language than with any database's stored procedure language. Advanced code editors, debuggers, and testing frameworks allow developers to work the way they're used to working on code. For example, writing tests with mocking techniques makes your tests faster and more stable. A modern deployment architecture uses multiple application servers, so you can deploy in a round robin or blue/green manner, using a dynamic load balancer to avoid sending to each application instance while it is restarting. This allows the deployment of changes to an application with no downtime.

Developers should implement more logic in application code to distribute the load better by making use of computing resources on the application servers. The SQL queries themselves still need to run centrally on the database server, but all the code that runs in between SQL queries, for example, to format queries and process query results, is better run on the application servers.

The illustration on page 295 shows the application servers and database server shown earlier in this chapter, with the load on each server distributed more evenly. All of the servers are giving good value, they have better performance on average, and they can handle occasional bursts of load without becoming a bottleneck.

The illustration shows a client/server architecture, but you might also use a more complex, multi-tier architecture. The benefit is the same: it's easier to scale out the workload over multiple servers, instead of concentrating the workload in stored procedures on the database server.

The case of using stored procedures is just one example of a software development habit. Instead of forming habits or traditions, it's better to validate assumptions, approach software architecture choices like an engineer, and make choices to use the best tools and technology for a given project.

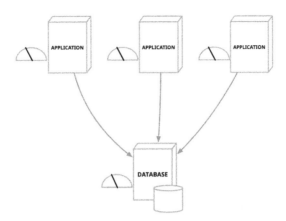

> If the only tool you have is a hammer, then every problem looks like a nail. It's better to expand your toolbox and use the right tool for the job.

Mini-Antipattern: Stored Procedures in MySQL

MySQL's implementation of stored procedures was introduced in version 5.0 in 2005. There wasn't much demand for improvements, because most developers who used MySQL during that time preferred to execute SQL queries from application code or ORM classes, instead of using stored procedures. Because of this history, using procedures in MySQL has some additional challenges, beyond those described in the preceding chapter. Even a developer who is accustomed to using stored procedures in other brands of SQL products should read the following points before deciding to use procedures extensively in MySQL.

Using Packages

MySQL's stored procedures don't have any support for packages, modules, or object-oriented features. This makes it more clumsy and difficult to organize large collections of procedures, or to deploy sets of procedures from multiple sources.

Debugging

Other brands of SQL databases have specialized development tools, but there is no IDE or developer tool for MySQL that supports debugging a stored procedure. Developers can't set breakpoints or inspect local variables directly. Some editors have tried to simulate debugging, by inserting lines of code into a procedure to log the state of variables, but this trick has to modify the code, which affects all clients who call the procedure.

Testing

Unit-testing code is done by isolating that code from other software components and executing it in a controlled environment. The code under test may call other functions, so mock objects are used to ensure the called functions are simulated and the function calls are tested for. MySQL stored procedures have no way to be run in a controlled environment; they are only run in the database server. They also have no support for calling the functions through mock interfaces; if they use SQL statements, those statements can only access real tables or procedures. Effectively, there is no standard support for unit-testing MySQL stored procedures; you have to develop those testing tools yourself. You can still perform system testing by calling stored procedures, but you need to do this in a real MySQL Server instance, and the procedures access real data during testing.

Compiling

MySQL does not save a compiled version of any procedure. Each session compiles a procedure the first time it uses it, but this compiled version isn't used by other sessions. When the client ends their session, the compiled versions of procedures they called are discarded. This implementation results in a lot of overhead to using procedures when sessions are short-lived, as they are in typical web applications.

Deploying

There is no support in MySQL for updating the code of a procedure without a risk of downtime. To deploy a change to a stored procedure, the developer must first DROP PROCEDURE, then CREATE PROCEDURE with the changed code. These steps can't be done atomically; there is a moment in between these two steps when the procedure is dropped, and the database returns an error to a client that tries to call it in that moment. This means that deploying a procedure is bound to cause at least brief downtime when using a single database server. If the procedure is called infrequently, the procedure might be dropped and recreated quickly enough that no one will notice. But if the application calls procedures during every request, the procedure call might fail hundreds of times, even if great care is taken to create the new procedure as quickly as possible.

Using Sharded Architecture

MySQL has limited support for tables accessed via a Linked Server (it requires a special storage engine called FEDERATED), so it's awkward to run stored procedures in a sharded architecture. One possible workaround is that the client knows in advance which server holds the shard of data they need, and calls the procedure using a session connected to the respective database server. Another workaround is that the client must call the same procedure on all of the shards, just in case partial data exists on some of the shards. The client then fetches results from all of these calls, some of which may be empty results.

Some projects implement distributed queries using a proxy middleware. Those middleware products are designed for queries against tables. They might not support calling stored procedures. For example, PlanetScale Vitess 14 is a great technology to supporting sharded architecture with MySQL, but it has does not support stored procedures that query sharded keyspaces.[1]

In general, developers using MySQL should write code in their client application to execute individual queries instead of using stored procedures. The exception case is when you need to reduce the impact of network latency between the application and the database when running many queries in rapid succession, but usually it's a better choice to run your application colocated with the database server on a fast network.

---

1. https://vitess.io/docs/14.0/reference/compatibility/mysql-compatibility/

Part V

Bonus: More Foreign Key Mini-Antipatterns

I've fielded a surprisingly large variety of questions about foreign keys. As a result, I've identified quite a few additional mini-antipatterns, and we decided to offer them here in their own part, as a bonus. They are divided into two chapters: mini-antipatterns about using foreign keys in general and mini-antipatterns specifically about using foreign keys in MySQL.

CHAPTER 26

Foreign Key Mistakes in Standard SQL

Foreign keys are part of the ANSI/ISO SQL standard, so many types of foreign key mistakes will be mistakes regardless of the specific brand of SQL database you use. This chapter is a collection of mini-antipatterns about those types of foreign key constraints, based on questions asked frequently by developers on public internet forums.

Each incorrect example is followed by the error returned by MySQL 8.0. The error message may be different in another version of MySQL, or in other brands of SQL databases. Following the description of the error and other consequences of the mistake, the correct way to implement the foreign key is shown or described.

In the following examples, a row in the Parent table may have zero, one, or many related rows in the Child table. A row in the Child table must be related to exactly one row in the Parent table. So, the tables have a one-to-many relationship (the many may also be zero or one). These tables aren't meant to model real-life family relationships, which are usually more complex.

Reversing the Direction of Reference

It might be hard to understand which table should have the foreign key constraint. If the developer is thinking of one-to-many relationships as "Parent can have many Children," they could assume the foreign key should be defined in the Parent table.

Foreign-Key-Checklist/has-many-reversed.sql
```
CREATE TABLE Child (
  child_id INT PRIMARY KEY
);

CREATE TABLE Parent (
  parent_id INT PRIMARY KEY,
```

```
  child_id INT NOT NULL,
  FOREIGN KEY (child_id) REFERENCES Child(child_id)
);
```

This is a misunderstanding. A given row in Parent can only have one value in the child_id column, so defining the foreign key constraint in the Parent table means that a given row in Parent can have only one Child, but zero, one, or many Parents can reference the same Child. That's the opposite of the intended relationship. No error is returned, but you can't use this design to store data with the relationship you need.

It might help to visualize the one-to-many relationship instead as "Child belongs to Parent," and define the foreign key in the Child table. This allows the Parent to be referenced by zero, one, or many children, whereas each Child row must reference exactly one Parent.

Foreign-Key-Checklist/has-many-correct.sql
```
CREATE TABLE Parent (
  parent_id INT PRIMARY KEY
);

CREATE TABLE Child (
  child_id INT PRIMARY KEY,
  parent_id INT NOT NULL,
  FOREIGN KEY (parent_id) REFERENCES Parent(parent_id)
);
```

Remember: the foreign key constraint should be defined in the table that is the "many" side of the one-to-many relationship.

Referencing Tables Before They Have Been Created

If the foreign key references a table before you have created that table, then you get an error.

Foreign-Key-Checklist/table-order-error.sql
```
CREATE TABLE Child (
  child_id INT PRIMARY KEY,
  parent_id INT NOT NULL,
  FOREIGN KEY (parent_id) REFERENCES Parent(parent_id)
);

CREATE TABLE Parent (
  parent_id INT PRIMARY KEY
);
```

The following error is returned as the first CREATE TABLE statement fails, before the second statement is run.

```
ERROR 1824 (HY000): Failed to open the referenced table 'Parent'
```

The order in which you create the tables is important. You must create the Parent table before you define a foreign key to reference it.

Foreign-Key-Checklist/table-order-correct.sql
```
CREATE TABLE Parent (
  parent_id INT PRIMARY KEY
);

CREATE TABLE Child (
  child_id INT PRIMARY KEY,
  parent_id INT NOT NULL,
  FOREIGN KEY (parent_id) REFERENCES Parent(parent_id)
);
```

If both tables have a foreign key that references the other (for example, the Child table references a Parent, and the Parent references its single favorite Child), then you must use three data definition statements instead of two. Create the first table without its foreign key constraint, then create the second table, then add the foreign key constraint to the first table with ALTER TABLE.

Foreign-Key-Checklist/table-order-mutual.sql
```
CREATE TABLE Parent (
  parent_id INT PRIMARY KEY,
  favorite_child_id INT
);

CREATE TABLE Child (
  child_id INT PRIMARY KEY,
  parent_id INT NOT NULL,
  FOREIGN KEY (parent_id) REFERENCES Parent(parent_id)
);

ALTER TABLE Parent
  ADD FOREIGN KEY (favorite_child_id) REFERENCES Child(child_id);
```

If a table contains a self-referential foreign key, you may define the foreign key in the CREATE TABLE statement.

As you get more tables, it becomes more complex to create the tables in the right order. You could create tables in a careful order, starting with those tables that themselves have no foreign key constraint. You could consider these tables "root" tables in an entity-relationship diagram. Then add tables that reference the root tables, and so on. This is not possible if there are any cycles of foreign key references among your set of tables, so an alternative is to create all the tables first, with no foreign key constraints, and then add the constraints after all tables exist.

Referencing No Key of the Parent Table

If referenced columns in the Parent table are not a PRIMARY KEY or UNIQUE KEY, then you get an error.

Foreign-Key-Checklist/no-key-error.sql
```
CREATE TABLE Parent (
  parent_id INT NOT NULL -- not a PRIMARY KEY or UNIQUE KEY
);

CREATE TABLE Child (
  child_id INT PRIMARY KEY,
  parent_id INT NOT NULL,
  FOREIGN KEY (parent_id) REFERENCES Parent(parent_id)
);
```

> ERROR 1822 (HY000): Failed to add the foreign key constraint. Missing index for constraint 'child_ibfk_1' in the referenced table 'Parent'

Notice the name of the constraint child_ibfk_1 is mentioned in the error message. An SQL constraint has a name, just like tables, indexes, and columns have names. The code examples in this chapter don't specify the constraint name, so MySQL generates a unique name automatically.

The column(s) referenced by the foreign key must be the PRIMARY KEY or a UNIQUE KEY of the Parent table.

Foreign-Key-Checklist/no-key-correct.sql
```
CREATE TABLE Parent (
  parent_id INT PRIMARY KEY
);

CREATE TABLE Child (
  child_id INT PRIMARY KEY,
  parent_id INT NOT NULL,
  FOREIGN KEY (parent_id) REFERENCES Parent(parent_id)
);
```

Creating Separate Constraints for Each Column in a Compound Key

If the primary key in the Parent table has multiple columns, but the foreign key is split into a separate constraint for each column, then you get an error.

Foreign-Key-Checklist/multi-column-error.sql
```
CREATE TABLE Parent (
  parent_id1 INT,
  parent_id2 INT,
  PRIMARY KEY (parent_id1, parent_id2)
);
```

```
CREATE TABLE Child (
  child_id INT PRIMARY KEY,
  parent_id1 INT NOT NULL,
  parent_id2 INT NOT NULL,
  FOREIGN KEY (parent_id1) REFERENCES Parent(parent_id1),
  FOREIGN KEY (parent_id2) REFERENCES Parent(parent_id2)
);
```

> ERROR 1822 (HY000): Failed to add the foreign key constraint. Missing index for constraint 'child_ibfk_2' in the referenced table 'Parent'

If the primary key in the Parent table has multiple columns, then you must create one foreign key that references both columns.

Foreign-Key-Checklist/multi-column-correct.sql
```
CREATE TABLE Parent (
  parent_id1 INT,
  parent_id2 INT,
  PRIMARY KEY (parent_id1, parent_id2)
);

CREATE TABLE Child (
  child_id INT PRIMARY KEY,
  parent_id1 INT NOT NULL,
  parent_id2 INT NOT NULL,
  FOREIGN KEY (parent_id1, parent_id2)
    REFERENCES Parent(parent_id1, parent_id2)
);
```

Using the Wrong Column Order

If the primary key in the Parent table has multiple columns, but the foreign key references them in the wrong order, then you don't get an error (provided the column data types are compatible), but you may not be able to add rows of data, because the columns are not referencing the correct columns in the Parent table.

Foreign-Key-Checklist/multi-column-order-error.sql
```
CREATE TABLE Parent (
  parent_id1 INT,
  parent_id2 INT,
  PRIMARY KEY (parent_id1, parent_id2)
);

INSERT INTO Parent (parent_id1, parent_id2) VALUES (1234, 5678);

CREATE TABLE Child (
  child_id INT PRIMARY KEY,
  parent_id1 INT NOT NULL,
  parent_id2 INT NOT NULL,
```

```
  FOREIGN KEY (parent_id2, parent_id1)
    REFERENCES Parent(parent_id1, parent_id2)
);

INSERT INTO Child (child_id, parent_id1, parent_id2) VALUES (1, 1234, 5678);
```

> ERROR 1452 (23000): Cannot add or update a child row: a foreign key constraint fails (`test`.`child`, CONSTRAINT `child_ibfk_1` FOREIGN KEY (`parent_id2`, `parent_id1`) REFERENCES `parent` (`parent_id1`, `parent_id2`))

The columns in the foreign key constraint must be in the same order they are defined in the PRIMARY KEY or UNIQUE KEY in the Parent table.

Foreign-Key-Checklist/multi-column-order-correct.sql
```
CREATE TABLE Parent (
  parent_id1 INT,
  parent_id2 INT,
  PRIMARY KEY (parent_id1, parent_id2)
);

INSERT INTO Parent (parent_id1, parent_id2) VALUES (1234, 5678);

CREATE TABLE Child (
  child_id INT PRIMARY KEY,
  parent_id1 INT NOT NULL,
  parent_id2 INT NOT NULL,
  FOREIGN KEY (parent_id1, parent_id2)
    REFERENCES Parent(parent_id1, parent_id2)
);

INSERT INTO Child (child_id, parent_id1, parent_id2) VALUES (1, 1234, 5678);
```

Using Mismatched Data Types

You must define the foreign key columns in the Child table using the same data types as the respective columns they reference in the Parent table. If the data types don't match, then you get an error.

Foreign-Key-Checklist/data-type-error.sql
```
CREATE TABLE Parent (
  parent_id INT PRIMARY KEY
);

CREATE TABLE Child (
  child_id INT PRIMARY KEY,
  parent_id VARCHAR(10) NOT NULL,
  FOREIGN KEY (parent_id) REFERENCES Parent(parent_id)
);
```

> ERROR 3780 (HY000): Referencing column 'parent_id' and referenced column 'parent_id' in foreign key constraint 'child_ibfk_1' are incompatible.

The difference between a signed and unsigned integer is enough to make the columns incompatible.

Foreign-Key-Checklist/data-type-int-error.sql

```sql
CREATE TABLE Parent (
  parent_id INT PRIMARY KEY
);

CREATE TABLE Child (
  child_id INT PRIMARY KEY,
  parent_id INT UNSIGNED NOT NULL,
  FOREIGN KEY (parent_id) REFERENCES Parent(parent_id)
);
```

> ERROR 3780 (HY000): Referencing column 'parent_id' and referenced column 'parent_id' in foreign key constraint 'child_ibfk_1' are incompatible.

The best choice is to make sure the data types are identical.

Foreign-Key-Checklist/data-type-correct.sql

```sql
CREATE TABLE Parent (
  parent_id VARCHAR(10) PRIMARY KEY
);

CREATE TABLE Child (
  child_id INT PRIMARY KEY,
  parent_id VARCHAR(10) NOT NULL,
  FOREIGN KEY (parent_id) REFERENCES Parent(parent_id)
);
```

However, as with most rules, there's an exception that seems to break the rule. Variable-length string columns may have different maximum lengths, but they're still compatible for purposes of foreign key references.

Foreign-Key-Checklist/data-type-length-correct.sql

```sql
CREATE TABLE Parent (
  parent_id VARCHAR(10) PRIMARY KEY
);

CREATE TABLE Child (
  child_id INT PRIMARY KEY,
  parent_id VARCHAR(20) NOT NULL,
  FOREIGN KEY (parent_id) REFERENCES Parent(parent_id)
);
```

If the foreign key column in the Child table has a shorter maximum length than the column in the Parent table it references, that's not an error, but then the rows in Child can only reference rows in Parent with a string value that is as short as the string in the Child row. So it's possible to store a long string in the Parent table that can't be matched in any row in the Child table.

It's not an error for a row to exist in Parent that is referenced by no rows in the Child table.

Likewise, the column in the Parent table may have a shorter maximum length than the referencing column in the Child table. That's not an error either. The strings in the Child table must reference a string in the Parent table, so you can insert only short strings into the Child table.

Using Mismatched Character Collations

This is related to the previous rule about data types. You might have string columns that seem to have identical types, except for the collation. If the referenced column has a different collation, then you get an error.

Foreign-Key-Checklist/collation-error.sql
```
CREATE TABLE Parent (
  parent_id VARCHAR(10) PRIMARY KEY
) CHARSET utf8mb4 COLLATE utf8mb4_unicode_ci;

CREATE TABLE Child (
  child_id INT PRIMARY KEY,
  parent_id VARCHAR(10) NOT NULL,
  FOREIGN KEY (parent_id) REFERENCES Parent(parent_id)
) CHARSET utf8mb4 COLLATE utf8mb4_general_ci;
```

> ERROR 3780 (HY000): Referencing column 'parent_id' and referenced column 'parent_id' in foreign key constraint 'child_ibfk_1' are incompatible.

To understand this problem, keep in mind what character sets and collations are. A character set is the way characters are encoded into bytes. A collation is the definition of how characters in that character set compare to each other; whether each pairing of characters compares as equal, less than, or greater than. The rules for character comparison in a foreign key column and the key column it references must be the same.

Make sure string columns have compatible character sets and collations (practically, this means the collations must be identical).

Foreign-Key-Checklist/collation-correct.sql
```
CREATE TABLE Parent (
  parent_id VARCHAR(10) PRIMARY KEY
) CHARSET utf8mb4 COLLATE utf8mb4_unicode_ci;

CREATE TABLE Child (
  child_id INT PRIMARY KEY,
  parent_id VARCHAR(10) NOT NULL,
  FOREIGN KEY (parent_id) REFERENCES Parent(parent_id)
) CHARSET utf8mb4 COLLATE utf8mb4_unicode_ci;
```

Creating Orphan Data

If you add a foreign key to a Child table that already contains data, you must be certain that every row in the Child table has a matching row in the Parent table.

Foreign-Key-Checklist/orphan-error.sql
```
CREATE TABLE Parent (
  parent_id INT PRIMARY KEY
);

INSERT INTO Parent (parent_id)
VALUES (1234);

CREATE TABLE Child (
  child_id INT PRIMARY KEY,
  parent_id INT NOT NULL
);

INSERT INTO Child (child_id, parent_id)
VALUES (1, 1234), (2, 5678);
```

In the preceding example, the Child table has a second row, which has no matching row in the Parent table. If there are any such orphans in your Child table, then adding the foreign key fails, and you get an error.

Foreign-Key-Checklist/orphan-error.sql
```
ALTER TABLE Child
  ADD FOREIGN KEY (parent_id) REFERENCES Parent(parent_id);

    ERROR 1452 (23000): Cannot add or update a child row: a foreign key constraint fails (`test`.`child`,
    CONSTRAINT `child_ibfk_1` FOREIGN KEY (`parent_id`) REFERENCES `parent` (`parent_id`))
```

Every value in the foreign key column(s) must match a value in the columns referenced. Use a query like the following to check for orphans:

Foreign-Key-Checklist/orphan-check.sql
```
SELECT CASE COUNT(*)
  WHEN 0 THEN 'Ready to add foreign key'
  ELSE 'Do not add foreign key, because orphan rows exist'
  END AS `check`
FROM Child
LEFT OUTER JOIN Parent ON Child.parent_id = Parent.parent_id
WHERE Parent.parent_id IS NULL;
```

This query is a generic example; substitute your table names and column names.

If you have orphan values in the Child table, then you can't add a foreign key to the table. First you must fix the data with one or more of the following:

- INSERT new rows to the Parent table until the none of the rows in the Child table have orphan values.

- UPDATE the rows in the Child table and set the orphan values either to NULL or a value that matches an existing value in the referenced column(s) of the Parent table.

- DELETE the rows from the Child table until none have orphan values.

Using the SET NULL Option for Non-Nullable Columns

You may add actions to the foreign key constraint, to execute if the values in the referenced column(s) of the Parent table change or if the referenced row in the Parent table is deleted. One of these optional actions is to SET NULL, so the values in the Child table become NULL instead of becoming orphaned.

If the columns of a foreign key are defined NOT NULL, and you try to define a foreign key constraint with the ON UPDATE SET NULL or ON DELETE SET NULL options, then you get an error.

Foreign-Key-Checklist/set-null-error.sql
```
CREATE TABLE Parent (
  parent_id INT PRIMARY KEY
);

CREATE TABLE Child (
  child_id INT PRIMARY KEY,
  parent_id INT NOT NULL,
  FOREIGN KEY (parent_id) REFERENCES Parent(parent_id)
    ON DELETE SET NULL
);
```

```
ERROR 1830 (HY000): Column 'parent_id' cannot be NOT NULL: needed in a foreign key constraint 'child_ibfk_1' SET NULL
```

The column(s) in the foreign key must be nullable if you want them to be set to NULL in the event of referential actions.

Foreign-Key-Checklist/set-null-correct.sql
```
CREATE TABLE Parent (
  parent_id INT PRIMARY KEY
);

CREATE TABLE Child (
  child_id INT PRIMARY KEY,
  parent_id INT NULL,
  FOREIGN KEY (parent_id) REFERENCES Parent(parent_id)
    ON DELETE SET NULL
);
```

Making Duplicate Constraint Identifiers

Foreign key constraints may optionally have identifiers, so you can use them later if you need to drop the constraint. Constraint identifiers must be unique within a whole schema. In other words, if two or more constraints in the same schema are given the same identifier, then you get an error.

Foreign-Key-Checklist/identifier-error.sql
```
CREATE TABLE Parent (
  parent_id INT PRIMARY KEY
);

CREATE TABLE Child1 (
  child_id INT PRIMARY KEY,
  parent_id INT NOT NULL,
  CONSTRAINT c1 FOREIGN KEY (parent_id) REFERENCES Parent(parent_id)
);

CREATE TABLE Child2 (
  child_id INT PRIMARY KEY,
  parent_id INT NOT NULL,
  CONSTRAINT c1 FOREIGN KEY (parent_id) REFERENCES Parent(parent_id)
);
```

```
ERROR 1826 (HY000): Duplicate foreign key constraint name 'c1'
```

Make sure each constraint identifier is unique if you specify them.

Foreign-Key-Checklist/identifier-correct.sql
```
CREATE TABLE Parent (
  parent_id INT PRIMARY KEY
);

CREATE TABLE Child1 (
  child_id INT PRIMARY KEY,
  parent_id INT NOT NULL,
  CONSTRAINT c1 FOREIGN KEY (parent_id) REFERENCES Parent(parent_id)
);

CREATE TABLE Child2 (
  child_id INT PRIMARY KEY,
  parent_id INT NOT NULL,
  CONSTRAINT c2 FOREIGN KEY (parent_id) REFERENCES Parent(parent_id)
);
```

If you choose to name the constraints, you should establish a naming convention that helps you to form unique constraint names. If you don't specify constraint names, typically unique names are are generated automatically.

Using Incompatible Table Types

In standard SQL, the Child table and the Parent table must be of the same table type. That is, both must be persistent base tables, or both must be global temporary tables, or both must be local temporary tables. See also Using Incompatible Table Types in MySQL, on page 319.

> Use this chapter as a checklist to resolve errors you experience while creating foreign keys in any brand of SQL database.

Success does not consist in never making mistakes but in never making the same one a second time.

> ➤ Josh Billings

## CHAPTER 27

Foreign Key Mistakes in MySQL

All implementations of SQL have enhancements and limitations, so there are a few types of foreign key mistakes that apply specifically to MySQL. This chapter is a collection of mini-antipatterns about those types of foreign key constraints, based on questions asked frequently by developers on public internet forums.

Each incorrect example is followed by the error returned by MySQL 8.0, and then the correct way to implement the foreign key.

Using Incompatible Storage Engines

MySQL supports multiple storage engines. When two tables are related by a foreign key constraint, they must use the same storage engine, and the storage engine must support foreign keys.

MySQL's default storage engine, InnoDB, supports foreign keys. Most other storage engines don't support foreign keys. If you try to define a foreign key in an InnoDB table, but the referenced table is not an InnoDB table, then you get an error.

Foreign-Key-Checklist/storage-engine-error.sql
```
CREATE TABLE Parent (
  parent_id INT PRIMARY KEY
) ENGINE=MyISAM;

CREATE TABLE Child (
  child_id INT PRIMARY KEY,
  parent_id INT NOT NULL,
  FOREIGN KEY (parent_id) REFERENCES Parent(parent_id)
) ENGINE=InnoDB;
```

```
ERROR 1824 (HY000): Failed to open the referenced table 'Parent'
```

There's a variation of this mistake: if the Child table's storage engine doesn't support foreign key constraints, it simply ignores the foreign key constraint. No error or warning is returned, but the resulting table will have no foreign key constraint.

Foreign-Key-Checklist/storage-engine-myisam.sql
```
CREATE TABLE Parent (
  parent_id INT PRIMARY KEY
) ENGINE=InnoDB;

CREATE TABLE Child (
  child_id INT PRIMARY KEY,
  parent_id INT NOT NULL,
  FOREIGN KEY (parent_id) REFERENCES Parent(parent_id)
) ENGINE=MyISAM;
```

The reason MySQL has this behavior is that in the early days, its designers wanted to allow importing SQL definition files from other brands of database, even if MySQL hadn't implemented all features of SQL yet.

Make sure both the Parent table and the Child table use the InnoDB storage engine. If you create a table without specifying the engine, then it should default to InnoDB.

You can check the storage engine of a table with the statements SHOW CREATE TABLE TableName, or by running a query against metadata tables such as the following:

Foreign-Key-Checklist/storage-engine-check.sql
```
SELECT ENGINE FROM INFORMATION_SCHEMA.TABLES
WHERE TABLE_SCHEMA = ? AND TABLE_NAME = ?;
```

In the preceding example query, substitute your schema name and table name for the "?" placeholders.

The NDB storage engine in MySQL Cluster also supports foreign keys. A similar restriction applies: if one table in the relationship uses the NDB storage engine, then the other table must also use NDB.

Using Large Data Types

In standard SQL, you can't define a PRIMARY KEY, UNIQUE KEY, or a foreign key on a BLOB, CLOB, TEXT, JSON, or ARRAY column.

In MySQL as well, it's not supported to define a key or an index for these large, variable-size columns, because an indexed data type must be no more than 3072 bytes (or 767 bytes in older versions). You can create a *prefix index* to make a key or index on the leading bytes of an indexed column. Even though this allows you to create a PRIMARY KEY or UNIQUE KEY on part of a long column, MySQL can't create a foreign key that references a prefix index, and you get an error.

Foreign-Key-Checklist/text-error.sql
```
CREATE TABLE Parent (
  parent_id TEXT NOT NULL,
  UNIQUE KEY (parent_id(40))
);

CREATE TABLE Child (
  child_id INT PRIMARY KEY,
  parent_id TEXT NOT NULL,
  KEY (parent_id(40)),
  FOREIGN KEY (parent_id) REFERENCES Parent(parent_id)
);
```

ERROR 1170 (42000): BLOB/TEXT column 'parent_id' used in key specification without a key length

Such a long column can't be a foreign key itself. A workaround in MySQL 5.7 or later is to create a *generated column* as a hash of the long column, and define a foreign key on that column. The generated column must use the STORED option to be referenced by a foreign key. The following example shows a definition of a stored, generated column to implement this workaround.

Foreign-Key-Checklist/text-workaround.sql
```
CREATE TABLE Parent (
  parent_id TEXT NOT NULL,
  parent_id_crc INT UNSIGNED AS (CRC32(parent_id)) STORED,
  UNIQUE KEY (parent_id_crc)
);

CREATE TABLE Child (
  child_id INT PRIMARY KEY,
  parent_id_crc INT UNSIGNED,
  FOREIGN KEY (parent_id_crc) REFERENCES Parent(parent_id_crc)
);
```

There is a small risk that two distinct texts result in the same hash value, and thus cause a duplicate error in the unique index. You might be able to use a hash function with a greater space, like MD5() or SHA1(), but the risk of collisions will never be eliminated. It would be better to use a pseudokey intead of a column with such long content as the unique key of a table.

MySQL Foreign Keys to Non-Unique Indexes

In standard SQL, the columns referenced by a foreign key must be the PRIMARY KEY or a UNIQUE KEY of the Parent table. InnoDB supports a non-standard feature: a foreign key does not have to include the whole set of columns in the referenced key. The foreign key is also allowed to reference a non-unique index in the parent table, instead of a PRIMARY KEY or UNIQUE KEY. The only rule is that the columns referenced by the foreign key must be the left-most columns of a key or index. Otherwise you get an error that tells you no index was found in the Parent table with those columns as the left-most columns.

Foreign-Key-Checklist/non-unique-error.sql

```sql
CREATE TABLE Parent (
  parent_id1 INT,
  parent_id2 INT,
  parent_id3 INT,
  PRIMARY KEY (parent_id1, parent_id2, parent_id3)
);

CREATE TABLE Child (
  child_id INT PRIMARY KEY,
  parent_id2 INT NOT NULL,
  parent_id3 INT NOT NULL,
  FOREIGN KEY (parent_id2, parent_id3)
    REFERENCES Parent(parent_id2, parent_id3)
);
```

ERROR 1822 (HY000): Failed to add the foreign key constraint. Missing index for constraint 'child_ibfk_1' in the referenced table 'Parent'

The columns of the foreign key must reference the left-most subset of columns of the key or index.

Foreign-Key-Checklist/non-unique-left-subset.sql

```sql
CREATE TABLE Parent (
  parent_id1 INT,
  parent_id2 INT,
  parent_id3 INT,
  PRIMARY KEY (parent_id1, parent_id2, parent_id3)
);

CREATE TABLE Child (
  child_id INT PRIMARY KEY,
  parent_id1 INT NOT NULL,
  parent_id2 INT NOT NULL,
  FOREIGN KEY (parent_id1, parent_id2)
    REFERENCES Parent(parent_id1, parent_id2)
);
```

Even though referencing a non-unique index or a subset of key columns is allowed, it's not recommended.

A foreign key that references a non-unique index or subset of key columns allows a given row in the Child table to reference values that can occur on multiple rows in the referenced Parent table. This leads to strange and ambiguous logical relationships, such as the following:

- Should the Child row be considered orphaned if one but not all of its Parent rows is deleted?

- If the foreign key is defined with the ON DELETE RESTRICT option, should it be an error to delete any Parent row, or only the last Parent row?

- If the foreign key is defined with the ON UPDATE CASCADE option, and you update the referenced value on one row of the Parent table, should it cascade the change to the Child row?

Any answers to these types of questions are subjective. They might be desired in one application, but not in another application. It's best to avoid these situations, by defining foreign keys only in the standard way. That is, the foreign key columns should reference the full set of columns of a PRIMARY KEY or UNIQUE KEY, so a Child row must reference only one row in the Parent table.

Foreign-Key-Checklist/non-unique-correct.sql
```
CREATE TABLE Parent (
  parent_id1 INT,
  parent_id2 INT,
  parent_id3 INT,
  PRIMARY KEY (parent_id1, parent_id2, parent_id3)
);

CREATE TABLE Child (
  child_id INT PRIMARY KEY,
  parent_id1 INT NOT NULL,
  parent_id2 INT NOT NULL,
  parent_id3 INT NOT NULL,
  FOREIGN KEY (parent_id1, parent_id2, parent_id3)
    REFERENCES Parent(parent_id1, parent_id2, parent_id3)
);
```

Using Inline References Syntax

Standard SQL and most implementations support syntax to define a foreign key for a single column on the same line as the column. However, MySQL doesn't support inline foreign key syntax. If you try to define a foreign key this way, you get no error, but the foreign key is not added to the table.[1]

Foreign-Key-Checklist/inline-ignored.sql
```
CREATE TABLE Parent (
  parent_id VARCHAR(10) PRIMARY KEY
);
```

---

1. https://bugs.mysql.com/bug.php?id=4919

```
CREATE TABLE Child (
  child_id INT PRIMARY KEY,
  parent_id VARCHAR(10) NOT NULL REFERENCES Parent(parent_id)
);
```

If you subsequently view the table definition by running SHOW CREATE TABLE Child, you see the foreign key constraint is missing, as if you had not defined it at all.

Foreign-Key-Checklist/inline-ignored.sql
```
CREATE TABLE `Child` (
  `child_id` int NOT NULL,
  `parent_id` varchar(10) NOT NULL,
  PRIMARY KEY (`child_id`)
) ENGINE=InnoDB DEFAULT CHARSET=utf8mb4 COLLATE=utf8mb4_0900_ai_ci
```

You must define a foreign key only with the table-level constraint syntax.

Foreign-Key-Checklist/inline-correct.sql
```
CREATE TABLE Parent (
  parent_id VARCHAR(10) PRIMARY KEY
);

CREATE TABLE Child (
  child_id INT PRIMARY KEY,
  parent_id VARCHAR(10) NOT NULL,
  FOREIGN KEY (parent_id) REFERENCES Parent(parent_id)
);
```

Using Default References Syntax

Standard SQL and most implementations allow a foreign key REFERENCES clause to omit the names of referenced columns, and they default to the primary key column(s) of the referenced table. However, MySQL doesn't support syntax for implicit referenced columns.[2]

Foreign-Key-Checklist/implicit-columns-error.sql
```
CREATE TABLE Parent (
  parent_id VARCHAR(10) PRIMARY KEY
);

CREATE TABLE Child (
  child_id INT PRIMARY KEY,
  parent_id VARCHAR(10) NOT NULL,
  FOREIGN KEY (parent_id) REFERENCES Parent
);
```

> ERROR 1239 (42000): Incorrect foreign key definition for 'foreign key without name': Key reference and table reference don't match

---

2. https://bugs.mysql.com/bug.php?id=35522

You can define a foreign key only by naming the referenced columns explicitly.

Foreign-Key-Checklist/implicit-columns-correct.sql
```
CREATE TABLE Parent (
  parent_id VARCHAR(10) PRIMARY KEY
);

CREATE TABLE Child (
  child_id INT PRIMARY KEY,
  parent_id VARCHAR(10) NOT NULL,
  FOREIGN KEY (parent_id) REFERENCES Parent(parent_id)
);
```

Using Incompatible Table Types in MySQL

In MySQL, neither the Parent table nor the Child table can be a TEMPORARY table or a PARTITIONED table.

Foreign-Key-Checklist/partition-error.sql
```
CREATE TABLE Parent (
  parent_id INT PRIMARY KEY
);

CREATE TABLE Child (
  child_id INT PRIMARY KEY,
  parent_id INT NOT NULL,
  FOREIGN KEY (parent_id) REFERENCES Parent(parent_id)
) PARTITION BY HASH(child_id) PARTITIONS 11;
```

> ERROR 1506 (HY000): Foreign keys are not yet supported in conjunction with partitioning

Foreign-Key-Checklist/temp-error.sql
```
CREATE TABLE Parent (
  parent_id INT PRIMARY KEY
);

CREATE TEMPORARY TABLE Child (
  child_id INT PRIMARY KEY,
  parent_id INT NOT NULL,
  FOREIGN KEY (parent_id) REFERENCES Parent(parent_id)
);
```

> ERROR 1215 (HY000): Cannot add foreign key constraint

You must use non-temporary, non-partitioned tables for both tables.

Use this chapter as a checklist to resolve errors you experience while creating foreign keys in MySQL.

Young man, in mathematics you don't understand things. You just get used to them.

> John von Neumann

Rules of Normalization

Relational database design isn't arbitrary or mysterious. You can use a number of well-defined rules to design a data storage strategy that avoids redundancy and helps make your application mistake proof, like the poka-yoke ideas mentioned earlier in this book. You've probably heard other metaphors for the same idea, such as *defensive design* or *fail early*.

The rules of normalization aren't complicated, but they are subtle. Developers often misunderstand how they work, perhaps because they expect the rules to be harder than they are.

Another possibility is that people are turned off by having to follow rules at all. Rules are the bête noire of developers who value newness, creativity, and innovation. Rules are, in a way, the opposite of freedom.

Software developers continually make trade-offs between simplicity and flexibility. You can make a lot of work for yourself by reinventing the wheel and developing custom data management software for every application. Or you can take advantage of existing knowledge and technology if you can conform to a relational design when you use a relational database.

The antipatterns in this book are described using their own merits (or faults) to avoid being too academic or theoretical. In this appendix, you'll see that theory can also be practical.

What Does Relational Mean?

This term *relational* doesn't refer to relationships between tables. It refers to the table itself, or rather, the relationship between columns within a table.

Mathematicians define a *relation* as the combination of two sets of values from different domains, with some condition applied that gives a subset of all the possible combinations.

For example, one set is the names of baseball teams, and the other set is cities. The combination of every team to every city is a long list of pairings. The relation has a particular subset of this list: the teams paired with their home city. Valid pairs include *Chicago/White Sox*, *Chicago/Cubs*, or *Boston/Red Sox*, but not *Miami/Red Sox*.

The word *relation* is used in two ways: as a rule ("this city is the home city of that team") and as the subset of pairings that comply with the rule. In SQL, you can store that result in a table with two columns, and one row per pair.

Of course, relations support more than two columns. You can combine any number of domains, one per column, into a relation. Also, you can use domains like the set of 32-bit integers or the set of text strings of a specific length.

Before you can begin normalizing tables, you need to be sure that they are proper relations. They have to meet the following criteria.

Rows Have No Order from Top to Bottom

In SQL, a query returns results in an unpredictable order, unless you use an ORDER BY clause to specify the order. Regardless of the order, the set of rows is considered to be the same.

Columns Have No Order from Left to Right

Whether we ask a developer to verify the product Open RoundFile against bug 1234, or whether we need to know if bug 1234 can be verified in product Open RoundFile by that developer, the result should be the same.

This is related to the antipattern in Chapter 19, Implicit Columns, on page 215, where columns are referenced by their position instead of by their name.

Duplicate Rows Are Not Allowed

Once you know a fact, stating it again doesn't make it any more true. Given the name of a baseball team, your data dictates the city. In this way, the city *depends on* the team name.

To prevent duplicates, you have to be able to tell one row from another and to address individual rows. To ensure this in SQL, declare a primary key constraint for a column or set of columns, whatever is needed to uniquely identify rows. You may alternatively declare a unique key constraint, if the column(s) named in the constraint are NOT NULL.

There might be duplication among non-key columns—for example, there are two teams in the city of Boston—but the row as a whole is still unique because the team names are different.

Every Column Has One Type, and One Value per Row

A relation has a *header* that defines the names and data types of the columns. Every row must have the same columns as those in the header, and a given column must have the same meaning on all rows.

You saw an antipattern break this rule in two ways in Chapter 6, Entity-Attribute-Value, on page 61. First, the EAV table models an entity that can have a custom set of attributes for every instance, so the entity is not bound by any header that defines its attributes.

Second, the EAV attr_value column contains all the entity's attributes, such as the bug's date reported, the bug's status, the account the bug is assigned to, and so on. A given value like 1234 in this column may be valid for two different attributes but mean something totally different.

The antipattern in Chapter 7, Polymorphic Associations, on page 77 also breaks this rule, because a given value like 1234 references the primary key of any of the multiple parent tables. You can't say 1234 on one row means the same thing as 1234 on another row.

Rows Have No Hidden Components

Columns contain data values, not physical storage indicators such as row IDs or object IDs. Chapter 22, Pseudokey Neat-Freak, on page 257 established that primary keys are unique, but they aren't row numbers.

Some databases bend this rule, giving you access to internal storage details with extensions to SQL (for example, the ROWNUM pseudocolumn in Oracle or OID in PostgreSQL). However, these values aren't properly part of the relation.

Myths About Normalization

It's hard to find a subject that is so widely misunderstood, despite having a precise definition. You are practically guaranteed to encounter developers who express with complete confidence untruths such as these:

- "Normalization makes a database slower. Denormalization makes a database faster."

False. It's true that you may need to use a join to retrieve attributes from separate tables after you apply normalization. If you denormalize data, you can avoid some joins.

For example, the comma-separated list in Chapter 2, Jaywalking, on page 9 stores products for a given bug. What if you also need a list of bugs for a given product? Denormalization usually helps convenience or performance for one type of query, but at great cost for other types of queries.

While there are legitimate uses for denormalization, you should model your database in normal forms first, before deciding to use denormaliziation. The *MENTOR* guide for indexing in Chapter 13, Index Shotgun, on page 141 applies to denormalization too: be sure you measure performance both before and after you implement a change for the sake of efficiency.

- "Normalization says to push the data out to child tables and reference it using a pseudokey."

False. You can use pseudokeys for the goal of convenience, performance, or storage efficiency, and those reasons are legitimate. However, it has nothing to do with normalization.

- "Normalization is where you separate attributes as much as possible, such as in the Entity-Attribute-Value design."

False. It's common for developers to use the word *normalization* inaccurately, implying that it makes data less human-readable or less convenient to query. In fact, the opposite is true.

- "No one needs to normalize past the third normal form. The other normal forms are so esoteric that you'll never encounter them."

False. One study showed that more than 20 percent of business databases contain designs that satisfy the first three normal forms but violate the fourth normal form. This is a minority, but it's far from insignificant. If you learn of a bug that potentially results in data loss and occurs in 20 percent of your applications, wouldn't you want to fix it?

What Is Normalization?

The following are the objectives of normalization:

- To represent facts about the real world in a way that can be understood

- To reduce storing facts redundantly and to prevent anomalous or inconsistent data

- To support integrity constraints

Notice that improving database performance is not on this list. Normalization will help you store data *correctly* and avoid getting into trouble when using SQL to query your data. It's practically inevitable that a database that is not normalized becomes a mess. You may have to develop a lot more code to clean up inconsistent or duplicate data. You will experience delays and expenses to the business from faulty data. If you include these scenarios, the benefits to performance from normalizing a database become clearer.

When a table satisfies rules of normalization, the table is in *normal form.* There are five traditional normal forms, describing progressive levels of normalization. Each normal form eliminates a specific type of redundancy or anomaly when you design a relation. Generally, if your table satisfies a normal form, the table also satisfies all the preceding normal forms. There are three additional normal forms that researchers have described. The progression of normal forms is shown here:

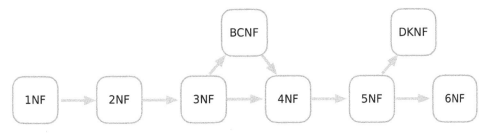

First Normal Form

The most fundamental requirement for first normal form is that the table must be a relation. If it doesn't meet the criteria for a relation described in the first section, then your table can't be in first normal form or any of the subsequent normal forms.

The next requirement is that the table must not have any *repeating groups.* Remember that each row in a relation is a combination between several sets, choosing one value from each set. A repeating group means that one row may have multiple values from the given set.

It also causes trouble to design a table with a set of similar columns, when these columns should be a single column on multiple rows. This design is sometimes informally called an example of repeating groups. It's not strictly the same as a repeating group, since each column contains a single value, but it leads to similar problems.

Two antipatterns in this book break first normal form:

- Multiple values from the same domain across multiple columns, in Chapter 8, Multicolumn Attributes, on page 89
- Multiple values within a single column, in Chapter 2, Jaywalking, on page 9

These antipatterns result in sparsely populated columns or comma-separated strings, like the following illustrations:

BugsTags

bug_id	tag_1	tag_2	tag_3
1234	crash		
3456	printing	crash	
5678	report	crash	data

Multi-Column Attributes

BugsTags

bug_id	tags
1234	crash
3456	printing,crash
5678	report,crash,data

Jaywalking

The proper design that satisfies first normal form is to create a separate table, so each value is on its own row, in a single column.

Bugs

bug_id
1234
3456
5678

BugsTags

bug_id	tag
1234	crash
3456	printing
3456	crash
5678	report
5678	crash
5678	data

In the preceding example, you can support multiple tags by inserting as many rows as needed.

Second Normal Form

The second normal form is identical to the first normal form, unless your table has a compound primary key. In the tagging example, keep track of which user chose to apply each given tag to a bug. The table also has an attribute to identify the user who first coined a given tag.

Normalization/2NF-anti.sql

```
CREATE TABLE BugsTags (
  bug_id  BIGINT UNSIGNED NOT NULL,
  tag     VARCHAR(20) NOT NULL,
  tagger  BIGINT UNSIGNED NOT NULL,
  coiner  BIGINT UNSIGNED NOT NULL,
  PRIMARY KEY (bug_id, tag),
  FOREIGN KEY (bug_id) REFERENCES Bugs(bug_id),
  FOREIGN KEY (tagger) REFERENCES Accounts(account_id),
  FOREIGN KEY (coiner) REFERENCES Accounts(account_id)
);
```

You can see that the identity of the coiner is stored redundantly (the following figure uses names instead of ID numbers for the user identities).

BugsTags

bug_id	tag	tagger	coiner
1234	crash	Larry	Shemp
3456	printing	Larry	Shemp
3456	crash	Moe	Shemp
5678	report	Moe	Shemp
5678	crash	Larry	Shemp
5678	data	Moe	Shemp

Redundancy

BugsTags

bug_id	tag	tagger	coiner
1234	crash	Larry	Shemp
3456	printing	Larry	Shemp
3456	crash	Moe	Shemp
5678	report	Moe	Shemp
5678	crash	Larry	**Curly**
5678	data	Moe	Shemp

Anomaly

This means someone might create an *anomaly* by changing the identity of the coiner on one row for a given tag (*crash*) without changing all rows for the same tag.

To satisfy second normal form, store the coiner for a given tag only once. That means you have to define another table, Tags, where the tag is the primary key, so there's bound to be only one row per distinct tag. Then you can store the coiner of that tag in this new table instead of in BugsTags and prevent anomalies.

Normalization/2NF-normal.sql
```
CREATE TABLE Tags (
  tag      VARCHAR(20) PRIMARY KEY,
  coiner   BIGINT UNSIGNED NOT NULL,
  FOREIGN KEY (coiner) REFERENCES Accounts(account_id)
);

CREATE TABLE BugsTags (
  bug_id  BIGINT UNSIGNED NOT NULL,
  tag     VARCHAR(20) NOT NULL,
  tagger  BIGINT UNSIGNED NOT NULL,
  PRIMARY KEY (bug_id, tag),
  FOREIGN KEY (bug_id) REFERENCES Bugs(bug_id),
  FOREIGN KEY (tag) REFERENCES Tags(tag),
  FOREIGN KEY (tagger) REFERENCES Accounts(account_id)
);
```

The following illustrates that each tag has only one user named as its coiner, so anomalies can't appear.

BugsTags

bug_id	tag	tagger
1234	crash	Larry
3456	printing	Larry
3456	crash	Moe
5678	report	Moe
5678	crash	Larry
5678	data	Moe

Tags

tag	coiner
crash	Shemp
printing	Shemp
report	Shemp
data	Shemp

Third Normal Form

In the Bugs table, you might want to store the email of the engineer assigned to work on the bug.

Normalization/3NF-anti.sql
```
CREATE TABLE Bugs (
  bug_id SERIAL PRIMARY KEY,
  -- . . .
  assigned_to BIGINT UNSIGNED,
  assigned_email VARCHAR(100),
  FOREIGN KEY (assigned_to) REFERENCES Accounts(account_id)
);
```

However, the email is an attribute of the assigned engineer's account; it's not strictly an attribute of the bug. It's redundant to store the email in this way, and you risk anomalies like in the table that fails second normal form.

In the example for second normal form, the offending column is related to at least *part* of the compound primary key. In the following example, which violates third normal form, the offending column doesn't correspond to the primary key at all.

Bugs

bug_id	assigned_to	assigned_email
1234	Larry	larry@example.com
3456	Moe	moe@example.com
5678	Moe	moe@example.com

Redundancy

Bugs

bug_id	assigned_to	assigned_email
1234	Larry	larry@example.com
3456	Moe	moe@example.com
5678	Moe	**curly@example.com**

Anomaly

To fix this, put the email address into the Accounts table. You can separate the column from the Bugs table, like this:

Bugs

bug_id	assigned_to
1234	Larry
3456	Moe
3456	Moe

Accounts

account_id	email
Larry	larry@example.com
Moe	moe@example.com

That's the right place, because the email corresponds directly to the primary key of that table, without redundancy.

Boyce-Codd Normal Form

A slightly stronger version of third normal form is called Boyce-Codd normal form. The difference between these two normal forms is that in third normal form, all non-key attributes must depend on the key of the table. In Boyce-Codd normal form, both key columns and non-key columns are subject to this rule. This would come up only when the table has multiple sets of columns that *could* serve as the table's key. These are called *candidate keys*. Some tables have multiple candidate keys, but only one of the candidate keys will become the primary key of that table.

For example, suppose you have three tag types: tags that describe the impact of the bug, tags for the subsystem the bug affects, and tags that describe the fix for the bug. Each bug must have at most one tag of each type. The candidate key could be the two columns bug_id and tag, but it could also be the two columns bug_id and tag_type. Either pair of columns would be specific enough to address every row individually, so these are both candidate keys for the table.

The following illustrates an example of a table that is in third normal form but not Boyce-Codd normal form.

BugsTags

bug_id	tag	tag_type
1234	crash	impact
3456	printing	subsystem
5678	crash	impact
5678	report	subsystem
5678	crash	impact
5678	data	fix

Multiple Candidate Keys

BugsTags

bug_id	tag	tag_type
1234	crash	impact
3456	printing	subsystem
5678	crash	impact
5678	report	subsystem
5678	crash	subsystem
5678	data	fix

Anomaly

To fix this table, refactor the tag_type attribute into the Tags table, like in the following illustration:

BugsTags

bug_id	tag
1234	crash
3456	printing
3456	crash
5678	report
5678	crash
5678	data

Tags

tag	tag_type
crash	impact
printing	subsystem
report	subsystem
data	fix

When the tag type is an attribute of the Tags table, anomalies are prevented. The table is now in Boyce-Codd Normal Form.

Fourth Normal Form

Now alter the database to allow each bug to be reported by multiple users, assigned to multiple development engineers, and verified by multiple quality engineers. A many-to-many relationship deserves an additional table:

Normalization/4NF-anti.sql

```
CREATE TABLE BugsAccounts (
  bug_id        BIGINT UNSIGNED NOT NULL,
  reported_by   BIGINT UNSIGNED,
  assigned_to   BIGINT UNSIGNED,
  verified_by   BIGINT UNSIGNED,
  FOREIGN KEY (bug_id) REFERENCES Bugs(bug_id),
  FOREIGN KEY (reported_by) REFERENCES Accounts(account_id),
  FOREIGN KEY (assigned_to) REFERENCES Accounts(account_id),
  FOREIGN KEY (verified_by) REFERENCES Accounts(account_id)
);
```

You can't use bug_id alone as the primary key. You need multiple rows per bug to support multiple accounts in each column. You also can't declare a primary key over the first two or the first three columns, because that would still fail to support multiple values in the last column. So, the primary key would need to be over all four columns. However, assigned_to and verified_by should be nullable, because bugs can be reported before being assigned or verified, All primary key columns standardly have a NOT NULL constraint.

Another problem is that the table may have redundant values when any column contains fewer accounts than some other column. The redundant values are shown in the illustration on page 332.

BugsAccounts

bug_id	reported_by	assigned_to	verified_by
1234	Zeppo	NULL	NULL
3456	Chico	Groucho	Harpo
3456	Chico	Spalding	Harpo
5678	Chico	Groucho	NULL
5678	Zeppo	Groucho	NULL
5678	Gummo	Groucho	NULL

Redundancy,
NULLs,
No Primary Key

All the problems shown previously are caused by trying to create an intersection table that does double-duty—or triple-duty in this case. When you try to use a single intersection table to represent multiple many-to-many relationships, it violates fourth normal form.

You can solve this by splitting the table into one intersection table for each type of many-to-many relationship. This solves the problems of redundancy and mismatched numbers of values in each column.

```
Normalization/4NF-normal.sql
CREATE TABLE BugsReported (
  bug_id       BIGINT NOT NULL,
  reported_by  BIGINT NOT NULL,
  PRIMARY KEY (bug_id, reported_by),
  FOREIGN KEY (bug_id) REFERENCES Bugs(bug_id),
  FOREIGN KEY (reported_by) REFERENCES Accounts(account_id)
);

CREATE TABLE BugsAssigned (
  bug_id       BIGINT NOT NULL,
  assigned_to  BIGINT NOT NULL,
  PRIMARY KEY (bug_id, assigned_to),
  FOREIGN KEY (bug_id) REFERENCES Bugs(bug_id),
  FOREIGN KEY (assigned_to) REFERENCES Accounts(account_id)
);

CREATE TABLE BugsVerified (
  bug_id       BIGINT NOT NULL,
  verified_by  BIGINT NOT NULL,
  PRIMARY KEY (bug_id, verified_by),
  FOREIGN KEY (bug_id) REFERENCES Bugs(bug_id),
  FOREIGN KEY (verified_by) REFERENCES Accounts(account_id)
);
```

Separating each many-to-many relationship into its own table would look like the following:

BugsReported	
bug_id	**reported_by**
1234	Zeppo
3456	Chico
5678	Zeppo
5678	Gummo

BugsAssigned	
bug_id	**assigned_to**
3456	Groucho
3456	Spalding
5678	Groucho

BugsVerified	
bug_id	**verified_by**
3456	Harpo

Fourth normal form doesn't seem so exotic now, and it's clear why it's important.

Fifth Normal Form

Any table that meets the criteria of Boyce-Codd normal form and does not have a compound primary key is already in fifth normal form. To understand fifth normal form, consider the following scenario.

Some engineers work only on certain products. You should design the database so you know the facts of who works on which products and which bugs, with a minimum of redundancy. Your first try at supporting this is to add a column to the BugsAssigned table to show that a given engineer works on a product:

Normalization/5NF-anti.sql
```
CREATE TABLE BugsAssigned (
  bug_id       BIGINT UNSIGNED NOT NULL,
  assigned_to  BIGINT UNSIGNED NOT NULL,
  product_id   BIGINT UNSIGNED NOT NULL,
  PRIMARY KEY (bug_id, assigned_to),
  FOREIGN KEY (bug_id) REFERENCES Bugs(bug_id),
  FOREIGN KEY (assigned_to) REFERENCES Accounts(account_id),
  FOREIGN KEY (product_id) REFERENCES Products(product_id)
);
```

This doesn't tell you which products may be assigned to the engineer to work on; it only lists which products the engineer is currently assigned to work on. It also stores the fact that an engineer works on a given product redundantly. This is caused by trying to store multiple facts about independent many-to-many relationships in a single table, similar to the problem in the fourth normal form. The redundancy is illustrated in the figure on page 334 (the figure uses names instead of ID numbers for the products).

BugsAssigned

bug_id	assigned_to	product_id
3456	Groucho	Open Roundfile
3456	Spalding	Open Roundfile
5678	Groucho	Open Roundfile

*Redundancy,
Multiple Facts*

The solution is to isolate each relationship into separate tables, as shown in the following code:

Normalization/5NF-normal.sql

```sql
CREATE TABLE BugsAssigned (
  bug_id       BIGINT UNSIGNED NOT NULL,
  assigned_to  BIGINT UNSIGNED NOT NULL,
  PRIMARY KEY (bug_id, assigned_to),
  FOREIGN KEY (bug_id) REFERENCES Bugs(bug_id),
  FOREIGN KEY (assigned_to) REFERENCES Accounts(account_id)
);

CREATE TABLE EngineerProducts (
  account_id   BIGINT UNSIGNED NOT NULL,
  product_id   BIGINT UNSIGNED NOT NULL,
  PRIMARY KEY (account_id, product_id),
  FOREIGN KEY (account_id) REFERENCES Accounts(account_id),
  FOREIGN KEY (product_id) REFERENCES Products(product_id)
);
```

The same change is shown in the following illustration:

BugsAssigned

bug_id	assigned_to
3456	Groucho
3456	Spalding
5678	Groucho

EngineerProducts

account_id	product_id
Groucho	Open Roundfile
Groucho	ReConsider
Spalding	Open Roundfile
Spalding	Visual Turbo Builder

Now you can record the fact that an engineer is available to work on a given product, even if the engineer is not currently working on a given bug for that product.

Further Normal Forms

Domain-Key normal form (DKNF) says that every constraint on a table is a logical consequence of the table's domain constraints and key constraints. Normal forms three, four, five, and Boyce-Codd normal form are all encompassed by DKNF.

For example, you may decide that a bug that has a status of *NEW* or *DUPLI-CATE* has resulted in no work, so there should be no hours logged, and also it makes no sense to assign a quality engineer in the verified_by column. You might implement these constraints with a trigger or a CHECK constraint. These are constraints between non-key columns of the table, so they don't meet the criteria of DKNF.

Sixth normal form seeks to eliminate all join dependencies. It's typically used to support a history of changes to attributes. For example, the Bugs.status changes over time, and you might want to record this history in a child table, as well as annotations about the change, such as when the change occurred, who made the change, and perhaps other details.

You can imagine that for Bugs to support sixth normal form fully, nearly every column may need a separate accompanying history table. This leads to an overabundance of tables, and it makes writing SQL queries laborious, because you have to join many tables back together to get the simplest result set. Sixth normal form is overkill for most applications, but some data warehousing techniques, for example Anchor Modeling,[1] use this form to implement *temporal databases*. You could use this form to query any data as it existed at a specific time in the past, or you could analyze how it changes over time.

Common Sense

Rules of normalization aren't esoteric or complicated. They're really just a technique resulting from common sense, to reduce redundancy and improve consistency of data.

You can use this brief overview of relations and normal forms as a quick reference to help you design better databases in future projects.

---

1. https://en.wikipedia.org/wiki/Anchor_modeling

Bibliography

[BMMM98] William J. Brown, Raphael C. Malveau, Hays W. McCormick III, and Thomas J. Mowbray. *AntiPatterns*. John Wiley & Sons, New York, NY, 1998.

[Bra11] Ronald Bradford. *Effective MySQL Optimizing SQL Statements*. McGraw-Hill, Emeryville, CA, 2011.

[BT21] Silvia Botros and Jeremy Tinley. *High Performance MySQL*. O'Reilly & Associates, Inc., Sebastopol, CA, 4th edition, 2021.

[Cel04] Joe Celko. *Joe Celko's Trees and Hierarchies in SQL for Smarties*. Morgan Kaufmann Publishers, San Francisco, CA, 2004.

[Cel05] Joe Celko. *Joe Celko's SQL Programming Style*. Morgan Kaufmann Publishers, San Francisco, CA, 2005.

[Cod70] Edgar F. Codd. A Relational Model of Data for Large Shared Data Banks. *Communications of the ACM*. 13[6]:377–387, 1970, June.

[Fow03] Martin Fowler. *Patterns of Enterprise Application Architecture*. Addison-Wesley Longman, Boston, MA, 2003.

[GHJV95] Erich Gamma, Richard Helm, Ralph Johnson, and John Vlissides. *Design Patterns: Elements of Reusable Object-Oriented Software*. Addison-Wesley, Boston, MA, 1995.

[Gol91] David Goldberg. What Every Computer Scientist Should Know About Floating-Point Arithmetic. *ACM Comput. Surv.*. 5–48, 1991, March.

[GP03] Peter Gulutzan and Trudy Pelzer. *SQL Performance Tuning*. Addison-Wesley, Boston, MA, 2003.

[HLV09] Michael Howard, David LeBlanc, and John Viega. *24 Deadly Sins of Software Security*. McGraw-Hill, Emeryville, CA, 2009.

[Mar08]   Robert C. Martin. *Clean Code: A Handbook of Agile Software Craftsmanship.* Prentice Hall, Englewood Cliffs, NJ, 2008.

[MC15]   Jason Myers and Rick Copeland. *Essential SQLAlchemy.* O'Reilly & Associates, Inc., Sebastopol, CA, Second edition, 2015.

[Nic21]   Daniel Nichter. *Efficient MySQL Performance.* O'Reilly & Associates, Inc., Sebastopol, CA, 2021.

[Rub22]   Sam Ruby. *Agile Web Development with Rails 7.* The Pragmatic Bookshelf, Raleigh, NC, 2022.

[Tro06]   Vadim Tropashko. *SQL Design Patterns.* Rampant Techpress, Kittrell, NC, 2006.

Index

Thank you!

How did you enjoy this book? Please let us know. Take a moment and email us at support@pragprog.com with your feedback. Tell us your story and you could win free ebooks. Please use the subject line "Book Feedback."

Ready for your next great Pragmatic Bookshelf book? Come on over to https://pragprog.com and use the coupon code BUYANOTHER2022 to save 30% on your next ebook.

Void where prohibited, restricted, or otherwise unwelcome. Do not use ebooks near water. If rash persists, see a doctor. Doesn't apply to *The Pragmatic Programmer* ebook because it's older than the Pragmatic Bookshelf itself. Side effects may include increased knowledge and skill, increased marketability, and deep satisfaction. Increase dosage regularly.

And thank you for your continued support.

The Pragmatic Bookshelf

A Common-Sense Guide to Data Structures and Algorithms, Second Edition

If you thought that data structures and algorithms were all just theory, you're missing out on what they can do for your code. Learn to use Big O notation to make your code run faster by orders of magnitude. Choose from data structures such as hash tables, trees, and graphs to increase your code's efficiency exponentially. With simple language and clear diagrams, this book makes this complex topic accessible, no matter your background. This new edition features practice exercises in every chapter, and new chapters on topics such as dynamic programming and heaps and tries. Get the hands-on info you need to master data structures and algorithms for your day-to-day work.

Jay Wengrow
(506 pages) ISBN: 9781680507225. $45.95
https://pragprog.com/book/jwdsal2

Design and Build Great Web APIs

APIs are transforming the business world at an increasing pace. Gain the essential skills needed to quickly design, build, and deploy quality web APIs that are robust, reliable, and resilient. Go from initial design through prototyping and implementation to deployment of mission-critical APIs for your organization. Test, secure, and deploy your API with confidence and avoid the "release into production" panic. Tackle just about any API challenge with more than a dozen open-source utilities and common programming patterns you can apply right away.

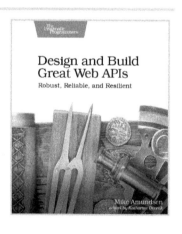

Mike Amundsen
(330 pages) ISBN: 9781680506808. $45.95
https://pragprog.com/book/maapis

Seven Databases in Seven Weeks, Second Edition

Data is getting bigger and more complex by the day, and so are your choices in handling it. Explore some of the most cutting-edge databases available—from a traditional relational database to newer NoSQL approaches—and make informed decisions about challenging data storage problems. This is the only comprehensive guide to the world of NoSQL databases, with in-depth practical and conceptual introductions to seven different technologies: Redis, Neo4J, CouchDB, MongoDB, HBase, Postgres, and DynamoDB. This second edition includes a new chapter on DynamoDB and updated content for each chapter.

Luc Perkins, Jim Wilson, Eric Redmond
(358 pages) ISBN: 9781680502534. $47.95
https://pragprog.com/book/pwrdata

Programming Ecto

Languages may come and go, but the relational database endures. Learn how to use Ecto, the premier database library for Elixir, to connect your Elixir and Phoenix apps to databases. Get a firm handle on Ecto fundamentals with a module-by-module tour of the critical parts of Ecto. Then move on to more advanced topics and advice on best practices with a series of recipes that provide clear, step-by-step instructions on scenarios commonly encountered by app developers. Co-authored by the creator of Ecto, this title provides all the essentials you need to use Ecto effectively.

Darin Wilson and Eric Meadows-Jönsson
(242 pages) ISBN: 9781680502824. $45.95
https://pragprog.com/book/wmecto

Pythonic Programming

Make your good Python code even better by following proven and effective pythonic programming tips. Avoid logical errors that usually go undetected by Python linters and code formatters, such as frequent data look-ups in long lists, improper use of local and global variables, and mishandled user input. Discover rare language features, like rational numbers, set comprehensions, counters, and pickling, that may boost your productivity. Discover how to apply general programming patterns, including caching, in your Python code. Become a better-than-average Python programmer, and develop self-documented, maintainable, easy-to-understand programs that are fast to run and hard to break.

Dmitry Zinoviev
(150 pages) ISBN: 9781680508611. $26.95
https://pragprog.com/book/dzpythonic

Data Science Essentials in Python

Go from messy, unstructured artifacts stored in SQL and NoSQL databases to a neat, well-organized dataset with this quick reference for the busy data scientist. Understand text mining, machine learning, and network analysis; process numeric data with the NumPy and Pandas modules; describe and analyze data using statistical and network-theoretical methods; and see actual examples of data analysis at work. This one-stop solution covers the essential data science you need in Python.

Dmitry Zinoviev
(224 pages) ISBN: 9781680501841. $29
https://pragprog.com/book/dzpyds

Modern Front-End Development for Rails, Second Edition

Improve the user experience for your Rails app with rich, engaging client-side interactions. Learn to use the Rails 7 tools and simplify the complex JavaScript ecosystem. It's easier than ever to build user interactions with Hotwire, Turbo, and Stimulus. You can add great front-end flair without much extra complication. Use React to build a more complex set of client-side features. Structure your code for different levels of client-side needs with these powerful options. Add to your toolkit today!

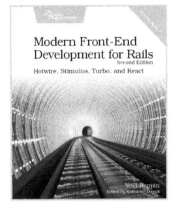

Noel Rappin
(408 pages) ISBN: 9781680509618. $55.95
https://pragprog.com/book/nrclient2

Build a Binary Clock with Elixir and Nerves

Want to get better at coding Elixir? Write a hardware project with Nerves. As you build this binary clock, you'll build in resiliency using OTP, the same libraries powering many commercial phone switches. You'll attack complexity the way the experts do, using a layered approach. You'll sharpen your debugging skills by taking small, easily verified steps toward your goal. When you're done, you'll have a working binary clock and a good appreciation of the work that goes into a hardware system. You'll also be able to apply that understanding to every new line of Elixir you write.

Frank Hunleth and Bruce A. Tate
(106 pages) ISBN: 9781680509236. $29.95
https://pragprog.com/book/thnerves

The Pragmatic Bookshelf

The Pragmatic Bookshelf features books written by professional developers for professional developers. The titles continue the well-known Pragmatic Programmer style and continue to garner awards and rave reviews. As development gets more and more difficult, the Pragmatic Programmers will be there with more titles and products to help you stay on top of your game.

Visit Us Online

This Book's Home Page
https://pragprog.com/book/bksap1
Source code from this book, errata, and other resources. Come give us feedback, too!

Keep Up to Date
https://pragprog.com
Join our announcement mailing list (low volume) or follow us on twitter @pragprog for new titles, sales, coupons, hot tips, and more.

New and Noteworthy
https://pragprog.com/news
Check out the latest pragmatic developments, new titles and other offerings.

Save on the ebook

Save on the ebook versions of this title. Owning the paper version of this book entitles you to purchase the electronic versions at a terrific discount.

PDFs are great for carrying around on your laptop—they are hyperlinked, have color, and are fully searchable. Most titles are also available for the iPhone and iPod touch, Amazon Kindle, and other popular e-book readers.

Send a copy of your receipt to support@pragprog.com and we'll provide you with a discount coupon.

Contact Us

Online Orders:	*https://pragprog.com/catalog*
Customer Service:	*support@pragprog.com*
International Rights:	*translations@pragprog.com*
Academic Use:	*academic@pragprog.com*
Write for Us:	*http://write-for-us.pragprog.com*
Or Call:	+1 800-699-7764

Lightning Source UK Ltd.
Milton Keynes UK
UKHW030144121122
412047UK00003B/10